WorldPerfect

The Jewish Impact
on Civilization

Ken Spiro

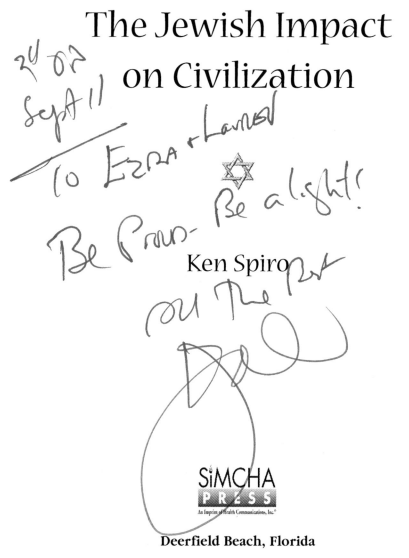

24 02
Sept 11
To Ezra + Laurel
Be Proud- Be a light!
all The Best

SiMCHA
PRESS
An Imprint of Health Communications, Inc.®

Deerfield Beach, Florida

www.simchapress.com

Library of Congress Cataloging-in-Publication Data

Spiro, Ken.
    WorldPerfect : the Jewish impact on civilization / Ken Spiro.
       p. cm.
    Includes bibliographical references.
    ISBN-13: 978-0-7573-0056-1
    ISBN-10: 0-7573-0056-1
    1. Civilization–Jewish influences. 2. Civilization, Classical. 3. Jews–
Civilization. 4. Jews–History. 5. Judaism–Relations. I. Title: World perfect.
II. Title.

    DS113 .S65 2002
    909'.04924–dc21

                                                                    2002070810

Simcha Press, its logos and marks are trademarks of Health Communications, Inc.

Publisher: Simcha Press
            An Imprint of Health Communications, Inc.
            3201 S.W. 15th Street
            Deerfield Beach, FL 33442-8190

R-09-07

Cover and inside book design by Lawna Patterson Oldfield
Cover photos ©PhotoDisc and ©Digital Vision Photography

What People Are Saying About
WorldPerfect: The Jewish Impact on Civilization . . .

"Ken Spiro, a historian and rabbi, offers a welcome antidote to the bad news blaring from most headlines. His readable *WorldPerfect: The Jewish Impact on Civilization* is a popular, unstuffy guide. . . . This is plainly history as unabashed advocacy, not the buttoned-down, objective variety most academically vetted tomes offer. Spiro makes no Gibbonian pretensions but rather presents a simple and passionate profession of faith in Jewish values that lies at the heart of Western culture."

The Jewish Press

"I just finished reading *WorldPerfect: The Jewish Impact on Civilization*, and I was enormously impressed. This is a book that everyone in the world should read. [It] document[s] so carefully and clearly that today's democratic values owe their existence to the Jewish people. Why has the world not recognized this?"

Kirk Douglas
actor and author of *My Stroke of Luck*

"Ken Spiro has given us a great gift with this inspired volume. He speaks directly to the role of faith, religion and life with no holds barred. The title *WorldPerfect* applies to a book whose words are perfect for this troubled world."

John F. Rothmann
talk-show host, KGO Newstalk

"Mr. Spiro clearly articulates a fascinating theory of the roots of modern morality and the strong connection to Jewish values. I really enjoyed reading this book, and as an added treat, I learned a great deal of history in a way that I could absorb and remember. Now, that's a great teacher! I will recommend this book as a 'must-read' for teachers coming into our center."

Debbie Seiden
Board of Jewish Education, Educational Resource Center, New York

To Ruth

Contents

Acknowledgments

This book is the result of an intellectual quest that began many years ago.

It started in 1980 at the Brandeis-Bardin Institute in California where I first met Dennis Prager who introduced me to the idea of ethical monotheism. It blossomed during my years of study at Yeshivat Aish HaTorah in Jerusalem where my Rosh Yeshiva, Rabbi Noah Weinberg, inspired me by deepening my understanding of the Jewish people's unique role and responsibility in human history.

It is my deepest hope that this book will, in some small way, contribute to bringing the world closer to the beautiful utopian vision that has been the longing of the Jewish people for thousands of years.

In addition to those mentioned above, I would like to express my deepest appreciation to the following people for making this book possible:

- To my wife Ruth and my children, Tzvi, Daniel, Chava, Sarah and Adina, and to my parents, for their love, support and for putting up with my crazy schedule.
- To Uriela Obst, my editor, who put countless hours into the manuscript and without whom this book would never have happened.

- To my agent Alan Nevins at AMG who tenaciously pursued the success of this project.
- To the staff of HCI and Simcha Press, especially Susan Tobias and Kim Weiss.
- To Danny Moskowitz for his research assistance.
- To the staff of Aish HaTorah Jerusalem and especially to Nechemia Coopersmith and the staff of the *www.aish.com* Web site where much of my material was first published and continues to appear.

And most importantly, I must express my gratitude to God without whose providence nothing is possible.

Introduction

While developing an idea for a lecture program, I conducted a series of surveys over a period of two years, asking people to list the fundamental values and principles they felt we needed to uphold in order to make our world as perfect as is humanly possible. In total, some fifteen hundred individuals were questioned. Overwhelmingly, my respondents—predominantly Westerners from the United States, Canada, South America, England, France, Germany, Austria, Switzerland, the Netherlands, Spain, Portugal, Italy, etc.—came up with remarkably similar answers, which could be grouped into these six categories:

1. *Respect for Human Life.* In a perfect world, all people would be guaranteed certain basic human rights, paramount among which must be the right to life. They should be able to live that life without constant fear of its loss and with certain basic dignity.
2. *Peace and Harmony.* On all levels—whether communal or global—people and nations should coexist in peace and harmony with respect for each other.
3. *Justice and Equality.* All people, regardless of race, sex, or social status, should be treated equally and fairly in the eyes of the law.

4. *Education.* Everyone should receive a basic education that would guarantee functional social literacy.

5. *Family.* A strong, stable family structure needs to exist to serve as the moral foundation for society and as the most important institution for socializing/educating children.

6. *Social Responsibility.* On an individual, community, national and global level, people must take responsibility for the world. This should include an organized social network to address basic concerns such as disease, poverty, famine, crime, and drug-related problems, as well as environmental and animal protection issues.

The respondents to my survey came from all walks of life, yet regardless of their backgrounds, they were in agreement. Indeed, they, and I venture to say most human beings the world over, deeply believe that a perfect world must include these universal values.

After I compiled the results of my survey and had some chance to think about them, I had to ask why.

Are these six basic ideas intrinsic to human nature? Have people always felt this way? And if not, where did we get these values? What is the source of this utopian world vision?

My search for answers to these questions has produced this book. Where did the values and principles of the modern world come from? The answer I found will surprise, perhaps even shock, the reader.

As the respondents to my survey were predominantly residents of democratic countries, they naturally assumed that the values they hold dear have originated—as did democracy—with the Greeks and, to a lesser extent, with disseminators of Hellenistic, or Greek, ideas: the Romans.

Indeed, this issue is subject to much debate in academic circles these days. Traditionalists continue to insist that the values of ancient Greece and Rome underlie all our learning, philosophy, art and ethics, while their opponents assert that their idealization of Greco-Roman standards of virtue, wisdom and beauty is sentimental if not downright unreal.

Reporting on this bitter controversy, the *New York Times*[1] asked in a headline:

THE ANCIENTS WERE:
A) BELLICOSE ELITISTS
OR B) THE SOURCE OF
WESTERN VALUES?

It would be pointless to negate that Greece and Rome, besides being among the most advanced civilizations of antiquity, have also been the most influential of civilizations on Western Europe and, by extension, the Americas. Without a doubt, many of our ideas about art, beauty, philosophy, government and modern empirical science do come from classical Greek thought. Western law, government, administration and engineering were also powerfully shaped by Rome. Indeed, we overwhelmingly get the lion's share of our culture from these civilizations.

But can the same be said about our values, ethics and principles?

Let me hasten to say that this is not a trick question; I am not hinting at some far-fetched notion that we really got our values from the Far East. With the recent interest in Eastern philosophies, a few voices have been raised advocating this view, but the undisputed historical fact is that only within the last few hundred years did the West have any significant interaction with the East.

So the question remains: How did we come to order our moral values in this particular way?

To answer this question, we shall begin our examination by taking a look at just how those civilizations—which, without a doubt, shaped our political and social systems—related to the values we hold dear today.

Part I

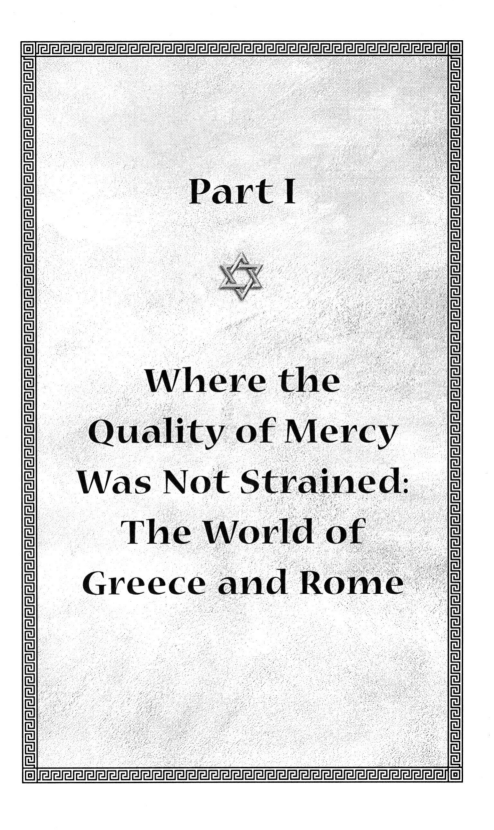

Where the Quality of Mercy Was Not Strained: The World of Greece and Rome

As we begin to trace the history of the values of our world, we shall first look at how the ancients who bequeathed to us so many of our ideas regarded the values we cherish today. Did they consider them essential to the making of an ideal world? Or was their world view considerably different from ours?

CHAPTER 1

Horror Show

Of all the principles we might list, the basic right to life seems certainly the most fundamental. We all want to live without fear of being arbitrarily deprived of life. We all want to live with a certain minimal amount of human dignity. We all want certain protection in the law against oppression by tyrants who might consider certain segments of society expendable simply because they are too weak or too poor to protect themselves.

As obvious and important as this concept seems to us today, it was not so obvious or important in the world of antiquity.

To begin with, Greeks and Romans—as well as virtually every ancient culture we know of—practiced infanticide.

By infanticide, I mean the killing of newborn children as a way of population control, sex selection (generally, boys were desirable and girls undesirable) and as a way of ridding society of potentially burdensome or deformed members.

A baby that appeared weak or sickly at birth, or had even a minor birth defect, such as a cleft palate, harelip or clubfoot, or was in some other way imperfect was killed. This was not done by some Nazi-like baby removal squad. This was done by an immediate member of the family, usually the mother or father, and usually within three days after birth.

The method of "disposal" varied, but generally we know that, in antiquity, babies were taken out to the forest and left to die of exposure, dropped down wells to drown, or thrown into sewers or onto manure piles.

The horror of a parent killing his or her child is shocking enough. But that this parent should have so little regard for the child as to unmercifully dump it where it might die slowly and painfully, or be picked up by someone to be reared into slavery or prostitution (as sometimes happened), suggests a level of cruelty beyond our modern imagination. In his essay "The Evolution of Childhood," Lloyd DeMause reports:

> *Infanticide during antiquity has usually been played down despite literally hundreds of clear references by ancient writers that it was an accepted, everyday occurrence. Children were thrown into rivers, flung into dung-heaps and cess trenches, "potted" in jars to starve to death, and exposed in every hill and roadside, "a prey for birds, food for wild beasts to rend." (Euripides, Ion, 504)*[1]

Gruesome evidence of this practice has been found in various archeological excavations. Most notably, in the Athenian Agora, a well was uncovered containing the remains of 175 babies thrown there to drown.[2]

Lest we assume that was the practice of the poor and ignorant, one of the most influential thinkers in Western intellectual history—none other than Aristotle—argued in his *Politics* that killing children was essential to the functioning of society. He wrote:

There must be a law that no imperfect or maimed child shall be brought up. And to avoid an excess in population, some children must be exposed. For a limit must be fixed to the population of the state.[3]

Note the tone of his statement. Aristotle isn't saying "I like killing babies," but he is making a cold, rational calculation: Overpopulation is dangerous, and this is the most expedient way to keep it in check.

Four hundred years after Aristotle, the practice of killing babies was firmly entrenched in the Roman Empire. This is an excerpt from a famous and much-quoted letter from a Roman citizen named Hilarion to his pregnant wife, Alis, dated June 17, circa 1 C.E.:

Know that I am still in Alexandria. And do not worry if they all come back and I remain in Alexandria. I ask and beg of you to take good care of our baby son, and as soon as I receive payment I will send it up to you. If you deliver a child [before I get home], if it is a boy, keep it, if a girl discard it.[4]

Hilarion, as we see, is very much concerned about his baby son, his heir. Indeed, a typical Roman family might be made up of two or three sons—to ensure succession should one son die—but seldom more than one daughter, who was considered a burdensome responsibility and was expendable. DeMause, one of many scholars quoting the Hilarion letter, adds:

Girls were, of course, valued little, and the instructions of Hilarion to his wife Alis are typical of the open way these things were discussed. . . . The result was a large imbalance of males over females. . . . Available statistics for antiquity show large surpluses of boys over girls; for instance, out of 79 families who gained Milesian citizenship about 228–220 B.C., there were 118 sons and 28 daughters.[5]

Of course, it could be argued that on other fronts the Greeks and the Romans were capable of refined thinking and an elevated approach to behavior. Seneca, the famed Roman philosopher and writer, developed a lengthy treatise on the control and consequences of anger. In it, he draws the distinction between anger and wisdom, using the following example:

Children also, if weak and deformed, we drown, not through anger, but through the wisdom of preferring the sound to the useless.[6]

Incidentally, Seneca, exemplifying the noblest ideals of Roman philosophy, condemned killing of human beings and even animals for sport. But he saw nothing wrong with killing babies for expediency. Indeed, infanticide was so common, so "natural" that playwrights made fun of it in the comedies of the time.[7] For example, the comedy *The Girl from Samos,* by the fourth-century B.C.E. Greek poet and playwright Menander, centers on two illegitimate babies, one of whom is exposed and whose mother ends up caring for the other child while fooling her lover that the baby is his.[8]

But then, the whole attitude toward the weak and helpless was totally skewed in ancient societies. Apart from thinking nothing of killing infants when they saw fit, the Romans engaged in the practice of mutilating unwanted children to make them at least "useful" for begging. (Incidentally, this horrifying practice is still seen today in India.)

Our morally minded friend Seneca, who was so concerned with the issue of useful versus useless, also came up with a tortured justification for this abomination:

Look on the blind wandering about the streets leaning on their sticks, and those with crushed feet, and still again look on those with broken limbs. This one is without arms, that one has had his shoulder pulled down out of shape in order that his grotesqueries may excite laughter. . . . Let us go to the origin of those ills—a laboratory for the manufacture of human wrecks—a cavern filled with the limbs torn from living children. . . . What wrong has been done to the Republic? On the contrary, have not these children been done a service inasmuch as their parents had cast them out?[9]

Today, we would view the killing of newborn babies because they were unwanted or the mutilation of tiny infants for profit as probably the most heinous act a person could commit. What is the weakest, most defenseless, most innocent member of society? A little child. Therefore, we believe that a child, a baby, deserves the protection of society even more than an adult. But in Greek and Roman thinking, rather than being accorded the most protection, children were given the least; this happened simply because, as totally powerless, they were the easiest people to trample on or get rid of.

William L. Langer, Harvard professor and former president of the American Historical Association, points out in his foreword to *The History of Childhood*:

Children, being physically unable to resist aggression, were the victims of forces over which they had no control, and they were abused in many imaginable and some almost unimaginable ways.[10]

So we see how very different the attitude of antiquity was to ours. The most basic right—to life (never mind life with dignity)—was by no means guaranteed.[11]

Another example, which clearly indicates this difference, is the practice of human sacrifice—killing people as a form of religious observance.

As with infanticide, virtually every culture we know of engaged in this practice: killing people in order to appease or pay homage to the gods. From the earliest recorded history to as late as the sixteenth century in the Americas and seventeenth century in Asia, human sacrifice was an accepted way of worship.

The Greeks and the Romans seemed generally more advanced on this one issue—with some exceptions—preferring to sacrifice animals to their phalanx of gods.

The Greeks practiced a custom where a human scapegoat was offered to the gods. Writes Sir James George Frazer in *The Illustrated Golden Bough,* his study of magic and religion:

> *The Athenians regularly maintained a number of degraded and useless beings at the public expense; and when any calamity, such as a plague, drought, or famine, befell the city, they sacrificed two of these outcast scapegoats. . . . They were led about the city and then sacrificed, apparently by being stoned to death outside the city. . . . But such sacrifices were not confined to extraordinary occasions of public calamity; it appears that every year, at the festival of the Thargelia in May, two victims, one for the men and one for the women, were led out of Athens and stoned to death.*[12]

Romans were more fond of sacrificing flocks of sheep; then, after the entrails and livers were extracted and reserved for godly consumption, they'd have a banquet and enjoy the rest themselves. Still, human sacrifice—of children, slaves and prisoners of war—was an accepted practice until the time of Hannibal,[13] and though it was officially outlawed in 97

B.C.E., it continued on a smaller scale, nevertheless, well into the first century C.E.

DeMause cites the following confirming sources:

> Dio said Julianus "killed many boys as a magic rite"; Suetonius said because of a portent the Senate "decreed that no male born that year should be reared"; and Pliny the Elder spoke of men who seek "to secure the leg marrow and the brain of infants."[14]

Probably, the practice was brought into the empire and nurtured by the various peoples the Romans conquered.

The Carthaginians, who represented a superpower in the region before being vanquished by Rome in the Punic Wars, were fond of human sacrifice to honor their most important god, Baal-Haman. Italian historian Indro Montanelli describes a Carthaginian religious ceremony in his book *Romans Without Laurels:*

> When it was a matter of placating or ingratiating themselves with Baal-Haman, they used babies, putting them in the arms of his great bronze statue and letting them fall into the fire blazing below. They were known to burn as many as three hundred a day while the blast of trumpets and the thunder of drums drowned out their screams.[15]

Similarly, Druidism, a Celtic religion that favored human sacrifice, entered the empire after the conquest of Gaul (which is now modern France and western Germany). The Romans went to the trouble of suppressing this cult, which, strangely, they considered "immoral." I say strangely, because while the Romans frowned on the slaughter of people for the purposes of worship, they thought it was perfectly fine to slaughter people for the sheer fun of it.

Surely, there can't be a better example of a total disregard for the value of human life than killing people for entertainment. And here the Romans take first prize. No civilization before or since was so blood-thirsty in this regard. Throughout the empire, more than two hundred stadiums were specifically erected for the exhibition of this particular "sport," which required that people and animals be housed and displayed in such a way that they couldn't escape before being murdered in front of a cheering and jeering audience.

The practice was extremely popular, and Emperor Augustus in his *Acts* brags that during his reign (29 B.C.E. to 14 C.E.) he staged games where ten thousand men fought and three thousand five hundred wild beasts were slain. While savage fights to the death between gladiators— who were usually slaves trained for the purpose—were the highlight, to keep up the novelty of death, Nero and Domitian even sent in women, children, blind people and dwarfs to fight each other. Anything went to keep the crowds happy.[16]

This form of entertainment reached its pinnacle with the inauguration, in the year 80 C.E. of the Coliseum, the ruins of which are today a big tourist attraction in Rome.

The Romans were justly proud of the engineering feat that the con-struction of the Coliseum represented. The giant 600-by-500-foot arena, built by Vespasian and completed by Titus, seated fifty thousand people. It had a removable roof and a floor that could be raised or lowered, depending on what the day's atmosphere demanded. Sometimes the Coliseum was transformed into a desert or into a jungle, and it could also be filled with water and turned into a lake so boats could sail in it.[17]

Why was this incredible place built? To feature death as an elaborate form of amusement for the masses.

On a typical day when the Coliseum was playing to a full house, the place was crowded with men, women and children—yes, the Romans thought nothing wrong with exposing children to this kind of grotesquerie. Admission was free, and a pillow for your seat, meat and wine were provided, also for free. The opening act to start off the morning was an exhibition of wild animals. The Romans went all over the empire to find wild, exotic beasts to astonish the crowds. Next, the arena was lowered to feature combat between them—Romans cheered as lions tore apart tigers, tigers went up against bears, leopards against wolves. It goes without saying that the Romans had never heard of animal rights.

Then came the bullfights, except that the toreadors, being slaves or convicts, had been given no chance to practice, so the bull usually gored them to death. The crowd roared. This is what they came to see.

You'd think that would be enough carnage for anyone. But no. That was only the warm-up act. Next came feeding people to the animals. Keep in mind that Rome was a very law-and-order-minded society and everything had to be done legally—you couldn't throw just anyone to the lions, just people convicted of a capital offense. But if they didn't have enough victims for a good day's fun, the Romans would conveniently condemn even minor criminals to death and replenish the supply. (Christianity, being a capital offense in Rome ever since the great fire of 64 C.E., for which its adherents were blamed, provided a steady supply of victims.)

During intermissions, giant fountains sprayed perfume in the air to reduce the stench of death. Entertainment did not stop, however. In between the spectacular killings were held run-of-the-mill executions by burning, beheading and flaying (that is, skinning people alive).

The main event was saved for the afternoon, and this was what the crowd was really waiting for—gladiatorial combat. The gladiators fought to the death, although the lives of particularly brave fighters could be spared by the emperor or the vote of the crowd.

In the year 107 C.E., during a four-month celebration of his conquest of Dacia, Trajan—who was perhaps trying to match Augustus's record—held a major tournament in which ten thousand gladiators and three thousand animals fought. This meant that whoever sat through that spectacle watched at least five thousand people die. Trajan was so fond of this kind of massacre—and he had a large supply of Dacian prisoners of war for the purpose—that apparently he sent twenty-three thousand people to their slaughter between 106 and 118 C.E.

It was all horrible and perverse, and if you thought it couldn't get worse, consider that Commodus (emperor from 180 to 192 C.E.) organized fights between crippled people and finished them off himself.

Of the Roman philosophers and great thinkers, only Seneca saw anything wrong with death as entertainment. He gives us the following grisly description of gladiatorial games. (Note that Seneca lived before the Coliseum was built and, therefore, in his day this "sport" had not yet reached full flower.) Seneca writes:

Now for the butchery pure and simple! The combatants have nothing to protect them. Their bodies are utterly open to every blow. Never a thrust but finds its mark. . . . The sword is not checked by helmet or shield. What good is armour? What good is swordsmanship? All these things only put off death a little. In the morning men are matched with lions and bears, at noon with their spectators . . . death is the fighter's only exit. . . . [The crowd yells:] "Kill! Flog Burn! Why does he jib at cold steel? Why boggle at killing? Why die so squeamishly?" The lash forces them on the sword. . . . There's

an interval in the display. [The crowd grows impatient:] "Cut a few
throats meanwhile to keep things going!"[18]

Other Roman greats were not as soft as Seneca. Cicero, for example,
thought that gladiatorial contests promoted courage and endurance,
although he was of the opinion that they were not all that entertaining.
Juvenal, who criticized everything, loved the games. And Pliny found
that watching people being massacred toughened the audience and therefore had educational value.

That about sums up the ancient world attitude toward the value of life.
The key thing to keep in mind, however, is that the Greeks or Romans
did think that law and order were essential to the efficient functioning of
society, and laws under both empires were many and strictly enforced.
But the idea that along with your status as a human being came the right
to life (forget about life with dignity) was not a given by any means.

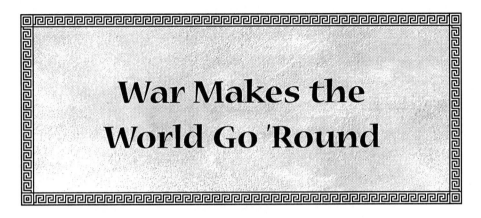

CHAPTER 2

War Makes the World Go 'Round

Today we understand that peace and harmony are vital to the future survival and development of humanity. The major world wars of this century, combined with frighteningly rapid technological advances in warfare, have brought home the realization that wars are something to be avoided at all costs. And while it is true that the world's nations have somehow accumulated enough nuclear weapons to kill each and every human being on the planet several times over, nevertheless, we see armament not as a preparation for war but as a deterrent to war.

Today, Western countries continue to develop arms not in order to conquer the countries weaker than they, but primarily to make sure that the few renegade dictators or fanatics—like Osama bin Laden, Slobodan Milosevic, Saddam Hussein or Muammar al Qaddafi, for example—don't try to realize their aspirations.

Even during the years of the Cold War when the Western world viewed the Communist bloc as a threat to democracy, a civilized dialogue was maintained between "enemies" within the confines of the United Nations. In short, no one doubts that peace is an ideal or that, if peace were somehow assured, the world would be a completely different place, with the resources now spent on armaments available for food, medicine, social programs and protection of the environment.

If the destructive nature of war is so obvious to us today, was it also obvious to the peoples of the ancient world?

We certainly can't claim that we're smarter than they were. You don't meet people like Plato, Aristotle, Socrates, Seneca or Marcus Aurelius nowadays. So if people were so smart back then, why is it that they were perpetually locked in warfare?

Three primary factors come to mind:

- For one, as we have already seen, human life had much less value. While laws for the orderly working of society existed, the stigma attached to killing people was far less. If you could kill people for sport, for the fun of it, how much more advantage to killing in war when you could get something material for your trouble—you could pillage the village, collect the spoils, rape the women and acquire the lands of the conquered for the empire.
- Another factor that encouraged war was the mentality of "might makes right." International law was the law of the jungle where the strong survive and the weak die. It was taken as an accepted fact that the strongest had the "natural" right to conquer.
- And finally, war was seen as glorious. The hero of antiquity was the warrior, and he was often chosen over others to lead the nation. He was glorified in song and poetry while still alive and memorialized in monuments and legends after his death.

The immortal *Iliad* by Homer, one of the greatest works of Greek literature, is exactly this kind of epic poem to the heroes of the Trojan Wars. In his *Hellenic Conceptions of Peace,* Wallis Caldwell analyzes the *Iliad,* pointing out the loopholes of the morality of the day:

> *Among the most interesting aspects of [Sarpedon's speech] is the*
> *absence of tension or contradiction between the warrior's pursuit*
> *of material gain (booty, land and privileged banquet portions) and*
> *his pursuit of glory.*[19]

It must be stressed that to the Greeks, the *Iliad* was more than a great tale, it was also a text for teaching values to the young. And what primary values does one learn in studying this classic? Well, the *Iliad* is one giant battle scene; the heroes are those who killed the most and greatest opponents. Thus the youth got the message: If you want to become a "star" in Greece, there is nothing better you can do with your life than to become a warrior. That was the one way open to all to achieve glamour, glory and immortality.

Since war (rather than peace) was a primary value in the ancient world, it is no wonder that every history book of the Greco-Roman period is filled with the seemingly endless recitation of battles, conquests and bloodshed.

From the arrival of the Greeks in the Mediterranean region in about 1000 B.C.E., the region was nearly constantly at war. The Greek city-states—Athens, Sparta, Corinth, Thebes—warred with each other when they weren't conquering and colonizing adjoining territories. Pericles—so famous for his principles of democracy and encouragement of art and culture—saw nothing wrong with rampant imperialism, a policy that led to the Peloponnesian War with Sparta lasting twenty-seven years.

The Greeks made war into an art form. The so-called "pitched battle"—with thousands of expendable foot soldiers colliding with the enemy, slaughtering and being slaughtered as they advanced—is a Greek invention. While we tend to think today of the Greeks as cultured and noble and of the Romans as roughshod, it is shocking to learn to what extent the Greeks abandoned all humanity when bent on conquest. As an example of their fighting style, let's consider the case of the island of Melos, which was neutral in the Athens versus Sparta conflict. Athens sought to subjugate Melos, and when it finally did so, it punished the Melians savagely, putting all the men of military age to death and enslaving the women and children. Did this bother the more elevated Athenians? Hardly. Aristophanes made fun of the poor Melians in his play *Birds*.

Granted, there were truce periods when one or the other of the city-states unquestionably dominated the region, but the Greeks could hardly be called lovers of peace. The peace of 362 B.C.E., for instance, came about because Athens, Sparta and Thebes had fought themselves into exhaustion, not because they had decided to renounce war. The peace lasted a mere seven years.

Plato, who lived and taught during those years, regarded it as "normal" for the city-states to be continually at war with each other, though he felt there had to be civilized rules to the fighting.

Then, of course, Phillip of Macedonia conquered the lot, becoming the supreme lord of all of Greece and creating a springboard for his son Alexander to conquer more—literally, the rest of the known world.

Trained by Aristotle, and heavily influenced by Homer, Alexander the Great came to power young, at age twenty, and went off to war—for the sheer glory of it. The Thebians revolted against him, so he razed their city and slaughtered or sold into slavery all its inhabitants. But we see moral progress in Alexander. He felt remorse for the bloody terror he had unleashed, and he repented in the temple of Apollo, the god of light and purification. Then he went off to war again.

After conquering the Middle East and chunks of Asia and North Africa, and spreading Hellenism wherever he went, Alexander died at age thirty-three of a fever.

Historians make much of the fact that Alexander's actions were all about ends justifying the means—that he conquered in order to unite all into a peaceful empire. If that was indeed true, then his method was never put to the test, because at the time of his death more wars were unleashed in a seemingly never-ending contest over succession.

Warring continued until the Romans came on the scene. A very pious people, the Romans believed that they were guided by their gods—particularly the trinity of Jupiter/Jove, Juno and Minerva—and could only go to war if the cause was just. They did not subscribe to the injunctions of might makes right or winner takes all.

So how is it that they set out to take over the world?

It all began with Rome wanting to safeguard its territories from takeover by another power. To keep Capua safe, you had to conquer Naples, then, of course, to keep Naples safe you had to conquer Beneveto, and so on and so on.

Serious land grabbing began in the third century B.C.E., when an internal conflict erupted on the nearby island of Sicily between the cities of Messina and Syracuse. Carthage, then a superpower whose interference Rome would not abide, came to the rescue of Messina, and Rome had to jump into the fray lest the Carthaginians got too close to Roman territory proper.

Thus was unleashed the first of the titanic struggles known as the Punic Wars, which, after much bloodshed over more than one hundred years (264 to 146 B.C.E.), led to the Roman domination of what had been the Carthaginian Empire.

Amidst the three Punic Wars came the Macedonian Wars, which pitted Rome against Greece. The rationale for these complicated conflicts arose when the Romans saw the Greeks—with whom they had a peace treaty—making alliances that they found potentially irksome, if not downright threatening. The Macedonian Wars ended in 168 B.C.E. with Rome victorious and in control of what had been Greece.

After that, nobody pretended that there was any just cause in conquest. When Julius Caesar conquered Gaul—a swath of land west of the Rhine and north of the Pyrenees that was then ruled by the Celts—he was motivated to do so by greed and ambition, and he openly used genocidal tactics. He himself summed it up best: *Veni, Vidi, Vici*—"I came, I saw, I conquered."

Caesar's ascent to power led to a civil war, and the Roman Empire was temporarily split between loyalists to Caesar and to his rival Pompey. That fight ended when Pompey was assassinated and Caesar became dictator in 44 B.C.E. He also met a violent end, stabbed to death on the Senate floor by a mob of "friends" just a few months after his ascent to absolute power, managing to utter the famous last words, *Et tu, Brute?* (or so Shakespeare tells us).[20]

Augustus Caesar, his successor, managed to bring about more political stability, and while he reigned as emperor, there was actually peace. This period from 27 B.C.E., and extending through the reign of Marcus Aurelius, until 180 C.E.—a whole two hundred years of peace—became known as Pax Romana. Of course, it came after all threats to the empire had been stamped out by the Roman boot. Everything that could be conquered had been conquered—Europe, the Middle East, Asia Minor,

Northern Africa, just about all of the Western world.

Some ambiguous scraps of land were still not firmly under Roman administration. Therefore, while there was no full-scale war during Pax Romana, annexation and consolidation of land, sometimes by force, naturally had to continue. But these forays via allies and mercenaries did not count as a breach of peace according to the way Rome looked at it, an attitude that might not match up exactly to the way we'd see it now.

CHAPTER 3

Even-Handed Injustice

Natives of liberal, democratic societies see justice and equality as the foundations upon which democracy is built. These are fundamental principles that ensure all citizens have the right to be treated equally before the law, regardless of their status in that society. These are the cornerstones of the U.S. Constitution and Bill of Rights.

Of course, the system is not 100 percent perfect, and we have seen cases where the wealthy (i.e., those who can hire the most expensive lawyers) do manage to get away with stuff the poorest folk (the ones with the public defenders) never seem to. Nevertheless, without a doubt, any "Joe Average" living in a democratic country today can say that he is protected under the law, which ensures him a measure of justice, equality, liberty and happiness.

Now let's look at Joe Average of antiquity (or for that matter of most of history). Could the same be said of him? Did he even come close?

Hardly.

He was usually a serf, a word that came into English usage from the Latin *servus* and that in the days of the Roman Empire meant "servant" or "slave"—in the ancient world there was no real distinction between the two.

The serf most often didn't own the land he farmed and had to pay rent for it in the form of percentage of crops grown. Sometimes he did own the land, in a manner of speaking, but had to pay a tax on it—also in the form of percentage of crops grown.

In Greece, specifically in Sparta, where the Spartans seem to have invented the idea, serfs were called "helots." The helots were a conquered people who were permitted to remain as state slaves on what was formerly their land. As such, they were bound to the soil and assigned to individual Spartans to till their holdings. In their munificence, the Spartans allowed the helots a limited right to accumulate property in exchange for half of the produce raised, according to Spartan poet Tyrtaeus, who compared the poor helots to asses worn down by heavy burdens.

Not surprisingly, the Spartans suspected that the slaves might revolt at any time. Therefore, laws existed permitting the murder of helots on any pretext, and secret police scoured the countryside for possible plots of sedition. Even the least rumor was instantly punishable by death.

In other parts of Greece, the serfs were called "hektermoroi," or sixth-partners, and they tilled the land of wealthy owners, paying a sixth of their produce for the privilege. In the years when the crop was bad, the peasants might not produce enough to feed themselves and thus accumulated an ever-growing debt to their masters. When Greece hit economic woes in the sixth century B.C.E., and antagonism between the filthy rich and the dirt poor threatened a near revolution, the Greek lawmaker (and poet) Solon annulled the huge debts of these poor peasants, but the system of wealthy men lording over a large number of humble dependents continued.

The Romans had a similar system of serfs called "coloni," or tenant farmers. Like the helots, the coloni were bound to the soil by debts that their children inherited and by laws restricting their freedom of movement. Although it was said that the coloni were not slaves, when the land was sold, they were sold along with it; and landlords were permitted to chain any of the hapless coloni suspected of wanting out of the arrangement.

The Romans bequeathed this tenant-farmer idea to Western Europe, where it blossomed as feudalism, a system that existed in France and Germany until the late eighteenth century, in Japan and Russia until the nineteenth century.

So the majority of average folk in antiquity tilled land that was not theirs, lorded over by an elite minority.

The power to determine the quality of life for thousands of people under their control was not vested in the nobility by virtue of integrity, education, competence or fairness, not by any stretch of the imagination. What gave the nobles power over the masses? The original "golden rule": He who has the gold makes the rules. The ability to rule was based almost exclusively on birth and wealth—the lineage of your family and what it owned were the sole determinants of your position in society. (In some cases, who managed to kill off who in order to get there also came into play.)

The vast majority of people were totally at the mercy of a small ruling class and could complain to no one if treated unjustly.

So what about democracy?

We certainly have to give credit where credit is due. Without a doubt, the Athenian Greeks invented the idea of government by the people. Not only that, theirs was the most efficient democratic system in history. Today, we only have representational democracy with each one of us voting for a representative who, we hope, will represent his or her constituency well. The Athenians, thanks to Pericles, had something better—each citizen voted directly.

But before we applaud the Greeks too much, we have to define who a citizen was. Today, a citizen means a resident or inhabitant of a place. In Athens, you could become a citizen only if you were an adult male and owned land and both your parents had been Athenians. This designation, it turns out, applied only to a small minority of people. (Hardly majority rule, which defines democracy today.)

Historians estimate several hundred thousand people were living in Athens, but—after women and children (who did not qualify as adult males), craftsmen and freedmen (none of whom owned land), slaves and resident aliens were deducted—only a few thousand Athenian males were eligible to vote. Thus, most of the residents of Athens were cut out of the "democratic" process. In the final analysis, the Greeks did not practice democracy as much as what we would call oligarchy—government by a few.

Incidentally, the Greeks discriminated across the board, so that even among citizens there were classes, or castes, and political privilege was proportional to your wealth.

While the Greek system was more advanced than anything else at the time and it served as the basis of our democracy, it was a far cry from our modern democratic vision of a true egalitarian system of one person one vote and equal justice for all. Henry Phelps-Brown, in his *Egalitarianism and the Generation of Inequality,* gives us an insight into the Greek mind:

The Greeks distinguished strongly between different types of persons and thought it only proper to treat them differently. This inequality of treatment they endorsed in the name of justice.[21]

It is in this context that we can better understand Aristotle when he tells us in his *Politics:*

It is thought that justice is equality; and so it is, but not for all persons, only those that are equal. . . . Again, as between male and female, the former is by nature superior and ruler, the latter inferior and subject. And this must hold good for mankind in general. Therefore, whenever there is the same wide discrepancy between human beings as there is between the soul and the body, as between man and beast, then those whose condition is such that their function is the use of their bodies and nothing better can be expected of them, those, I say are slaves by nature. It is better for them, just as in the case mentioned, to be ruled thus.[22]

Now it must be said that in Aristotle's society even freedmen, who did not qualify as "citizens," were no better off than slaves in some respects. Artisans, laborers and tradesmen had no legal rights and were the victims of those who were deemed superior to them and who ruled over them.[23]

Distinctions in one's legal standing carried through into the courts of law, where a killer of a citizen was treated differently from a killer of a slave. In the former instance, he was put to death. In the latter, he paid remuneration to the slave's owner. The reason is obvious. Slaves were not considered human. Slaves were rather like animals, i.e., property of the owner. [24]

In Athens, a slave could not testify in court because he was expected to say only things that would favor his master's case. Therefore, if his testimony was vital, he first had to be tortured so that the court could be sure his word could be trusted. Page DuBois in *Torture and Truth,* recounts the horror of it:

> *The party in a trial who wished a slave to be tortured would put his question in writing, specifying which slaves he wished to have tortured and the questions they were to be asked, and also agreeing to pay the slave's owner for any permanent damage inflicted on the slave.*[25]

Note that the slave's feelings about what terrible mutilation might be done to him were not considered. But if he lost a limb and could not work, then his master had suffered a loss, and *his master* would be compensated.

The Athenian "democratic" system underwent a major upheaval in 404 B.C.E., when Athens lost the Peloponnesian War to its sister city-state, Sparta. The citizen body was reduced to three thousand privileged men and some one thousand five hundred political opponents were killed for holding the wrong views. A few years later, even the famed Socrates was condemned to death for his teachings. As we know, he died by drinking hemlock.

Not long after, Alexander the Great came to power and, perhaps taking Aristotle's lessons in superiority versus inferiority a little too much to heart, had himself declared a god.

It was a natural progression really. The Greeks long believed that the gods interacted with humans, had sexual relations with them and produced offspring. Indeed, from time immemorial, there had existed a widespread belief among pagan peoples the world over that their rulers were offspring of the gods. They took it as a given that their monarch was begotten by a god who visited his mother one starry night.[26]

The Greeks had no trouble swallowing this one wholesale, and from Alexander's time on, their political system was a divinely ordained monarchy, or perhaps it should be more accurately described as a divinely ordained dictatorship.

So much for Greek democracy.

We must not leave the Romans out here and also must give them credit where credit is due.

In the early sixth century B.C.E., the Romans overthrew the tyrant Traquinius Superbus, dispensed with monarchy and established *libertas*. Thus the Roman Republic was born, proclaiming a government by the people, which translated to rule by a few special people, the *nobilitas*. The Romans were just as picky as the Greeks regarding who was a citizen.

Much is made of the political organization of the republic with a Senate (where the "patricians," i.e., aristocrats, had a voice), and an Assembly (where the "plebeians," i.e., commoners, had a voting voice). But the plebeians, far from what we might think of as commoners today, were, in fact, the rich who were relative newcomers to Rome and not of the original aristocratic *paterfamilias*.

In Rome, according to Montanelli, "the poor man counted for nothing."

Eventually the masses, the *proletariat* in Latin (though certainly not the slaves), came to have some voice in the councils of the plebs, but that was a long way from having real political power, as all the decisions of importance were made in the Senate.

Additionally, the practical matter of protection under the law did not improve for the poor man; if anything, his rights were even further reduced.

In his study of the Roman legal system, Peter Garnsey writes that when the aristocrats committed heinous crimes, the worst punishment they could suffer would be exile, while others would lose their lives for the very same offense:

> *"Deportation" and "relegation," two forms of exile, were standard penalties in the first group [upper class penalty]. . . . The most serious "lower class penalty" is called by the jurists* summum supplicium *("the highest punishment"). The term stood for aggravated forms of the death penalty, including exposure to wild animals, crucifixion and death by fire. Next, condemnation to hard labour in the mines was for life, and the condemned was reduced to a status akin to slavery. Condemnation to live and fight as a gladiator was just as degrading and carried a greater risk of death. . . . Torture was, by tradition, applied only to slaves. But legal texts which forbid the use of torture for certain classes of free men indicated both that free men were not immune from torture in the middle and late second century, and that only well-connected free men were considered worthy of protection against it.*[27]

The pretense of justice and of representational government in Rome went out the window by 133 B.C.E. That was when, following an argument over land redistribution, Tiberius Gracchus—a duly elected tribune whose job was to protect the rights of the plebeians against encroachment by the patricians—was clubbed to death on the floor of the Assembly. A period of tyrannical repression followed, and political murder and martyrdom—hardly the values of democracy—became regular features of Roman politics. Self-interest, self-indulgence and extortion for political gain were the order of the day between the major scandals, coups and assassinations. Law and order vanished as the ruling aristocrats challenged each other in bloody feuds.

During this time, the famed orator Cicero defended the republic—at the same time arguing *against* democracy. Like Aristotle, Cicero saw equality as illogical and even undesirable:

> *What is called equality is really more inequitable. For when equal honor is given to the highest and the lowest—for men of both types must exist in every nation—then this very "fairness" is most unfair; but this cannot happen in states ruled by their best citizens.*[28]

But the matter was no longer up for debate. The vestiges of the Roman Republic collapsed in 44 B.C.E. when Julius Caesar declared himself dictator. Although his reign was short-lived (as we mentioned earlier, he was stabbed to death in the Senate the same year), others followed in his precedent-setting footsteps. After that, the Roman emperors were self-defined gods to be worshipped and obeyed without question.

So much for Roman democracy.

Before we leave the subject of equality, another word has to be said about the human being who was totally without rights, who was considered subhuman, but whose labor held up the world of antiquity—the slave.

The slaves actually were the majority of the population of Athens and Rome. For example, in the year 331 B.C.E., it is estimated that the ratio of slaves to citizens was almost 5:1. In Rome, in the year 100 C.E., 90 percent of the population (!) consisted of non-Italians of slave origin (though some now were freedmen). Important Romans averaged as many as five hundred slaves apiece, according to Michael Grant's *The*

World of Rome.[29] Elsewhere in Italy, the slaves numbered as many as two million wretched souls, who, owing to their terrible work conditions, could hope to live to the ripe age of twenty-one. The treatment of Roman slaves, writes Grant, "was frightful and unspeakable, one of the worst blots on the history of the human race."

As a result, there were slave revolts, mercilessly put down. Diodorus, the Roman historian, records such a revolt on the island of Sicily in the first century B.C.E.:

> *The Slave War broke out from the following cause. The Sicilians, being grown very rich and elegant, in their manner of living, brought up large numbers of slaves . . . and immediately branded them with marks on their bodies. . . . Oppressed by the grinding toil and beatings, maltreated for the most part beyond all reason, the slaves could endure it no longer. . . .* [30]

The most famous slave revolt, led by Spartacus in 73–71 B.C.E., pitted ninety thousand slaves against the imperial Roman army and was put down with much difficulty and six thousand slaves crucified along the Apian Way.[31]

It must be said that, subsequently, various voices spoke up for a better treatment of slaves (the Stoics being the most prominent advocates of natural equality of all men), and laws were passed to protect slaves from murder and the worst kinds of cruelties. But Rome still was what Rome was. Grant writes:

> *The visible and practical sign of Roman will to power was Roman cruelty. This found expression in savage primitive floggings, often resulting in death, crucifixions, tortures, burnings and*

buryings alive, hurling from the Tarpeian rocks, drowning in sacks, brutal punishments by heads of families and schoolmasters. It was not for nothing that the axe and rods were the emblems of Roman authority. And although certain Romans, rising above the blood-stained world in which they lived, protested against this cruelty and legal improvements followed, the slaves were always the worst sufferers.[32]

CHAPTER 4

Ignorance As Bliss

Today we view education as one of the most basic responsibilities of any government toward its citizens. More than that, we realize that educated populations are good for any country. Ignorant people are generally limited in what they can achieve personally or contribute to their community, and a society comprised of uneducated people will be backward. The benefits of education are obvious to us. The question then arises: Were they also obvious to people of antiquity?

Historians estimate that less than 1 percent of the people of ancient times were literate. In the more advanced civilizations of Greece and Rome—which eventually came to need widespread literate bureaucracies to run their empires—the situation was much better, with about 5 percent of the general population and 15 percent of the adult male population able to read and write.[33] (Today, literacy in the world is at 77 percent, and in the Western nations is close to 100 percent.[34]) Greece boasted museums (where scholars could study disturbed only by the muses) and libraries (equipped with *libers,* or books, for the same purpose). The grandest of the Greek libraries was at Alexandria and by some estimates held seven hundred thousand papyrus scrolls. But your average Tom, Dick or Horatio could not stop by and take out a book, because these volumes were reserved for the intellectual elite.

So we are forced to ask another question: If education is such an important factor in the productivity of a society and such a significant advantage in terms of personal advancement, then why is it that so much of humanity in ancient times was uneducated? Not even the most advanced societies, such as Greece and Rome, which did have rudimentary education systems, had free public education for the masses.

There are two main reasons for mass illiteracy in history. One has to do with practical realities of life and the other has to do with deliberate policies of government.

Today, we take our privileged existence for granted. We may not be millionaires, but we don't realize how well off we are. Most of us living in the Western world live in houses with heat, electricity and indoor plumbing. We sleep through the night in peace (unless we have small children). We wake up in the morning, have a hot shower and then go to the kitchen, which is stocked with a vast amount of food (most of which we don't eat anyway because we are on diets). We get in a car or on a bus or train and go to work. We come home after our eight-hour day, eat supper, relax and watch TV. We have time for recreation and vacations. We expect to live long enough to enjoy retirement. And we take our way of life for granted.

But the Joe Average of antiquity did not enjoy our standard of living. He was concerned with sheer survival. He worried that an enemy would attack his village, burn down his house, rape his wife, kill him and take his children into slavery. If he was lucky to live in peaceful times, he worried that his wife would die in childbirth and that his kids would not survive the usual childhood diseases, which accounted for much of the 50 percent child mortality rate. And if his family was happy and healthy, he worried about droughts, floods and plagues. He worked from dawn to dusk without weekends off, never heard of the concept of vacations, and died before he could imagine such a thing as retirement.

When the name of the game was survival, who could afford to send his kids to school? The ones who managed to grow up without dying had to work in the fields.

Now, Greece and Rome did have schools, but they weren't for the peasants. They were generally for the children of the ruling minority, who as we saw, owned the land.

We know that by about the middle fourth century B.C.E. in Greece, there existed schools where boys (and later, in limited numbers, also some girls) were taught reading, writing, gymnastics, and in the higher grades, also mathematics, literature and rhetoric. Additionally, competitions were organized to test their knowledge of these subjects as well as recitation, singing and lyre playing.

The elementary schools were privately run and paid for by the parents of the students. The secondary schools were controlled by the government but were not free,[35] and at least for a time, were seen as preparation for military service. (It is no wonder that the works of Homer were studied in minute detail.)

Rome had a somewhat different approach to education than did Greece, but later adopted the Hellenistic approach. Right through the time of the Punic Wars, Roman fathers taught their sons the basics of culture and discipline, and subjects such as reading, writing, history and arithmetic. Of course, to teach his son, the father had to be literate, and only the higher strata of society could make that claim. Boys were also apprenticed to leading men who became their teachers and mentors.

Later, with the decline of the family, it became fashionable to send children away to private schools (to get rid of them, says Montanelli). The girls "majored" in music and dancing, the boys in literature and philosophy.

However, these schools did not approximate anything that we have today. Stanley E. Bonner, in his *Education in Ancient Rome,* describes the reality of the day:

> *The Roman state neither created an educational system itself nor gave anything like adequate financial support to the system which developed of its own accord. Education was not made compulsory even at the primary stage, and the acquisition of literacy was haphazard. There was no provision for the training of teachers. There was no school-building programme, and most of the instruction was given in premises never designed for teaching purposes. It is true that some of the more enlightened rulers gave help and encouragement here and there, and the state eventually allowed municipalities to appoint and pay a certain number of teachers, granted exemptions from civic burdens, and gave a more permanent, though limited, patronage to the higher learning. . . . There was, clearly, inequality of opportunity, and the children of the well-to-do classes benefited most.*[36]

Incidentally, from the time of Alexander the Great, when Greek became the world language (much the way English is now), the Greek educational system prevailed. The gymnasium—where athletics and rhetoric were stressed—inculcated Greek values to the children of the privileged. Graduating from the gymnasium was a prerequisite for entry into the government bureaucracy (which was vast) and a gateway to material success.

Of course, the masses were not educated, and for this there is another reason—one more sinister. Education represented power. Knowledge was dangerous; it could destabilize society. (As indeed it has in more modern history—revolutions seemingly begin with students.) Ignorant people were far more easy to control.

Harvard scholar William V. Harris in *Ancient Literacy* draws the picture for us:

> *It should be obvious that in Greece and to an even greater extent in the Roman Empire the illiteracy of the masses contributed to the stability of the political order. . . . The written culture of antiquity was in the main restricted to a privileged minority—though in some places it was quite a large minority—and it coexisted with elements of an oral culture. This written culture certainly helped to widen class differences, as well as having the overwhelmingly important effect of enabling empires to build. Access to the privileged world of writing was automatic for some and variously difficult for others. The Greeks and Romans would have become very different people if,* per impossibile, *they had achieved mass literacy.*[37]

Maybe.

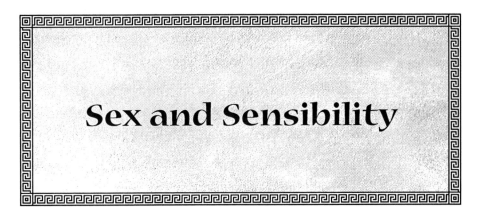

CHAPTER 5

Sex and Sensibility

We appreciate today that having a stable family structure is one of the basic building blocks for a healthy society. Where a stable family structure does not exist, or where such a structure is falling apart, the society is in trouble (which is why this topic is so hot in America today).

Every civilization that ever existed has had some sort of family structure. What we want to examine now is not so much the institution of family, but rather how family values in antiquity were affected and came to be dominated by an obsession with sexuality.

To begin, we have to understand the ancient attitude toward modesty and intimacy.

In Greece, the public exhibition of one's genitalia was not deemed immodest, because it was simply not a social taboo. Men socialized naked in bathhouses all the time. Public toilets were benches with holes in them, set out in the open along the streets, visible to any passersby.

The body—more precisely, the perfection of the body—was revered. The more perfect, the more beautiful. The Olympics—originally a Greek religious event held in honor of Zeus at Olympia—were conducted in the nude, as were all athletic competitions in the gymnasium.[38] How you looked, every bit of you, was incredibly important. One merely has to look at the idealized Greek sculpture, particularly of nude youths, to realize this.

Romans, on the other hand, viewed the Olympics with disgust—to compete nude in public was degrading in the eyes of the Romans, whose idea of entertainment, as we saw earlier, was vastly different. This is not to say, however, that the Romans had a vastly different idea of modesty. They also socialized nude in bathhouses, but it was athletic competition that they found demeaning. (In any case, the idea eventually grew on them, and various nude sports did catch on in Rome as well.)

In both Greece and Rome, the attitude toward sexuality was liberal, to say the least. Basically, anything was acceptable. There were only two serious taboos. Incest was frowned upon because it weakened society and created social tumult. (For example, Caligula, who cohabited with his sister, was generally considered mad; he is remembered in Roman history for a chaotic and bloody reign that undermined the empire.) Adultery was also forbidden when committed by, or with, a married woman. Fidelity of one's wife was needed to ensure clear lines of succession with no doubt of the paternity of the heirs. Beyond that, nothing was really restricted.

The concepts of homosexuality and heterosexuality were nonexistent, as these distinctions were not operational. No one ever had to worry about coming out of the closet; there was no closet to come out of.

The chief issue in a sexual relationship was not whether it was between members of the opposite sex or of the same sex, but who was the active and who was the passive partner.

In Roman society, it was perfectly acceptable for freeborn males to be actively bisexual, as long as in their liaisons they did not violate norms pertaining to social hierarchy. The older, higher-born male had to play the active, dominant role, because it was believed that the Roman male was meant to dominate the world. To be passive was to be wimpy. The passive partner had to be socially subservient and thus could be a slave, a boy, a woman or girl, an animal, or even an inanimate object. Archeologist Lawrence E. Stager, writing in *Biblical Archeology Review,* notes that:

> *Because of his dominant status and power, it was considered a gross violation of the moral order for a Roman male to perform fellatio or cunnilingus on his sexual partner.*[39]

The emperor Elagabalus, who ruled about one hundred years before the collapse of the empire, made the fatal mistake of ignoring the moral macho code.[40] It wasn't the fact that the young emperor prowled the public bathhouses at night looking for male lovers that caused a scandal. It was that he then rewarded the sexual prowess of his partners by appointing them to high government office. Furthermore, he developed a habit of wearing mascara and heavy rouge. He was "removed" from office—murdered—after only four years in power.[41]

Today, religion is seen as putting the brakes on licentious sexual behavior, but the religions of the Greeks and Romans (and of many other ancient cultures) were permeated with sexuality. Indeed, this was a ubiquitous feature of virtually all the mythologies of the ancient world. The gods were involved in rampant sexual activity. For example, in Greek mythology, which the Romans adopted wholesale, the god Uranus, the personification of heaven, cohabited with Gaia, the personification of

Earth, to give birth to a phalanx of gods. Zeus, the most important of their descendants, was depicted as promiscuous, having more than two dozen divine and human consorts. Among his better known sexual conquests was the rape of Europa and the abduction, when overcome by erotic passion, of the beautiful boy Ganymede.[42]

With the gods setting such a sexually active example, human beings were bound to follow suit. Needless to say, temple orgies and fertility rites were regular features of religious observance. Phallic worship was universal. In Rome, it was not uncommon for houses to sport large phallic statues in the front yard, cakes to be baked in the shape of genitalia, and even small children to wear amulets in the shape of such organs around their necks.[43]

Pedophilia and pederasty were out in the open and accepted as commonplace. A sexual relationship between an adult man and a boy was not the serious felony it is today, but rather was viewed as the highest form of love in Greece. It was also considered a fundamental part of the education and socialization of a boy. Writes Tharkil Vanggaard in *Phallus: A Symbol and Its History in the Male World*:

> *An older man would take a young boy "under his wing." This was an honor that gave the boy a permanent higher status in society. If no one wanted the boy it was considered a dishonor. This was not considered feminine but rather a sign of manliness and part of the noblest education.*[44]

Imagine the mentality of an aristocratic Greek citizen. If your middle-aged neighbor didn't make advances toward your young son, you'd have to hang your head in shame: "No one wants our Demetrius!" Today, if your neighbor would do this to your son, you'd make sure he faced criminal prosecution. What a change in attitude!

Bernard I. Murstein, in *Love, Sex and Marriage Through the Ages,* gives us a further rationale for the Greek point of view:

> *It was considered natural that an educated masculine man would want to create a copy of himself in his student, whereas a baser person would simply procreate with women in the ordinary biological manner. . . . A man who energetically wooed women was regarded as effeminate, since only an effeminate person would want to spend time with such inferior creatures.*[45]

Once we understand the prevailing mentality, it is easy to see why the greatest writers and philosophers—such as Sophocles, Aeschylus and Plato—were active pederasts. Plato made his feelings on the subject known in his *Symposium:*

> *I, for my part, am at a loss to say what greater blessing a man can have in earliest youth than an honorable lover . . . if we could somehow contrive to have a city or an army composed of lovers and their favorites, they could not be better citizens in their country . . . no man is such a craven that love's own influence cannot inspire him with valor that makes him equal to the bravest born.*[46]

The Spartans and Thebians took Plato's ideas to heart and created special military units—the Sacred Band was one of them—comprised of older men and their youthful lovers. They fought more fiercely than other soldiers because no one wanted to die ingloriously in front of his lover. This was how the Greeks defined machismo and romance.[47]

But what about love of women?

Since the Greeks were famous for their adoration of female goddesses, including Isis, Aphrodite, Athena and Minerva, and since they wrote a goodly amount of erotic poetry about women (as well as men), we are astonished to find the pervading attitude quite different.

The Greek poet Propertius gives us a hint: "May my enemies fall in love with women and my friends with boys."[48]

Not what you'd call an early feminist writer. Neither was Hesiod, whose poems *Theogony* and *Works and Days* portray the creation of women as punishment for men.[49] Hesiod's women are creatures whose seductive beauty only conceals their baseness and uselessness:

> *A wife can exhaust a man sexually and age him prematurely; and like a drone, she drains his hard-won accumulation of agricultural wealth. . . . Yet a wife is a necessary evil because without her a man cannot have a son to inherit his property.*[50]

But let us go to the great Aristotle, one of the more elevated minds of the day, and see what he had to say on the subject of women:

> *The female is, as it were, a sterile male. . . . The female is, as it were, a castrated male. . . . A female, in fact, is female on account of inability of a sort, viz., she lacks the power to concoct semen.*[51]

Additionally, Aristotle did not think that women were 100 percent rational beings, and Plato believed that women were usually inferior to men, though, being broad-minded, he allowed that there could be exceptions in individual cases.[52]

There were laws on the books that specified that a man might lose his right to pass on his inheritance if he was not of a sound mind. What could bring on a diminishment of a man's intelligence in Athens? "Madness, old age, drugs, disease, madness, and the influence of women."[53]

That being the opinion of the legislators and philosophers, it should not surprise us that no one in antiquity ever heard of women's rights, or that a woman, being viewed as subservient to a man, was generally considered his property. As such, she was scarcely better than a slave, at least as far as the law was concerned.

Xenophon, the Greek historian who was a disciple of Socrates, wrote of his wife, "She knew that it was her job to be neither seen nor heard. What more could I want?"[54]

There were exceptions to be sure. A few women did rise to prominence and are remembered in history: the poetess Sappho from the island of Lesbos; Hagnodice, the first female physician; Agesistrata, the richest woman in Sparta, where women were allowed to own property; Arsinoe, the daughter of Ptolemy I and wife of Ptolemy II who ran the empire with her husband-brother; and several successive queen Cleopatras who ruled from about 180 B.C.E. to 30 B.C.E.

Generally, however, the average Greek woman didn't have power or legal rights. Writes Michael Massey in *Women in Ancient Greece and Rome:*

> *Athenian law, like the law of most Greek communities, made very clear the differences between the various groups of women. There were freeborn women and slave women; there were citizen women and metic women (resident noncitizens from another polis); there were upper-class women and lower-class women. But whichever group they belonged to, they all had one thing in common: They had no political rights of any kind.*[55]

In Rome, this went so far as to literally efface women from society. Women had no identity apart from their husbands or fathers. Indeed, they had no personal names! Their names were merely feminized versions of their father's names. For example, Marcus Tullius Cicero's daughter was called Tullia. If a man had more than one daughter (which was rare as girls were usually killed right after birth), they were both given the same name with "the Younger" or "the Second" tacked on to prevent confusion.[56]

Neither in Greece nor Rome could a woman pick her husband and instead was usually given away by her father to a mate of his choice.

Once married, a Greek woman spent her life in seclusion, relegated—in the words of Plato—to a "submerged and shadowy existence."[57] Her life was totally confined to the women's quarters, the most remote and protected part of the house, which she could not leave. A decent woman simply did not walk around the town in Greece; her slaves did all the errands for her.

From the archeological excavations on the north slope of the Areopagus in Athens, we get a glimpse of what a woman's life was like. The men's quarters on the north side of the house and the women's quarters on the south side each had their own entrance; there was no access to the men's quarters from the women's quarters![58]

Secluded in her house, disdained by her husband, legally insignificant, what was a woman to do but bear children or die trying. (This was a real hazard. The lifespan of an average Greek woman was thirty-five; her husband usually outlived her by ten years.)[59] If she was abandoned by her husband for another woman, the Greek woman had no recourse under the law, but should she commit adultery, her husband could kill her without trial.[60]

The same was true of the average Roman woman. Writes Censor Cato:

The husband is the judge of his wife. If she has committed a fault, he punishes her; if she has drunk wine, he condemns; if she is guilty of adultery, he kills her.[61]

In the eyes of her husband, the wife of antiquity had only one real purpose—to bear legitimate heirs to his estate. And to some that was a
mighty slim reason to marry.

Zeno of Citium, the founder of Stoicism, was in favor of the Platonic
idea of a community of wives "on the grounds that the truly wise man
would find a matrimonial household quite unnecessary."[62]

Others shared his view, though perhaps not for the same reason.
Marriage was simply not something a man looked forward to. It only
cramped his style. As a rule, men delayed marrying as long as possible.

Plutarch relates that the Greek wedding night could better be described
as rape, after which the bridegroom retired to a night of lovemaking with
other men.[63]

As time passed, the birthrate in Greece plummeted, which, combined
with the losses in war, became a source of worry. In the sixth century
B.C.E., the great lawmaker Solon passed a law making marriage
mandatory.

This wise decision was later imitated by the Romans. In the Roman
Empire, a man was not only required to marry but also to have a minimum number of legitimate children if he wanted to bequeath his
property.

Additionally, to encourage women to bear children, laws were passed
freeing them from male guardianship and gradually extending their
rights and responsibilities. The degree of women's freedom depended on
the number of children she had. Massey tells us:

The laws of Augustus (emperor from 27 B.C.E. to 14 C.E.) stated
that a freeborn woman with three children need not have a
guardian: Men must have thought that a woman who had given

birth to three children deserved to be taken seriously! Augustus was
keen to encourage the birth rate and was ready to offer this reward
to women with larger families.[64]

But these laws were too little too late—by then social mores to the
contrary were too deeply ingrained.

Rome had built an empire with one of the greatest military machines in
human history. But as time passed, the empire was forced to hire merce-
nary soldiers to maintain its fighting force. By the time Rome collapsed,
it could not field an army—all of its soldiers were mercenaries, and no
empire could be maintained by hired guns, so to speak. Why did this happen? Because the birth rate had so dropped through the floor that the
Romans had no people left to fight for them. In 200 C.E. the population of
the Roman Empire was estimated at about fifty million people; by 600
C.E. (just when the Mohammedan forces were advancing) the population,
which should have been expanding exponentially, was only twenty-six
million people.[65]

Greece had come to a similarly unhappy end several hundred years
earlier, when, with its population grossly diminished due to war and
misogyny, its forces could no longer defend the motherland. You'd think
the Romans would have learned.[66]

The two greatest civilizations in history certainly collapsed, in part,
because of the sexual licentiousness of their citizens and their societies'
disregard for the value of the family.

If a man had to be *forced* into marriage and into having children, then
we don't need to wonder at his attitude toward the family unit. Indeed, if
you were a man in Greco-Roman society, just how would you define your
"family" values? Here's a possible list:

- Learn sex at an early age from the man next door.
- Marry as late as possible.
- Avoid your wife (lest you should fall under her influence and lose stability of mind) and continue to enjoy the sexual company of other men.
- Rear sons (your heirs).
- Discard (kill) girl babies (maybe keep one).
- Send your sons off to school.
- Marry off your daughter early (that is, if you had decided to keep one).
- Personally introduce your neighbor's young son to sex with men.
- Eat, drink and be merry, and watch your civilization rot into oblivion.

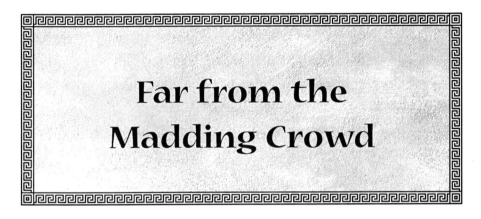

Far from the Madding Crowd

By now it should be obvious to us that societies that did not value life, that were continually locked in warfare, that did not grant equal rights to all their inhabitants, and that preferred to have a huge percentage of their populations uneducated were not going to put much effort into social welfare programs.

We take for granted today that the government is obligated to provide social welfare programs. But virtually all such programs that exist in the Western world today came into being during the last few hundred years, mostly as an outgrowth of the spread of liberal democracy. In the ancient world, if you were destitute and had no family support, the government wasn't going to help you.[67]

In addition to national social welfare programs, we also have the contemporary concept of international responsibility. When another country experiences a natural disaster or some other misfortune, the developed world is quick to respond with foreign aid. This, too, is a very recent phenomenon in world history.

Imagine asking Rome for assistance if your country were rendered temporarily defenseless by a flood or famine; the empire would promptly respond—and send more than fifty thousand Roman soldiers to rape and pillage your country.

It would be ridiculous to expect the Greeks and the Romans to feel pity for the unfortunates of another land when they couldn't muster a smidgen of such feeling for their own people.

The third century B.C.E. saw a deep recession in Greece following the conquests of Alexander the Great. The gulf between rich and poor widened, and the city-states faced serious threat of a revolt. But even though it would have been in their best interest to placate the poor, the idea of giving anything away for free out of a sense of charity did not seem to spring to the otherwise fertile Greek mind.

Grant writes that the Greeks, in response to food shortages and the like, were "able to think of nothing better than to ask for contributions from the rich, who, however, thought it more glamorous to spend money on buildings and festivals."[68] While a few of the coastal cities organized grain doles, the Greek mainland did not see fit to imitate them.

"Pity for the poor," writes Grant, "had never had much place in the Greek character."[69] Indeed, the Stoics regarded pity as a weakness, and although Aristotle favored kindness and generosity, he stopped at talking about it. The same can be said for some of the other writers and poets who, while deploring the terrible conditions, seemed to see poverty as a subject for satire rather than sympathy. Plutarch summed up the prevailing attitude:

But if I gave to you, you would proceed to beg all the more. It was
the man who gave to you in the first place who made you idle and
so responsible for your disgraceful state.[70]

The Roman attitude mirrored the Greek. Writes A. R. Hands in
Charities and Social Aid in Greece and Rome:

At Rome the poor were described as leves, inquinati, improbi,
scelerati, etc., terms implying dishonesty. Indeed, even those who
work for their living but are without land of their own in Rome may
so be described, as they are by Cicero . . . [who] felt appropriate to
describe them as sardem orbis et faecam, the poverty-stricken scum
of the city.[71]

However, the Romans were much more savvy when it came to dealing with the social problem the poor posed than the Greeks. This was for
them not a problem of conscience, but a problem of control. They wanted
to keep the masses out of politics and also realized that a large starving
population presented a danger to national security.

Indeed, the fury of the Roman mob has been much written about.
P. A. Brunt in his essay on the subject talks about the reasons for the constant turbulence among the city population—misery and squalor:

The houses of the poor must have been ill-lit, ill-ventilated and
unwarmed; facilities for cooking were inadequate; water had to be
fetched from the public fountains, and the supply cannot have been
abundant. . . . We may fairly assume that most of the inhabitants of
Rome lived in appalling slums. They offered shelter but no more. As

for furniture, Cicero speaks of the poor man as having no more than
a stool and a bed where he lived, worked and slept. (Cic., in Cat.,
iv. 17.)[72]

To live under such conditions was bad enough, but to go hungry as well was too much to bear and the Roman mob would erupt like a powder keg.

This is why the state instituted a calculated program of bread and circuses—amusing the poor with bloodsports at the forums and chariot races at the circuses and subsidizing the cost of grain when necessary.

Augustus in his *Acts* brags that he made twelve distributions of grain at his own expense, and he lists the many games and wild beasts he presented for the amusement of the proletariat. This was the Roman idea of a social welfare program.

Likewise, in the late first century C.E., Emperor Nerva instituted a fund whereby money was loaned on easy terms to farmers in trouble and the low interest collected sent into a fund for poor children.

The mistake should not be made that the poor in Rome were "taken care of." Far from it. Grain doles were organized only when times were dire and revolt seemed imminent.

Thus the motivation for these acts of kindness was not social responsibility nor social obligation, not by any stretch of the imagination. In fact, the Romans had not heard of the concept of charity. Rather, they fed the poor only when absolutely necessary as a calculated means of keeping them quiet so that the wealthy elite could stay safely in power.

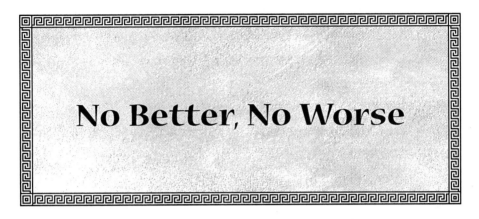

CHAPTER 7

No Better, No Worse

I do not mean to judge the Greeks and Romans too harshly. The sad fact is that virtually every ancient society behaved like them and did no better on the values scale we assume to be the universal standard of decent human behavior.

For example, infanticide was ubiquitous. As Kohl points out:

> *Infanticide has been customary in high civilizations as well as primitive and small-scale societies. In imperial China, Japan and Europe it was used as a method of controlling population growth and avoiding starvation and social disruption. . . . Females were not valued and were selected for infanticide first, as males were preferred to perpetuate the family line.*[73]

In Japan, infanticide was called *mabiki;* the same word is used to describe the thinning of a field of vegetables, giving a clue to how it was viewed in society and how common it was.[74]

In India, the practice was also very common, even if the means of death was a bit more creative and perhaps more merciful than we have seen in Greece and Rome. For example, a child was smothered in milk, or opium was smeared on the mother's breast in quantity sufficient to cause immediate death.[75]

As for other attitudes toward the value of life, it must be noted that the Indians sacrificed human beings up to the period of the Brahmans, around 900–700 B.C.E. Sacrifices included burying five heads under an altar, those of a man, a horse, an ox, a sheep and a goat.[76] The altar was shaped like a firebird that would carry the sacrifice to heaven.

The Chinese practiced human sacrifice much longer than the Indians— well into the sixteenth century. They believed that earthly prosperity could not continue without it. As an example of how far they would go, we have an excavation at An-yang where archeologists unearthed an entire company of soldiers, including horses and chariots.[77]

On the other side of the globe, ancient societies were no better. When the Spanish conquered Central and South America in 1519, they found a particularly grisly form of human sacrifice *still* in full flower in Mexico. The Aztecs—a highly advanced people in many ways—went to war with nonlethal weapons in order to take large numbers of captives. These prisoners were brought back to the Aztec capital city, Tenochtitlan, where, one by one, they were dragged up pyramids for the sacrifice, which involved ripping out the hearts of the victims while they were still alive. Since the Aztecs believed that if the blood stopped flowing, the world would cease to exist, they engaged in perpetual human sacrifice on a scale that is hard to fathom.[78]

As for peace and harmony, historians have long romanticized the Chinese attitude toward war and have seen in it tendencies toward pacifism. However, the sad fact is that the Chinese made war and lots of it. Writes Harvard fellow Frank A. Kierman Jr. in *Chinese Ways in Warfare:*

No people before modern times has left so extensive a record of military institutions and exploits. After the appropriately titled Warring States were unified by force in 221 [B.C.E.], each of the dozen major dynasties and an equal number of smaller ones were all founded by military means. Central power grew out of the sword.[79]

Indeed, during the period from 403 to 221 B.C.E. when the various independent states of mainland China were warring with each other, "no fewer than 110 states" were swallowed up by their mightier neighbors.[80]

However, in their military tactics the Chinese differed vastly from other ancient societies. As early as the fifth century B.C.E., generals such as the famed Sun Tzu—author of the classic *The Art of War*—taught how to intellectualize war. They studied insidious ways of attacking the enemy mind and winning through fear and superstition. But, of course, the end goal was the same—to conquer and to win.[81]

Unfortunately, the Great Khan of Mongolia, better known as Genghis Khan, later adopted these Chinese tactics; adding to them the brute force of a barbarian, he was able to lay waste to China (where he is estimated to have murdered eighteen million people), and to sweep from the Pacific to the Mediterranean in a short six years. His credo?

The greatest happiness is to vanquish your enemies, to chase them before you, to rob them of their wealth, to see those dear to them bathed in tears, to clasp to your bosom their wives and daughters.[82]

As for India, Hindu political philosophy *required* the king to fight. It advocated, "Make peace with the powerful, war with equals and conquer the weak."[83] A king who died in his bed was a disgrace to the kingdom, and only a king who fought could make it into heaven.

It is amazing that with that kind of background the Indians managed to win independence from the British through a strategy of nonviolence.[84] Unfortunately, immediately upon achieving victory, they went to war with each other—Hindus against Moslems—and before it was over, more than one million people had died.

Justice and equality? Asian societies were notorious for their caste systems and oppression of the masses. Writes Craig J. Reynolds in *Feudalism: Comparative Studies:* "Western academic historians more or less agree that . . . Asian social systems functioned with ties of bondage, subordination, and even vassalage."[85]

India's system was perhaps the worst of any caste society. Because Hindu philosophy held that a man was born not only to his job but to his employer as well, it doomed a person to officially sanctioned life-long oppression if he had the misfortune to land low on the totem pole.[86] A person could do nothing to escape his caste and could not marry outside of it. Of course, if you were lucky to be born to the brahmans (priests and scholars) or kshatriyas (the military and rulers), life was good; it was harder if you were among the vaisyas (farmers and merchants) or sudras (peasants and laborers); but it was miserable if you were one of the untouchables, a total outcast. This was such a terrible fate for a human that the latter was legally, if not socially, outlawed in 1949.

During the Chinese classical period (1027–256 B.C.E.) when the Chou Dynasty ruled China, a system existed of dukes, counts and earls (called *kung, hou, po, tzu* and *nan*) who ruled an essentially "feudal" society.

This system made for an orderly, even if unjust society, which, due to warfare, had deteriorated by the time the famed moralist, Confucius, entered the picture circa 551–479 B.C.E. Confucius—rather than preaching equality and justice for all—advocated returning to the old system to ensure safety and good government and integrity of the realm. Emphasizing loyalty—of son to father, of subject to ruler, of wife to husband, etc.—the Confucian model was well suited to anyone looking for moral justifications for demanding obedience.[87]

Even during the heights of Chinese imperial society—as in the Tang and Sung dynasties (600–1200 C.E.)—the feudal system persisted, though repeatedly reformed. Writes J. S. Critchley in *Feudalism:*

> *[Land ownership was] concentrated in large units, worked by landless vagrants and* chuang k'o, *personal tenants of the owner. By Sung times, political disorder and commendation, debt and poverty had reduced these people to serfs. Whether as tenants or labourers, they were personally dependent upon and subject to the authority of the landowners to whom they "belonged."*[88]

Ditto for Japan.

Indeed, in Japan, the oppressive feudal system lasted the longest of any modern nation—until 1881![89] Japan also holds the record for being the last civilized nation to give up the belief that their emperor was god. This happened on January 1, 1946, when Emperor Hirohito, after Japan's defeat in World War II, publicly acknowledged that he was not divine.

Education for all? Not in Asia. Yes, it is true that China had a very advanced civilization that experienced several periods of cultural and technological creativity equal to or even greater than those in the West. But even though the Chinese valued wisdom and education, they did not value it for the masses. Indeed, the mandarin elite preferred the masses to be ignorant and controllable. Thus the Chinese never achieved a rate of literacy any greater than the Greeks (who boasted a measly 10 percent).

Similarly, in India only the upper classes were literate, and although their literacy rate rivaled that of the Greeks, this, again, is not saying that much.[90]

Of course, in Asian societies women were seldom educated. In every respect they were treated abominably, as they were seen as nothing more than the property of their husbands.

In nineteenth-century Japan, for example, only 15 percent of women could read. Women served men, and when they could no longer work, they were discarded. In the city of Nagano, there is a large rock in the middle of a rice terrace where old women of the valley were left to die after they had outlived their usefulness.[91]

How the Chinese viewed women can be summed up with this Chinese proverb: "Ten fine girls are not equal to one cripple boy."[92] In later years (beginning with the tenth century C.E.), neo-Confucianism—a metaphysical system that combined the teachings of Confucius with the beliefs of Taoism and Zen Buddhism—brought many reforms and advances into Chinese society. But it inexplicably encouraged the practice of *ch'an chu,* the binding of feet of little girls to prevent their growth. Why promote something so cruel? Neo-Confucians were concerned with separation of the sexes and with restricting the woman to the home; a woman whose feet were dwarfed and crippled could hardly get far away from her husband.[93]

In India, as in China, the birth of a boy was a cause for celebration, the birth of a girl a cause for dismay. Explains Edward Blunt in *Social Services in India:*

The birth of a son is ardently desired, because he is necessary to the performance of the sraddha *ceremony, whereby his father's salvation is secure. . . . On the other hand, the birth of a daughter is a matter of positive regret, for sooner or later she must be married and . . . it is on the bride's father that will fall the heavy wedding expenditure.*[94]

Once married, the Indian woman became her husband's property and responsibility—so much so that upon his death she literally ceased to have reason to exist.[95] She was then burned alive on his funeral pyre. Even after the Indians discontinued human sacrifice, the practice's second cousin, widow burning, persisted and was not outlawed until 1829, and then only due to British efforts.[96] (Occasionally, reports surface that in rural villages the practice continues to this day.)

As for the notion of social responsibility,[97] the concept was totally foreign to Asian peoples. Largely to blame was the concept of "karma," a fundamental belief of Hinduism (since fourteenth century B.C.E.) and Jainism and Buddhism (since sixth century B.C.E.). Under this doctrine, your troubles—poverty, disease, suffering—were seen as resulting from your evil deeds in a past life. Confucianism and neo-Confucianism reinforced this with the maxim "Reward good, punish evil." Practically, this meant that when you hit hard times, nobody was going to help you out since whatever you got, you not only deserved, but your misfortunes branded you as an evil person.[98]

* * *

In short, the Greeks and Romans were not alone. The Asian civilizations, just like the European ones, were largely devoid of the values we hold precious. They had human sacrifice, infanticide and caste systems, and their societies were marred by tremendous inequality, poverty and oppression of the disadvantaged.

Yes, they had beautiful philosophies, but we must make a distinction between cultural and technological sophistication and the moral and ethical reality of a society. The two are in no way connected.

Some practices, such as widow burning, child mutilation or human sacrifice, we consider especially horrifying and barbaric today. But we should not confuse barbarism with lack of sophistication. The Asian civilizations were highly sophisticated, made up of intelligent and ingenious people capable of great feats in engineering, lofty cultural aspirations and great love of beauty. In other words, people could build magnificent buildings, love beauty and culture and art, write great works of poetry and literature, develop new ideas in philosophy, and yet lack basic—or what today we consider basic—moral concerns.

CHAPTER 8

Conclusions: Part I

So that is the ugly underside of the Greek and Roman (and other ancient) civilizations. There was little regard for human life, a conquest mentality, rights for the privileged few, and no pity for the have-nots. We are batting zero in our quest to find a source for the values we cherish in the Western world.

So why do we look to these ancient cultures when we think of the values of modern democracy?

It is probably because we equate the values of our world with democracy, which did indeed originate with the Greeks. Another reason we make this mistake is because historians—particularly those of the eighteenth and nineteenth centuries—have given us a lopsided, romanticized picture of the contributions of Greece and Rome, while ignoring many of the negative aspects of these cultures. We think of the classical Greeks sitting under olive trees outside beautiful cities, discussing philosophy.

It's true that they did do that, but that is only a small part of who they were. Other ancient cultures, the Chinese in particular, have been often presented in a similarly distorted fashion.

In summary, let me stress again that I am not saying that all human beings of antiquity were evil creatures who went around killing babies, waging war and reveling in bloodsports. Joe Average was just trying to make it through the day. But he lived in a society that had a different way of looking at the world than we do today. The people of antiquity operated on an entirely different value system than the citizens of the modern liberal, democratic world. And while a few individuals back then may have spoken about the importance of peace and education, the vast majority of humanity believed and practiced otherwise.

Likewise, I am not saying that these civilizations contributed nothing positive to the world. Indeed, they were brilliant in engineering, astronomy, literature, law, art, science, mathematics, philosophy and politics, and we have inherited much from them.

But I am saying that what we did *not* inherit from them are their morality and values. The universal vision of world peace, harmony, justice and equality is not the product of Greece, Rome, the Far East or any other civilization of the ancient world.

If the ideas we hold so dear today did not spring, along with democracy, from the Hellenistic world, where did they originate? That is the puzzle we shall attempt to unravel now.

Part II

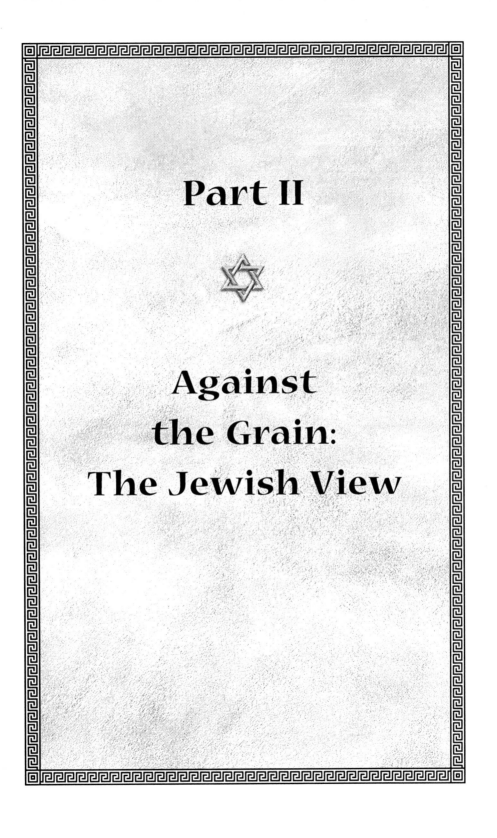

Against
the Grain:
The Jewish View

I will insist that the Hebrews have done
more to civilize men than any other nation . . .
fate had ordained the Jews to be the most essential
instrument for civilizing the nations.[1]

John Adams,
second president of the United States

Certainly, the world without the Jews
would have been a radically different place. Humanity
might have eventually stumbled upon all the Jewish
insights. But we cannot be sure. All the great conceptual
discoveries of the human intellect seem obvious and
inescapable once they had been revealed, but it requires
a special genius to formulate them for the first time.
The Jews had this gift. To them we owe the idea of
equality before the law, both divine and human;
of the sanctity of life and the dignity of human person;
of the individual conscience and so a personal
redemption; of collective conscience and so of social
responsibility; of peace as an abstract ideal and
love as the foundation of justice, and many other items
which constitute the basic moral furniture of
the human mind. Without Jews it might
have been a much emptier place.[2]

Paul Johnson,
Christian historian, author of A History of the Jews
and A History of Christianity

Could that be true?

Is it really possible that our moral values do not originate in one of the great civilizations but have been bequeathed to us by a small, otherwise insignificant nation inhabiting a tiny piece of real estate in the Middle East?[3]

I venture to say that the ancient Hebrews (who later came to be known as the Israelites and still later as the Jews) would have disagreed with the statements of Adams and Johnson. They would have insisted that they had nothing personally to do with inventing the values that ran against the grain of the world around them and were indeed totally unknown to other peoples. They would have insisted that these values came from God, and that they were merely the people chosen to disseminate them worldwide.

This was the story they told from the time they appeared on the world scene around 1300 B.C.E., hundreds of years before the ascent of Greek civilization. Back then, they were still a newly emerging nation that functioned more like a large extended family, with all family members tracing their ancestry to a man named Abraham who had lived sometime around 1800 B.C.E.[4] They were a strange people with an even stranger religion:

- They believed in only one God—all-powerful, infinite and invisible—who had created everything known to man, a notion totally foreign to every ancient people that preceded them.
- They claimed that all of them—some six hundred thousand men and an untold number of women and children—had miraculously escaped from slavery in Egypt, then the mightiest empire on Earth, through the miraculous intervention of their God.

• They claimed that after their great escape, they reached a mountain in the wilderness, Mount Sinai, where they *all* had an encounter with God; during that encounter, and through the person of their leader Moses, they supposedly received a code of behavior—compiled in a holy book known as the "Torah"—which they scrupulously followed.

It was a story bound to raise more than a few eyebrows in the ancient world. Of course, the ancient people believed all sorts of wild things about divine relationships with human beings, so the Jews' story was not in itself all that outlandish. Nor was a society governed by laws so strange; after all, previous law codes, the Code of Hammurabi[5] being the most famous, set forth rules governing property rights and the like. What the ancient world couldn't fathom was *this particular code.* Indeed, it was a code that to the ancient mind seemed irrational.

"The Jews are distinguished from the rest of mankind in practically every detail of life," wrote Roman philosopher Deo Cassius, expressing his disapproval. "In particular . . . they do not honor any of the usual gods, but show extreme reverence to only one God."[6]

Part of that "extreme" reverence translated into following that God's law, a law that could not be altered as was convenient. It was an absolute, God-given standard, and by that fact alone it stood apart from any law of any other society.

But there was more about the Jews that was strange, besides their God and their law. The Torah—or the *biblos,* as the Greeks would call it—was like no holy book of any people before or since. It made the Jews look *bad.* In it, they are shown as shirkers and complainers, often sinning against their own God and his law. And yet they insisted that they needed to carry around with them the history of their failures as well as their successes in order never to lose sight of their mission to elevate humanity.

We shall now take a look at how the ancient Jews viewed our six fundamental principles essential to the building of a perfect world and see how close they came to our standard.

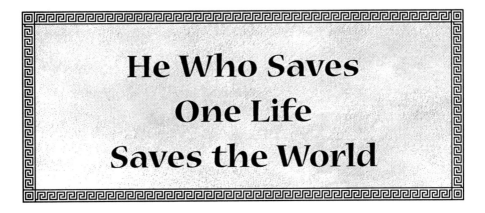

CHAPTER 9

He Who Saves One Life Saves the World

The Torah teaches that all humanity was created in the image of God. Indeed, the Book of Genesis, the first of the five books of the Torah, specifically states:

> God said: "Let us make a human in our image, as our likeness." . . . And thus God created the human being in His image. In the image of God, He created the human being; male and female, He created them.[7]

It naturally follows that if *every* human being has been created in the image of God, then every human life has infinite value and must be safeguarded and protected. That means everyone, no matter how young, no matter how old, no matter how poor, no matter how smart, no matter how deficient mentally or physically—in other words, every human being on the face of the Earth.

Indeed, Jewish law makes no distinction whatsoever between infants and adults (though notably it does permit abortion in certain, though limited, circumstances). Martin Kohl in *Infanticide and the Value of Life* remarks:

> *[In Jewish law] the title to life is absolute, and equal to that of any other person, from the moment of birth . . . it spells out the sanctity of life in very specific terms, attributing infinite value to every innocent life.*[8]

Lloyd DeMause in *The History of Childhood,* after describing the horrible treatment of children in antiquity, notes: "Philo [the Jew] was the first person I have found who spoke out clearly against the horrors of infanticide [in Rome]."[9]

It then should be no surprise that sanctity of life is one of the most important concepts in the Jewish worldview.

This idea is most clearly expressed in the sixth of the Ten Commandments: "Thou shall not murder."[10]

The Hebrew of the original is often mistranslated as "Thou shall not kill," but the Torah does permit killing when necessary to destroy evil. The reasoning is that if you don't destroy evil, evil will destroy you. Judaism does not believe in pacifism and does have a death penalty, but because life is considered so precious, it is actually near-impossible to sentence someone to death. For example, two *eyewitnesses,* relating the same exact account of the crime, are required for capital punishment to be carried out. According to the Talmud, any court that pronounced the death sentence more often than once every seven years was considered a "murderous court."[11] (According to the famed Roman-era teacher and martyr Rabbi Akiva, any court could be so branded if it handed down the death penalty more often than once every seventy years![12])

In the case of accidental killing, special provisions further underscore to what lengths the Jews would go in their reverence for life. The hapless offender was allowed to flee to one of six specially designated "cities of refuge." This was to prevent a relative of the deceased from taking revenge in the heat of grief and passion and thus extinguishing another life. This was also meant to impress upon the perpetrator of the accidental killing that he had deprived the world of a precious God-given life, and though unintentional, his act required repentance just the same.[13]

Needless to say, infanticide, human sacrifice and killing for sport are all prohibited by the Torah.[14]

Indeed, the most dramatic story of the Book of Genesis, the first book of the Torah, is the test of Abraham in which God tells him to offer his son Isaac as a sacrifice. Even though Abraham knows by then that the God he believes in does not need or want human sacrifice, he shows his total obedience by his willingness to do anything God wants, even if he doesn't understand it. However, at the crucial moment, after he ties up his son and places him on a pyre, and just as he is poised with knife in hand, God tells him in no uncertain terms, "Stop!"[15] Abraham is restrained from harming his son, and he sacrifices a ram in his place. Jewish scholars have drawn many lessons from this story, among them that obedience to God and his law must come above all else, and also that, by preventing the sacrifice of Isaac, God thereby decreed unequivocally that he does not want human sacrifice.[16]

By the time the Israelites settled the Promised Land and made their capital in Jerusalem, the practice of human sacrifices by other nations was so abhorrent to them that the site of Canaanite child sacrifices, the Valley of Hinnom, in Hebrew *Ge Hinnom,* gave rise to the name for hell:

gehenom.[17] Although located close to the site of Solomon's Temple, the valley was never settled and remains undeveloped to this day.

To emphasize the infinite value of human life, the Torah admonishes that no expense or effort be spared to save a single life and permits the violation of almost all of its more than six hundred commandments to do so.[18]

In the same period of time that the Romans were having fun watching the slaughter of thousands of people in the Coliseum, the rabbis wrote in the *Mishna:*

> *He who saves one life . . . it is as if he saves an entire universe.*
> *He who destroys life . . . it is as if he destroys an entire universe.*[19]

CHAPTER 10

When the Lion Lies Down with the Lamb

The most eloquent expression of
the longing for peace is found in the writings
of the ancient Hebrews.[20]

Anatol Rapoport in
Peace: An Idea Whose Time Has Come

Today, the best testimony to the Jewish vision of world peace can be found at the headquarters of the international institution dedicated to world peace—the United Nations. As it happens, the United Nations has never been accused of being pro-Jewish; since the Palestine partition vote, the UN has passed more than a thousand resolutions condemning Israel, even going so far as to declare Zionism to be racism.[21] But, nevertheless, on the wall outside the General Assembly headquarters in New York City, the UN has chosen to borrow the words of the Jewish prophet Isaiah to define its vision of peace:

And they shall beat their swords into plowshares and their spears into pruning hooks, nations shall not lift up sword against nations. Neither shall they learn war anymore.[22]

The following didn't make it onto the UN wall, but a few verses later Isaiah makes this much misquoted statement:

The wolf shall dwell with the lamb, the leopard lie down with the kid, the calf and the beast of prey shall feed together with a little child to herd them.[23]

This is the Jewish vision of peace, brotherhood and harmony—a vision that is better known as the Messianic vision because it is expected to become reality upon the coming of the Messiah, the "anointed one," a Jewish leader who will usher in world peace.[24]

Although that time is yet to come for the Jews (the Christians call it the "Second Coming"), it is useful to see how the ancient Jews related to the issues of conquest, war and peace while they awaited the utopian time described by the prophets. Explains Maimonides, the great medieval Jewish scholar:

The sages and prophets did not long for the Messianic era in order to rule the world, nor to subdue the nations . . . but to be free to pursue Torah and its wisdom. . . . [They longed for a time when] there would be no hunger and no war, no jealousy and no strife . . . and the entire world would be entirely occupied to acquire the knowledge of God.[25]

The Jewish sages constantly reminded the people of the importance of peace—in the world and in their personal lives:

- "By three things is the world preserved: by truth, by judgment, and by peace."[26]
- "Great is peace, since all blessings are comprised therein, as it is written: 'The Lord will give strength unto His people; the Lord will bless His people with peace.'" (Psalms 29:11)[27]
- "Be the disciples of Aaron, loving peace and pursuing peace, loving one's fellow man and drawing them near the Torah."[28]
- "The whole of Torah is for promoting peace."[29]

The emphasis on peace was so strong, so fundamental, that the everyday greeting of the Jews became "Shalom," or "Peace."[30]

If they placed such a high value on peace, did the Jews never go to war in the days of the Israelite kingdom, when they were a power to be reckoned with?

The answer is no, and for a number of reasons.

First, as noted above, the sixth of the Ten Commandments is "Don't murder" *not* "Don't kill." Since Judaism believes that it is sometimes necessary to fight evil, there are times when it is deemed appropriate to go to war, namely, to defend one's country and preserve one's society and values.

However, even war of this kind was considered a matter of last resort. The only exception involved the settling of the Promised Land (and how this came about is explained in detail in Part III).

The Israelites laid claim to all of the Promised Land by the year 1258 B.C.E. The conquest was completed by the famed King David, author of the Psalms, who conquered the city of Jerusalem—*Yerushalayim* in Hebrew, meaning "City of Peace"—and made it the capital of Israel. King David had wanted to build a beautiful temple to God on a hill overlooking the city, the site on which Abraham had offered to sacrifice his son Isaac. But the Bible tells us that God prevented him because David, as a result of his participation in the conquest of the Promised Land, had blood on his hands.[31] We thus learn that anyone who has engaged in war—even justified war—is unacceptable for certain very holy tasks.

The Temple was built in the tenth century B.C.E. by David's son, King Solomon, whose forty-year reign was known as a golden age of peace. (Forty years of peace in the Middle East is a truly amazing accomplishment when one looks at the four thousand–year history of the region.)

Other than settling the land, the Israelites did not engage in any type of conquest, although for a time they certainly had the ability and power. But they understood that the real goal of their existence—as described in the Bible—has always been peace, harmony and unity of mankind.

It is interesting to note that whereas the high point of other great empires is usually identified as the climax of their power and physical conquest, the zenith of ancient Israel is characterized not by expansion and domination but by peace. Not only that, but the Bible relates[32] that rulers from all over the world—rather than feeling threatened by Israel's cultural imperialism—came there to seek wisdom from King Solomon.

We might add that another characteristic that distinguished the Israelites during this era was the conspicuous absence of war-hero worship. Warriors such as David and Joshua, for example, were seen as divinely inspired liberators who provided leadership while God worked the miracle and vanquished the enemy. While their qualities were admired, the real hero in Judaism was always the scholar and prophet—the wise man, not the strong man.[33]

Glorification of war was alien to the Israelites. War was nothing to be proud of. The Jewish sages preached a different lesson: "Who is a mighty man? One who conquers his own evil inclination."[34]

To get that point across, numerous parables were taught comparing the insignificance of warfare with a human enemy to the fierce battle that rages within one's self between the evil inclination and the good inclination. One such parable is attributed to King Solomon:

> *Once there was a small city with a few inhabitants. A great king came upon it and surrounded it and built huge fortresses within it. But a poor sage found to be living there rescued the city with his wisdom, though no one remembered him.*[35]

In this story, the human being is represented by the "small city" since a man is a world in miniature.[36] His attributes are "a few inhabitants." The king who surrounds the city while at the same time building huge fortresses within is the evil inclination that surrounds a person but also establishes a stronghold inside him or her. The poor sage—the wise man, who has only a few resources—nevertheless is shown as the victor. The final lesson is a hopeful one—in the end, the battle will be won, and "The evil will bow down to the good."[37]

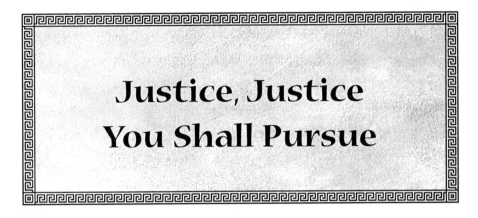

CHAPTER 11

Justice, Justice You Shall Pursue

If we look in the Torah or the other writings of the Hebrew Bible, the word "justice" appears over and over again—a total of 120 times. A great deal of space and care is devoted to explaining what justice is, what law is, what equality is and how they are to be administered fairly among people. While the idea of justice was not unique in the ancient world, the Jewish interpretation of what it meant was nothing short of revolutionary. Justice was justice only when it was administered equally to all people, regardless of their status within society, as the Torah states:

> *You shall not commit a perversion of justice; you shall not favor the poor and you shall not honor the mighty; with righteousness you shall judge your neighbor.*[38]

In Judaism, no one is above the law: not the rich, not the poor, not even the king. Jewish kings, while vested with special privileges and powers, were accountable to God and *to their subjects,* something unheard of in

the ancient world.[39] Further, they were saddled with a tremendous responsibility—to be role models for the rest of the nation. While every Jew was
commanded to copy a Torah scroll as a way of learning the law of God,
the king was required to copy two. The second he had to carry with him
wherever he went, so he would remember he was constantly bound by law
given by God—the King above all kings—and so that he would be ever
mindful of his many responsibilities.[40]

But then again, the Jewish government was not a monarchy, nor, as is
often erroneously stated, a theocracy. It was a sophisticated system of
checks and balances including the king (or the executive branch); the
high priest (the religious branch); and a supreme court, the Sanhedrin
(the judicial branch), whose job was the administration of justice. (There
was no need for a legislative branch because the interpretation of the
Torah and its application to new situations was taken care of by the
Sanhedrin.)

The Sanhedrin was a unique body of seventy-one men. And, as odd
as it may sound, one could not become a member unless one had children, the Torah's reasoning being that only a parent truly understands
the concept of mercy. Every offender is someone's child; a parent would
not forget that.[41] Other qualifications included an encyclopedic knowledge of secular and religious subjects (especially, of course, Jewish
law), fluency in all the languages of the region, and a reputation for
integrity and honesty beyond question. Basically, each judge had to be
good and smart, but he didn't have to be a landowner; social status was
not one of the criteria.[42]

Interestingly, the Torah—which stresses the equality of all people—
makes no provisions for a representational form of democracy in which
people vote for their government. Rather, it strongly implies that a

political system comprised of individuals who rise to a position of leadership based on knowledge, integrity and dedication is superior to any other, such as, for example, a government put into power by a popularity contest based on clever rhetoric and partisan politics.

Amazing as it may seem today, the Jewish system worked in the days when all saw themselves as subservient to God and Torah law; at that time, members of the Sanhedrin were often poor people whose only claim to fame was their wisdom.

In the days of the Roman Empire, the president of the Sanhedrin was the famed Hillel, who was one of the poorest of Jews. Hillel is remembered for his debates of religious questions with Shammai, another brilliant rabbi who just happened to be one of the richest people of the time. Yet we don't see that Shammai's opinions held sway just because he was wealthier. Just the opposite. Interestingly, in Jewish heritage, the opinions of Hillel have come to dominate interpretations of most laws.[43]

Above all, the Sanhedrin was seen as a body that dispensed justice tempered by compassion. As noted earlier, putting offenders to death was almost unheard of, as was sending them to prison—in point of fact, prisons did not exist in ancient Israel. The wise men of the Sanhedrin reasoned that while prisons might remove a prisoner from society, they were unlikely to improve the person's behavior. (As we well know from more modern experience, it's a form of punishment that tends to produce embittered people and hardened criminals.) Since Judaism was concerned with justice and fixing the world, the best way to correct a criminal's mistake would be to send him to work for a good family who would take responsibility to see that he mended his ways.

Such an offender was called an *aved,* which is sometimes translated as "slave," but the idea is closest to that of an indentured servant. However, it is true that an *aved* was "sold" to a family willing to take responsibility for him as a way of paying back money that he had stolen, embezzled or owed in some other way.[44] During his servitude, which could never exceed seven years, the fruits of the *aved*'s labor went to his employer until he paid off his debt, at which time he had to be freed with severance pay to help him start a new life.[45]

There was yet another kind of *aved* in Hebrew society—*aved Canaani*—that is, an *aved* who came from an idolatrous people and who did not want to convert to Judaism. The general attitude toward an *aved Canaani* was a cautious one. Indeed, the Talmud states:

> *The Merciful God requires that your slave be your equal. You should not eat white bread and he black bread . . . you should not sleep on a feather bed and he on straw. Hence it was said, "Whoever acquires a slave acquires a master."* [46]

Anyone who might have thought of exploiting the labor of an *aved Canaani* was forewarned by Jewish law: The responsibility for another human being is awesome. It was forbidden to abuse the *aved Canaani* in any way. If any harm came to him, his master had to pay him damages and free him immediately. If his master killed him, he was tried for murder. States Paul Johnson in *A History of the Jews*:

> *It is no accident that slavery among the Jews disappeared during the Second Commonwealth [middle of the fourth century B.C.E.] . . . as God was the true judge in a court of law, all were equal there: king, high priest, freeman, slave.* [47]

Thus we see that equality was a paramount Torah value. As an extension of this concept, any non-Jew who respected Torah law and followed the seven basic Noahide laws[48] was considered equal to a Jew and received all protection under the law. Indeed, unlike many other religions, Judaism holds that it is not necessary to be Jewish to get to heaven. God judges you by your actions and not by your beliefs. All you have to do is be a pursuer of goodness and justice in the eyes of God.

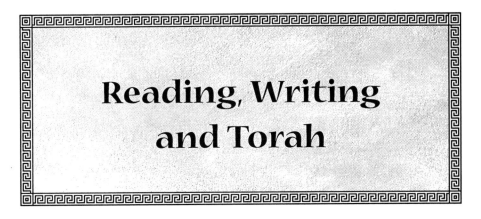

CHAPTER 12

Reading, Writing and Torah

As mentioned ealier, one of the main reasons for the low level of literacy in the ancient world was the desire of the ruling classes to keep the masses ignorant and controllable. Paradoxically, while many ancient cultures valued wisdom, they didn't translate that into educating the population.

Judaism had the exact opposite perspective. It held that it is every human being's obligation to take an active role in being responsible for the world. This could only be done effectively if one were educated. As Rabbi Moshe Avigdor Amiel explains in *Ethics and Legality in Jewish Law:*

> *In most societies, there is no direct connection between law and the educational system. . . . Our [Torah] laws, however, are given over to the entire nation, who are obligated to learn them, as they are considered a religious duty. The laws are oriented to educate the populace, and to inculcate a feeling of justice in their hearts.*[49]

Therefore, Judaism made education the top priority for the entire people. The obligation was squarely placed on each individual to educate his children:

> *You shall love the Lord, your God, with all your heart, with all your soul and with all your might. Let these words, which I command you today, be upon your heart. Teach them diligently to your children and speak of them while you sit in your home, while you travel on the road, when you lie down and when you arise.*[50]

To teach his child, each parent had to be literate. That meant that *every Jew* had to be literate. Additionally, it made perfect sense that the obligation to educate one's children could be fulfilled in the best possible way by professional masters, scholars or teachers. We have evidence from the reign of King Hezekiah (who ruled in the late eighth century B.C.E.) that among the Jews there existed a system of schools for every single child. A unique result of this was that the Jews became the only people in the ancient world with a virtual 100 percent rate of literacy.[51] British historian Cecil Roth, in *The Jewish Contribution to Civilization,* notes:

> *Education was considered a religious duty. Illiteracy was almost unknown, and even the illiterate had the profoundest respect for learning. The Jews, as a result of their respect for a written code of religious law, were the first of all peoples to institute an elementary school-system. A universal scheme of education had existed in Palestine since the first or second century B.C.*[52]

So important was this obligation to educate that Rabbi Joshua Ben Gamla, high priest in the first century C.E., ordained that "teachers of young children should be appointed in each district and each town and that children should enter school at age of six or seven."[53]

Maimonides, one of the greatest medieval Jewish scholars, put it even more strongly when he admonished the Jewish population:

> *Appoint teachers for the children in every country, province and city. In any city that does not have a school, excommunicate the people of the city until they get teachers for the children. If they don't, destroy the city.*[54]

The result of an attitude such as this, which placed education of the children as the highest moral responsibility of every adult, had a visible impact on the Jewish population and naturally was noticed and remarked upon by outsiders. It is no wonder that the Arabs referred to the Jews as *ahl al-kitab*, "the people of the book."

Peter Abelard, a French medieval monk, wrote in the twelfth century:

> *A Jew, however poor, even if he had ten sons, would put them all to letters, not for gain as the Christians do, but for understanding of God's law. And not only his sons, but his daughters.*[55]

(One of the most interesting discoveries about the Cairo Genizah—a collection of two hundred thousand fragments of discarded books, letters and other writings dating from 1025 to 1897 C.E.—is the tremendous amount of material written by women, indicating a high level of literacy among both men and women.[56])

We also have more recent records—for example, from seventeenth-century Poland[57] and eighteenth-century Italy[58]—indicating that even small Jewish communities, as small as fifty families, maintained free schools staffed with professional teachers, and provided, besides books and education, free hot meals and clothing to the students.

But education did not end with graduation from school. Adults continued to study Torah—a project that the rabbis considered a lifetime duty. The results were astonishing. To follow the same example from eighteenth-century Italy, the literacy rate among the Jews there was 94 percent, whereas the overall population had a literacy rate of 55 percent.[59]

A record survives also from Poland, once a thriving Jewish center. In Poland in the seventeenth century, we are told:

There was hardly a single house in which they did not study. Either the householder himself was a scholar, or else his son or his son-in-law studied perpetually: Or, at the very least, he gave hospitality to some young student.[60]

A Christian scholar adds:

Once I noticed a great many coaches on a parking place, but with no drivers in sight. . . . A young Jewish boy showed me the way: In a courtyard, on the second floor, was the shtibl *[study hall] of the Jewish drivers. It consisted of two rooms: one filled with Talmud volumes, the other a room for prayer. All the drivers were engaged in fervent study and religious discussion. . . . It was then that I found out and became convinced that all professions, the bakers, the butchers, the shoemakers, etc., have their own* shtibl *in the Jewish district; and every free moment which can be taken off from their work is given to the study of the Torah.*[61]

As additional evidence of the above,[62] there are books and placards that survived those bygone days. One book, preserved at YIVO Library in

New York, bears the stamp "The Society of Wood-Choppers for the Study of Mishnah in Berditchev." A shingle photographed in Warsaw reads, "Society of Wagon Drivers for the Study of Talmud." All testify that not only children's education but also continuing adult education were thus taken as a matter of course among Jews, centuries before the concept had begun to penetrate the outside world.

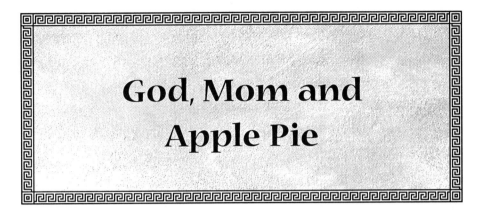

CHAPTER 13

God, Mom and Apple Pie

From the Torah—specifically from the story of creation of Adam and Eve—the Jews learned that the first human being was both a man and a woman who was split in two.[63] Thus, a man and a woman who marry are unifying two halves of a whole, and not just creating a partnership or a team. This underlying assumption gave rise to a radically new attitude toward women, marriage and family, one completely at odds with the norms of the ancient world and truly precedent-setting in human history.

A famous Jewish blessing reads, "Blessed are you, Lord, Our God, King of the Universe, who created the human being."[64] This blessing is not said at the birth of a child as might be assumed, but at a wedding because a human being is not considered complete until married. Judaism teaches that your spouse is your other half, your soul mate, the being to whom you dedicate your life.

From this attitude stem myriad Torah laws intended to preserve the sanctity of marriage and family.[65]

Judaism requires that a man control himself physically and focus his sexual and emotional energy on his wife. Sex is not a male power tool for establishing domination, but rather a vehicle for love and intimacy. In a dramatic departure from the practices of virtually all ancient societies (and some modern), a husband has the *legal* obligation to sexually satisfy his wife before seeking his own satisfaction. Not doing so is grounds for divorce.[66]

This is seen as such an important duty of the husband that the Talmud actually spells out how often men of various professions are required to have sex with their wives to keep the women happy:

- men of independent means, every day
- laborers, twice a week
- donkey drivers (who must travel away from home), once a week
- camel drivers (whose caravans are away from home longer than those of donkey drivers), once a month
- sailors (for obvious reasons), once every six months[67]

To drive the point home most vehemently, the Talmud gives an illustration of a man who was neglectful of his marital duties and caused his wife to shed tears; soon after, he was killed in a tragic accident.[68]

Not only is a husband not permitted to cause his wife pain, but he is required to respect her in all ways. We see numerous examples of the high regard for women and their superior judgment in the Torah. Abraham is instructed by God to follow his wife's wishes: "Whatever Sarah has said to you, listen to her voice."[69] Rebecca is portrayed as being wiser than her blind husband, Isaac, and of possessing prophetic insights regarding their twin sons, Jacob and Esau. While the Israelites are enslaved in Egypt, it is the women who act heroically: The midwives Shifra and Puah refuse to follow the orders of Pharaoh to murder male babies at birth; Miriam, the sister of Moses, literally risks her life to help save her baby brother; the compassionate Egyptian princess, Batya, fishes Moses out of the Nile and adopts as her own son this Israelite child sentenced to death by Pharaoh, her father. Later, while in the wilderness, the Israelite women do not participate in the sin of the Golden Calf and refuse to believe the report of the spies who try to dissuade the escaped slaves from entering the Promised Land.

Most significantly, God is portrayed in Judaism as neither male nor female, but as having both male and female characteristics. Although the masculine Hebrew verb forms—when God acts, creates, etc.—have led to the use of the masculine pronoun "he" in English translation, there are numerous references in Jewish literature (particularly the *Zohar,* the chief work of the Kabbalah) to the *Shechinah,* God's warm, loving and decidedly feminine presence.[70]

Therefore, it is not surprising that Jewish women have had a unique position in their society. Not only were they not second-class citizens as everywhere else, but they even had legal rights. The *Ketubah,* the marriage contract, specifies what a man is obligated to do for his wife; her obligations to him are not listed.[71]

The Greek poet Palladas wrote of the Greek attitude:

Marriage brings a man only two happy days: the day he takes his bride to bed and the day he lays her in her grave.[72]

Rabbinical sages wrote in the Talmud of the Jewish attitude:

Love your wife as you love yourself and honor her more. . . . He who is without a wife dwells without blessing, life, joy, help, goodness, peace and without defense against temptation.[73]

Later in Jewish history, according to Cecil Roth, marriage was consistently regarded by the Jews as a natural and praiseworthy state—not as in the Christian Church, where it was considered a concession to human weakness:

> *In the 12th and 13th centuries, when in the general world wife-beating was not only customary among all classes but expressly permitted by Canon Law and by the statutes of some small towns (as it was indeed by Francis Bacon long after this) the Rabbis could declare, "It is not the way of our people to beat their wives as the Gentiles do." The practice was, indeed, regarded in the Codes as justifiable ground for divorce.* [74]

While some opinions expressed in the Talmud have been interpreted as taking a negative view of women, they are the exception rather than the rule and are often unfairly quoted out of context.

To be sure, the Torah view of women is quite different from today's liberal/feminist view prevailing in Western democratic countries. The fundamental principle that could best describe Judaism's attitude toward men and women is "different but equal"; as two halves of a whole, each possesses distinct strengths and abilities. That is, men and women are different creatures both physiologically and psychologically (as in, "Men are from Mars, and Women are from Venus").

Men are seen as externally motivated aggressors. This is why Judaism believes that men require far more control and training to actualize their potential than women. Women are seen as internally driven, intuitive, more sensitive, disciplined and focused. This is part of the reason why Jewishness is passed on through the mother—the eternal essence of a child's soul comes from the woman. And therefore it follows that the mother's role is stressed. In *Too Many Women? The Sex Ratio Question*, Marcia Guttentag points out:

> *[Jewish] families have been highly stable, and great value has always been placed on the Jewish wife and mother. . . . Modern feminists have emphasized the negative side of the roles of women in Judaism, though usually to the neglect of the positive values connected with traditional roles. . . . But evidence is overwhelming that Jewish women were loved, respected, valued, admired, and cherished within the traditional role. Only our modern eyes see these women as second-class citizens.*[75]

This is not to suggest that in Israelite society women were only wives and mothers. While leadership was seen as much more a "male thing," if the best person for the job was a woman, she got the responsibility. The best example of this was judge and prophetess Deborah, who ruled the Israelites for some forty years circa 1100 B.C.E. and even led them in battle.[76]

Another powerful prophetess was Hulda, whom the king and the high priest consulted on authenticity of a Temple scroll found during renovations. Hulda also delivered an ominous prophecy that God's "wrath had been incited against this place (the Temple) and it will not be extinguished"[77] more than a hundred years before the Temple's actual destruction. These two women were so revered that it is written in the *Zohar* of them:

> *There were two women in the world who sang praises to the Holy One that all the great men in the world never said. Who are these women? Deborah and Hulda. And all the verses that Deborah sang are rooted in higher wisdom.*[78]

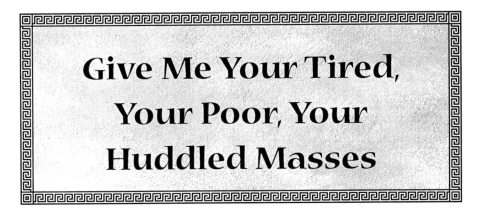

CHAPTER 14

Give Me Your Tired, Your Poor, Your Huddled Masses

From the Torah concept of justice springs a whole list of responsibilities of one person to another.

To begin with, in Hebrew "charity" is called *tzedakah,* which literally means "justice." In Jewish law, giving to those who needed help was not seen as a voluntary response to a loving feeling toward others; it was a legal obligation.[79]

The concept of the tithe—a donation of one-tenth—originates in the Torah, which requires each person (even a beggar) to contribute to the welfare of the poor, sick, widows, orphans and whoever else was needy.[80] This obligation was not limited to the Jewish community, but extended to all righteous strangers.[81]

If the Torah could legislate charity to this extent, it should not surprise us that it would also legislate love. Thus, in the Book of Leviticus, we find this remarkable sentence, which, in today's world, we have come to take for granted: "You shall love your neighbor as yourself."[82]

The Torah then continues, laying out the basic ethics that today are the foundation of all the liberal and democratic principles we cherish. Indeed, Leviticus 19 is possibly the most concise enumeration of just about every major principle of social behavior and social responsibility:

- You shall not deal deceitfully with one another.
- You shall not swear falsely.
- You shall not lie to one another.
- You shall not cheat your fellow.
- You shall not steal.
- You shall not rob.
- You shall not withhold a worker's wages.
- You shall not insult the deaf (which includes inflicting damage verbally).
- You shall not place a stumbling block before the blind (which includes prohibitions against deceiving or tricking others, as well as giving bad advice).
- You shall not be a gossipmonger among your people.
- You shall not hate your neighbor in your heart.
- You shall not take revenge.
- You shall not bear a grudge.
- You shall rise before the aged and show deference to the old.
- You shall love the stranger.[83]

And that's by no means a complete list. In Leviticus, we also find this remarkable prescription: "You shall not stand idly by while your neighbor's blood is shed."[84]

This commandment dictates that when you see a human being in distress, physical or otherwise, you have a *duty* to help him or her—

another unheard-of concept in the ancient world.

While every civilization in human history had legal systems designed to keep individuals from damaging society, Judaism insisted that refraining from doing damage is merely the starting point for decent behavior.

Some half a century before the great civilizations whose legacy we cherish, Jews were already setting a standard higher than the one we have today. Even in modern America we do not have a law that makes it a crime to be a bystander to someone's suffering.[85] Under Jewish law, you couldn't watch—and you had to act. Many people today would say, "I'm a good person. I wouldn't hurt anyone." That's not the Jewish understanding of a good person. A good person can't just be "not bad." A good person can't be neutral. A good person has to actively do good and prevent harm by others. If you are not part of the solution, you are part of the problem.

The idea of social responsibility, incidentally, extends not just to people but to animals and the environment as well. Under Jewish law, you cannot eat until you have fed your animals. You're not allowed to be cruel to animals. You cannot hunt animals for sport. If you see an animal in distress, you must help it. You can't destroy the environment in any way—you can't cut down a fruit tree, not even in time of war. The first environmental and animal rights are, unbelievably, found in the Torah and dating back thirty-three hundred years![86]

In other words, you have to take responsibility for the whole world. Why? Explains Amiel:

The source of Jewish universalism lies in the unity of God. This is the basis of Judaism and the source of the Jewish soul. The unity of God means that not only has "One God created all of us," but "there is but one Father for all of us." (Malachi 2:10)[87]

The Jewish mantra, which all are required to repeat twice each day and to proclaim at the moment of death, is this: *Shema Israel, Adonai Elehainu, Adonai Ehad.* "Hear O Israel, the Lord is Our God, the Lord is One." Dr. Avraham Altmann, the late chief rabbi of Trier, expounds further on the awesome responsibility conveyed by this idea in his essay "The Meaning and Soul of 'Hear O Israel'":

> *If no one else hears the silent cry of the humiliated, the power-less hidden victims, the Jew must hear it; that is the noblest ethical significance of "Hear, O Israel." Through the silent walls of hard prison cells, hear the sighs, Israel; out of the lonely huts of deserted widows and orphans, from the bed of pain of the sick and suffering, from the silently borne anguish of those rejected or denied justice; from the mute looks of the timid and sorrow-laded, from the pale lips of the starving and needy, you as a Jew must hear the cries of pain, without their having to be emitted. The cry of the suffering is the cry of God, calling out from its victims to you. As the Psalmist [Moses] lets God speak: "I am with the oppressed in his suffering." (Psalm 91:15)*[88]

Ample evidence exists that throughout history Jews took this responsibility very seriously. In Rome during the seventeenth century, when Jews were particularly oppressed and confined to a ghetto, there existed thirty benevolent associations in a population of less than five thousand Jews. Even the smallest, poorest ghetto in Europe had a lodging house for indigent strangers, a salaried physician so medical assistance was available to all and a free educational system.[89]

Despite poverty and the pressure of life in the segregated zone of White Russia known as the Pale of Settlement, where all the Russian

Jews were shunted in the nineteenth century, Jewish charitable activities flourished unabated. Some provinces were so poor that more than 20 percent of the residents depended on the largesse of their neighbors to exist, and still money was found to supply poor students with clothes, soldiers with kosher food, the poor with free medical treatment, poor brides with dowries and orphans with technical education.[90]

This pattern of giving continued when the Jews of the Pale began to emigrate to America at the turn of the century. A study of immigrants by Dr. Edmund J. James, president of the University of Illinois, and four associates from Philadelphia, Chicago and New York, reports:

> *Beyond any other nationality, the Jew in America cares for his own and needy. . . . There are practically no Jewish street beggars. . . . And there is a further fact of the utmost significance and consequence, there are practically no American-born Jewish poor.*[91]

Roth, after citing example after example in his *Jewish Contribution to Civilization,* goes so far as to conclude:

> *With this tradition [of charity as justice] in the background it was natural that the Jews should have played a conspicuous part, once they were given the opportunity, in every modern humanitarian movement. Indeed, the western world owes a recognizable part of its charitable organizations and outlook—apart from individual benefactions and personal participation—to Jews.*[92]

CHAPTER 15

Conclusions: Part II

The ideals of social justice, which western
reformers are endeavouring to carry into practice
in our own day, are the ideals taught by
[the Jewish prophets] Isaiah, Amos and Micah,
now become part of the common heritage of mankind.
It would be absurd to claim that the affirmation
of righteousness as a fundamental principle in the
conduct of human affairs is peculiar to the Hebrew:
It is to be found in the teachings of Buddha,
of Confucius, of the Greek philosophers.
These, however, made their protest against superstition
and plea for righteousness, almost simultaneously,
some two hundred years later than Amos and Hosea
had sounded the call . . . in the eighth century B.C.,

and this, according to the traditional view, was nearly
a thousand years after those same ideas
had been proclaimed at Sinai.[93]

Cecil Roth in
The Jewish Contribution to Civilization

I have to follow the above statement with one disclaimer. Just as I did not set out to prove that all human beings of antiquity were evil creatures who went around killing babies, waging war and reveling in bloodsports, I did not set out to prove that the Jews were the perfect role models of our ideals.

The world has seen its share of wicked Jews, while there have been many righteous non-Jews in history. Certainly it's true that the Jews, as a people, have not always lived up to the values of the Torah; indeed, many turned away from their own religion.

But there's no question that the Jews have been the moral giants of human history, and that their ethical vision has served as the model for the rest of humanity.

Thomas Huxley, the nineteenth-century biologist and thinker who described himself as an agnostic and a humanist, remarked on Jewish ideals:

The [Torah] has been the Magna Carta of the poor and of the oppressed; down to the modern times no State has a constitution which the interests of the people are so largely taken into account, in which the duties so much more than the privileges of the rulers are insisted upon, as that drawn up for Israel in Deuteronomy and Leviticus.[94]

To summarize, the real message that the Jews introduced to humanity is that we are each responsible for the world.

It is an idea that initially was confined to the Jews alone, largely because to the societies of the Middle East, these concepts were simply too outlandish. Interestingly, the Greeks were the first to be fascinated by the Torah and ordered it translated into Greek.

So now, we have come to an interesting puzzle:

We have first examined the Greco-Roman society and found it almost totally bereft of the essential human values we uphold today, though to be fair, they were no better or worse than any other ancient society. But we did find in that seemingly barbaric world the first major steps taken by humankind toward true democracy.

We then looked at the Jewish society, a tiny group that, in comparison to the major civilizations, would be but a speck in the world continuum. But we found among the Jews a groundbreaking approach to how human beings, always treating each other as equals, should relate to each other. The very values we consider essential today to making a perfect world originated in the Torah/Hebrew Bible. Yet the Jews seemingly did not believe in democracy.

So how is it that we, who are products of liberal western democracies, have come to accept Jewish values as our own?

The answer is as fascinating as it is complicated. Now we begin to tell the story of the progress of history, which brought us today to this time and place, and which grafted Jewish ideas onto a new vision of democracy such that they pervade the very consciousness of our world.

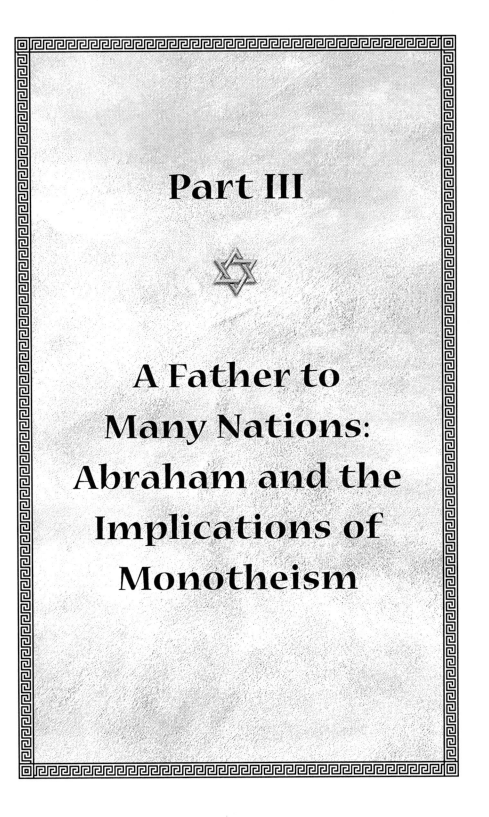

Part III

A Father to Many Nations: Abraham and the Implications of Monotheism

It is not difficult to see how we came to be influenced in so many different respects—art, philosophy, science, law, government—by Greece and Rome. They were the most advanced civilizations of their times. They built vast empires that dominated a large part of the world for centuries. And hand in hand with their physical control over millions of people came a cultural imperialism that exerted tremendous influence over their domains and beyond.

The question of Jewish influence is far more puzzling. The Jews of antiquity never built anything more than a prosperous little kingdom—about the size of Massachusetts—and the major events of Jewish history pale in comparison to the earth-shaking events of the great empires that surrounded this tiny nation.

It is true that following the destruction of Jerusalem by the Romans in 70 C.E., Jews were dispersed throughout the world, and over two thousand years of their exile they came to interact with numerous peoples. But the Jewish role in these interactions was almost always submissive, the role of the victim of unceasing, intense hostility. It is difficult to imagine how such a people, who were so despised by different cultures and so much at the mercy of others, could possibly have been in a position to exert any significant influence on those with whom they interacted, much less inculcate them with the universal values we have defined.

So how did it happen?

CHAPTER 16

Keeping Up with the Morality of the Joneses

The world of antiquity teemed with religions. Everyone believed in the supernatural world inhabited by many divine beings, and it often seemed the more gods the merrier.

Many people in the Western world don't realize that the concept of a secular culture—divorced from any particular religion or belief in a god or gods—is relatively new in history. It is the product of the Enlightenment and first appeared as a major force in Western civilization at the end of the eighteenth century. Prior to that time, religion was a ubiquitous feature of every culture. Since the dawn of civilization (that is, the dawn of written language and city building some six thousand years ago), a huge number of religions have come and gone, comprising a tremendous range of beliefs and practices.

For example, the Mesopotamian religion, as practiced by the Sumerians and Akkadians around 3000 B.C.E., consisted of the worship of humanlike gods with supernatural powers who were said to control natural events. There was Anu, the god of heaven; Ea, the god of water; Enlil, the god of the Earth; Adad, the god of storms; Tammuz, the god of fertility and so forth. An idol, that is a statue of the deity, was dressed, "fed," and waited upon by the collection of priests who comprised his royal court. (Indeed, the mythology of the Middle Eastern people taught that people were created in order to serve the gods and provide them with food.) The will of the gods was deduced by the reading of the entrails of animals that were routinely sacrificed to keep the gods happy.

The Egyptians worshipped gods—some two thousand of them—who were at first thought to reside in the bodies of the animals, but were later humanized. Thereafter, they were often depicted as having a human body but the head of an animal. Hathor, the goddess of love, had a human body but the head of a cow; Amon, the fertility god, had the head of a ram; Ra, the sun god, had the head of a hawk. Amon and Ra were later linked as the supreme god Amon-Ra and identified with Zeus and Jupiter. A massive temple, one of the largest ever built by the Egyptians, was dedicated to this god at El Karnak somewhere between 1570 and 1070 B.C.E. and is a major tourist attraction to this day.

The Babylonians, around 600 B.C.E.—at the time of Nebuchadnezzar and the famed Hanging Gardens, one of the Seven Wonders of the Ancient World—had more than fifty temples dedicated to their various gods. The most acclaimed was the magnificent ziggurat where Marduk, their chief god, was worshipped. Marduk was at first the god of thunderstorms, but later was promoted to the god of Heaven and Earth. Another impressive temple was dedicated to Ishtar, the goddess of fertility and love, whose worship called for prostitution; a Babylonian woman was required to come to Ishtar's temple at least once in her life-time and offer herself to a stranger who would pay for the service.

It suffices to say that eventually, due to Hellenistic influence on Rome, the many gods of Greece and Rome became interchangeable so that Roman Jupiter, god of Heaven and Earth, became identified with the Greek equivalent Zeus; Roman Venus, the goddess of love, beauty and fertility, became identified with Greek Aphrodite; Roman Mars, god of war, with Greek Ares; Roman Minerva, goddess of arts and crafts, with Greek Athena; Roman Neptune, the god of water, with Greek Poseidon.

As diverse as these religions were, they all had one thing in common—they were all polytheistic. And whatever the age, civilization or religion, the polytheistic theology was remarkably similar.

Each major power in nature was viewed as a distinct deity.[1] Therefore, every polytheistic religion had its sun god, moon god, earth god, sea god, fertility god and so forth. Although these gods were all endowed with supernatural powers, they looked and acted suspiciously all too human. They ate, drank, slept, loved, hated, made love and war—just about everything humans did.[2]

The relationship between mortals and the gods was complex. It was perceived that the gods interfered in the affairs of humankind and manipulated people to get what they wanted and needed. But the mortals, through magic and sacrifice, could also manipulate the gods to act on their behalf.[3] Trying to figure out what the gods were up to and how to bribe them for the best possible outcome for oneself weighed heavy on ancient minds.

Polytheistic theology directly affected the ancients' understanding of morality and ethics—that is, what was considered correct or incorrect behavior within a given society. But since every religion had a profusion of gods, there was no absolute source for right or wrong. People might conclude that god X wanted them to do one thing while god Y wanted them to do something else.[4] The correct course of behavior was not based on an absolute standard of right or wrong but rather on each person's perception of the will of the gods, with no small measure of his or her own desires thrown in.

So how did Joe Average decide between the will of god X versus the will of god Y? He looked over the fence at his neighbor—whatever everybody else was doing must be the right thing. What was socially acceptable, i.e., the local custom, was considered morally correct.

The direct connection between ethics and custom in the ancient world is reflected in the vocabulary of Greece and Rome. The word "ethics" is derived from the Greek word *ethos,* meaning "custom." The word "moral" comes from the Latin word *mores,* which means "customs" or "habits."[5]

Customs are social habits that evolve more or less arbitrarily within a community, and they vary tremendously from culture to culture. As people are swayed by the winds of expediency—i.e., by whatever is self-serving and convenient—customs tend to change. Most significantly, they are not based on any absolute standard of correct behavior, but rather on what is accepted among people.

To be sure, throughout history, there arose numerous philosophers—Plato and Marcus Aurelius were two such giants—who devised "objective" ethical systems for the benefit of society. But the impact of their lofty ideas was limited. First of all, their teachings usually reached only a limited group of sophisticated disciples and were not disseminated to the masses. And second, and perhaps more significantly, their teachings didn't carry the weight of a divine commandment behind them. Rather, they were seen as the personal opinions of some smart human authors, and as such could be changed or rejected by others who didn't wholeheartedly agree or who didn't feel like inconveniencing their lives to suit someone else's idealistic vision.[6]

This does not mean that ancient polytheistic civilizations were devoid of morality or justice. They all had systems of laws, often quite detailed, specific and strictly enforced. (For example, Greece's Draconian laws from seventh century B.C.E. have given us a name for harsh justice.) The ancients knew that a society that allows murder, theft and the like will not survive for very long. But what motivated the polytheistic world to devise its codes of moral behavior was logic (i.e., society must be protected) rather than the compulsion to live by an absolute standard of right and wrong.

Now we might ask this: Does it really matter all that much if there is an *absolute* standard?

To answer that question, let's take the example of murder, which was universally outlawed in ancient societies.

In the polytheistic world the logical foundation for prohibiting murder was based on the concept that murder, if not prohibited, is disruptive to society and leads to anarchy. As a consequence of this logic of expedience, an individual could be punished for killing his neighbor. But that same individual could kill his own child—as an act of expediency, i.e., sex selection or population control—without fear of any consequences. Indeed, as was noted earlier, infanticide was a completely acceptable practice in virtually every polytheistic society known. To forbid the murder of a child would require an absolute standard that life is sacred and was decreed such by some absolute authority—say, the Creator of Life.

This distinction between a legal code based on a logical imperative versus an absolute standard has practical implications in virtually every area of law and largely explains the very different and often shocking practices of the ancient world.

In the final analysis then, the combination of trying to figure out what the gods wanted one to do, plus keeping up with the morality of the Joneses, created for the people of antiquity a culture that was essentially ruled by what was "politically correct" at the moment. In today's world, we'd call that kind of culture amoral.

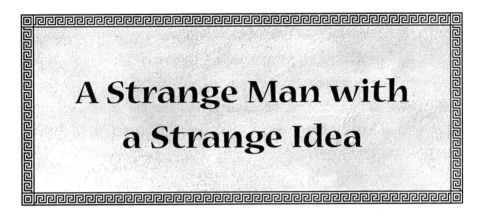

A Strange Man with a Strange Idea

Into just such a world—ancient Mesopotamia at the end of the nineteenth century B.C.E., to be specific—was born an individual whose strange idea would alter history forever. We have come to know this strange man as Abraham, and his idea as monotheism.

What we know about Abraham is confined to a few chapters in the Book of Genesis,[7] to the first book of the Bible, and to the Jewish oral tradition. It is not within the scope of this book to take up various issues of Biblical criticism; suffice it to say that there is much debate on this subject among Biblical scholars. Nevertheless, some three billion Christians, Muslims and Jews accept as part of their theology that monotheism arose at this juncture in history, was confined for a long time to the followers of Abraham who later came to be called Jews, and then finally, over the course of the last two thousand years, was disseminated widely throughout the world.

At the time of Abraham's birth in the city of Ur (which has now been excavated in Iraq), the Mesopotamian civilization was highly sophisticated with its own art and literature, even boasting libraries of clay tablets. Ur was a religious center and home to a number of magnificent ziggurats dedicated to the various Mesopotamian gods.[8]

According to the Midrash, which is part of the Jewish oral tradition, Abraham's father, Terach, was an idol maker by profession, and so Abraham (then called Abram) grew up in an environment steeped in polytheistic beliefs. Yet, even as a boy Abraham came to the conclusion that the statues his father manufactured and sold had no supernatural power. The Midrash relates that young Abraham smashed the idols in his father's shop and then blamed the act on one statue, which he left standing with an ax in its hand. When his furious father shouted that he was a liar because the idol was incapable of any movement or action, young Abraham retorted, "Should not your ears listen to what your mouth is saying?"[9]

Abraham went on to conclude that polytheism was an illusion. Another Midrashic tale illustrates his search for the real thing. First Abraham reasoned that if the Earth was a god, it was not the most powerful because it could not make things grow without rain. But if the rain was a god, surely the sun, which chased rain clouds away, was more powerful. But then the sun had to move over from the sky for the moon, so the moon was more powerful than the sun. But the moon shone only by night. On and on, he tried to deduce which was the supreme power. Finally, by observing the regular rhythm of day and night, of the seasons, and of all natural laws, he concluded that there was a single higher intelligence that was directing the whole show.[10]

But his was not merely a discovery of one God versus many gods. The God of Abraham was radically different from any idea of a god then existing in the ancient world: He was all-powerful, all-knowing, benevolent, infinite and invisible. Since he was infinite, everything was contained within him; there was nothing that he didn't have already. This infinite God was complete and perfect; he did not eat, drink or sleep—in fact, he had no needs whatsoever.[11]

Abraham's conclusions and worship of only one God responsible for all of creation led him to a dialogue with the divine. And thus Abraham came to learn that, unlike the assumptions of his polytheistic neighbors, the infinite being he had discovered required nothing and could not be manipulated by mere mortals. But the one God clearly communicated to Abraham that he desired a relationship with all of his creation and was actively involved in overseeing the affairs of humanity.

Abraham's revelation did not earn him a standing ovation in his day and age.

The average person in the twentieth century would not have any trouble comprehending Abraham's description of one, invisible, benevolent God; today, some three billion people worldwide ascribe to a belief in one God as the basic tenet of their faith. But in his time, Abraham was fighting against a culture that gave rise to a "creation epic" that read in part:

Marduk summoned the great gods to Assembly . . .
Who was it that contrived the uprising?
The Igigi, the great gods, replied to him:
"It was Kingu who contrived the uprising. . . .
They bound him, holding him before Ea.
They imposed on him his guilt,
and severed his blood vessels.
Out of his body they fashioned mankind."[12]

To the Mesopotamians, the God of Abraham must have seemed like a totally insane idea. One invisible God who existed alone, supreme, infinite; the un-created creator of the universe was an alien concept that had no parallel in any other belief system in the world.[13]

So it is no wonder that monotheism encountered significant hostility in ancient times. In addition to being entirely different and incomprehensible, monotheism was also a totally exclusive belief system. Other polytheistic cultures were magnanimously pluralistic—"You worship my god; I'll worship yours." Indeed, it was considered common courtesy for foreigners and heads of state to worship the gods of the countries they visited. Some invaders even made it a practice to "steal" the gods of conquered nations to be held as "hostages" and to be worshipped as well.[14] And, as we saw earlier, blending of gods was also common—for example, the Egyptian Amon was merged with Ra, then was identified with Greek Zeus who, in turn, was identified with Roman Jupiter.

In stark contrast to these practices, Abraham flatly asserted that the worship of any god save the one God was prohibited. In Abraham's eyes, it would be nothing less than the negation of reality.

To be totally different was bad enough, but to try to tell the rest of the world that it was wrong must have seemed outrageous.

And yet that is what Abraham set out to do.

The uniqueness and true greatness of Abraham was *not* that he was the first person on Earth to believe in one God. Indeed, he was not the first. If we take the opening chapters of Genesis literally, then Adam knew only one God and so did his early descendants. We are also told that Noah was a monotheist and Jewish oral tradition maintains that Noah's son Shem (the father of the Semites) carried on his father's tradition.[15] But by the time of the Tower of Babel, that tradition was lost, and

Abraham had to rediscover it for himself. This was certainly a testament to the clarity and independence of his thinking, but Abraham went further. He committed himself to spreading the idea of monotheism in order to build a world whose moral and ethical foundation would spring from the belief in an all-powerful, just and loving God.

Along with his commitment came a vision, a mission—which he passed on to his son Isaac, who passed it on to his son Jacob, who passed it on to his twelve sons, the twelve tribes of Israel. The mission of Abraham's descendants was to bring the concept of one God into the consciousness of all humanity and along with it a universal, absolute, divinely given standard of morality, a standard that we have come to call "ethical monotheism."

This ethical monotheism that started out as the mission of one lone individual almost four thousand years ago was destined to become one of the most influential and powerful ideas in human history.

As Ronald Green concludes in *Religion and Moral Reason*:

When all prescriptions for human life are traced to God's will, morality obtains enormous authority. . . . When the moral law is objectified as expressing God's will, the law ceases to be subject to any of the reasoned criticism provoked by regarding it as an instrument of human reason alone.[16]

CHAPTER 18

One for All and All for One

So how did we get from Abraham to the modern worldview that cherishes his ideas? Let us follow history and see.

From the time of Abraham to the time of his grandson Jacob and Jacob's twelve sons, who were the progenitors of the twelve tribes of Israel, the story of monotheism is essentially a story of a family.

By the end of the book of Genesis,[17] we learn that a famine hits the area where Jacob is living (near Hebron in modern Israel), and the family migrates to Egypt. Coincidentally, Jacob's son Joseph attained there a high position as grand vizier to the pharaoh and is in charge of grain distribution. Joseph settles the clan in the land of Goshen, on the eastern delta of the Nile River. At that time they number "seventy souls."[18] They are not a large group of people by any means, certainly not large enough to make a dent in the picture of the world.

Yet, they are an unusual, highly productive people, and they prosper dramatically in Egypt, as the Bible recounts in the Book of Exodus. All that prosperity, the Jewish oral tradition tells us, makes them forget the mission of Abraham, Isaac and Jacob as they begin to take on Egyptian ways and worship Egyptian gods.[19]

Despite their efforts to act as loyal citizens of Egypt, Pharaoh begins to perceive them as a threat—a group of foreigners whose loyalty lies in question should war with the Assyrians or the Hittites break out—and he takes steps to enslave them. Thus, they are forced to build the cities of Pithom and Ramses, amid much ill-treatment and oppression, which includes, at one point, the drowning of all newborn Israelite boys.[20]

This is, of course, the place where the famous story of Moses comes in. He is the Israelite baby saved from drowning by the ingenuity of his mother, who floats him on the Nile in a basket, and by the kindness of Pharaoh's daughter, who fishes out the basket and adopts the baby. Brought up as a prince in Pharaoh's palace, Moses leaves his life of luxury one day and witnesses the suffering of his brother slaves. Seeing an Israelite beaten by an Egyptian overseer, he kills the Egyptian and then flees for his own life.[21]

Skip ahead sixty years, and Moses, who has been leading the life of a shepherd for all this time, now has a startling encounter with the burning bush from which a voice speaks to him:

> *Do not come closer. Remove your sandals from your feet, for the place on which you stand is holy ground. I am . . . the God of your father, the God of Abraham, the God of Isaac, and the God of Jacob.*[22]

God commands the reluctant Moses to return to Egypt to lead his people out of slavery to the Promised Land so they may continue the mission undertaken by their ancestors.

All this we know from the Bible; Egyptian records on this score are mum,[23] though the ruins of the cities of Pithom and Ramses still stand in silent testimony to the slave hands that built them. There is also a record—a painting in a rock tomb west of the royal city of Thebes, depicting slaves at work, described by Werner Keller in *The Bible As History:*

> *The detail shows the manufacture of Egyptian bricks, the most notable features being the light-skinned workmen, who are clad only in linen aprons. A comparison with the dark-skinned overseers shows that the fair-skinned men are probably Semites, but certainly not Egyptians. . . . The picture is an impressive illustration of the Biblical words: "And the Egyptians made the children of Israel to serve with rigour, and they made their lives bitter with hard bondage in mortar and bricks." (Exodus 1:13–14)[24]*

After living in Egypt for 210 years, 116 of them as slaves, the Israelites, now numbering 603,550 men and an untold number of women and children, are led out by Moses.[25] They are no longer a family—they are a nation.

They will bear witness forever to their miraculous escape from slavery. The story of the ten plagues that broke the resolve of Pharaoh to keep them will be retold over and over to graphically illustrate to the polytheistic world—which believed every force in nature to have its own god—that the one God has complete mastery over all creation.

This story they will retell every year at Passover for thousands of years, obeying the commandment to do so: "Remember this day, on which you went free from Egypt, the house of bondage, how the Lord freed you from it with a mighty hand."[26] Other commandments will also be linked to it:

- "You shall have no other gods besides Me . . . [for] I am the Lord, your God who brought you out of the land of Egypt, the house of bondage."[27]
- "You shall not oppress a stranger, for you know the feelings of the stranger, having yourselves been strangers in the land of Egypt."[28]
- "You shall love the stranger as yourself, because you were strangers in the land of Egypt."[29]

The giving of these commandments—as well as the famous Ten Commandments—takes place shortly after the miraculous crossing of the Reed/Red Sea, which parted to allow the Israelites to flee the Egyptian army in hot pursuit. The Egyptian forces, caught by returning waves, drown, and the Israelites break into a song of gratitude for their miraculous escape to freedom.

Interestingly, although they were enslaved by Egypt and the forces that pursued them to the Reed Sea were bent on revenge, the Israelites were prohibited by a specific Torah commandment from hating the Egyptians. To this day, Jews spill a little wine during the Passover Seder to signify that pleasure at the celebration is diminished by the remembrance of the death of these human beings, even if they were the enemy.[30]

Having escaped the Egyptians, the Israelites arrive at Mount Sinai and are told to prepare for an encounter with God. What God intends has already been communicated to them through Moses:

"You saw what I [God] did to Egypt and how I carried you on wings of eagles and brought you to Me. And now if you listen diligently to My voice, and preserve My covenant, you shall be My special treasure among all the peoples, for all the Earth is Mine.

You shall be to Me a kingdom of priests and a holy nation."... And
they had replied: "All that the Lord has spoken we will do." [31]

But the climactic event is yet to come. The Bible sets the stage for the
momentous event when a nation of escaped slaves will encounter the
Creator of the Universe:

> *On the third day, as morning dawned, there was thunder and*
> *lightning, and a dense cloud upon the mountain, and a very loud*
> *blast of the horn; and all the people who were in the camp*
> *trembled. Moses led the people out of the camp toward God, and*
> *they took their places at the foot of the mountain.* [32]

What happens next is related as a unique event in human history—a
revelation to all those present. Every man, woman and child heard the
voice of God.

At that moment they were transformed into a nation with a mission.
They recommitted to the task undertaken by Abraham and reconfirmed
the covenant Abraham had made. They did so by stating, *"Naseh*
v'nishma," literally meaning "We will do and we will hear." [33] The
acceptance was unconditional.

The Bible relates that like Abraham—whom God didn't randomly
elect to be his messenger but only assigned him the task once Abraham
discovered God for himself—so too the Israelites chose God and took
upon themselves the responsibility to change the world. And thus they
became "God's chosen people," but the more accurate description would
be "the people who chose God." [34]

In their tradition and writings, they will see this not so much a privilege as a responsibility—a national obligation of what the prophet

Isaiah would later call being "a light unto the nations."[35] By their covenant, they have become a people dedicated to the responsibility of creating a just and moral society based on the idea of one God, whose qualities they are to emulate—"Just as He [God] is merciful, so too shall you be merciful. Just as He is compassionate, so too shall you be compassionate."[36] This society, in turn, served as the model for the rest of humanity.[37]

In his classic comparative study, *The Religions of Man*, Huston Smith remarks on the uniqueness of this "gift" the Jews brought from Mount Sinai to the world:

> *It is here that we come to the supreme achievement of Jewish thought; not in its monotheism as such, but in the character it ascribed to the God it discovered to be One. The Greeks, the Romans, the Syrians, and most of the Mediterranean peoples would have said two things about their gods' characters. First, the gods tend to be amoral; second, toward man they are preponderantly indifferent. The Jews reversed the thinking of their contemporaries on both points. Whereas the gods of Olympus tirelessly pursue beautiful women, the God of Sinai watches over widows and orphans. While Mesopotamia's Anu and Bannan's El were going their aloof ways, [the God of Sinai] is speaking the name of Abraham, lifting his people out of slavery, and seeking his lonely, heart-sick exiles in Babylon. God is a God of righteousness whose loving kindness is from everlasting to everlasting and whose tender mercies are over all his works.[38]*

As they set off on this mission, the Israelites are promised a land of their own—henceforth, the Promised Land—where they will be able to create this model society. But, a year later, when they stand poised on the border, astonishingly, they balk at entering it. Their reluctance—which is seen as the sin of not trusting sufficiently in God—is punished with forty years of wandering in the desert.[39] When the Israelites are finally allowed to enter the Promised Land, they are told that as further punishment they now must fight to possess it. That is the only time that conquest is commanded—to settle the land within specifically delineated borders.

The way this happens is described in the Bible and contains numerous lessons for humankind.

First, when they finally enter the land of Israel, it is said that the waters of the Jordan River parted to allow them entry and the walls of the city of Jericho fell down when they blew their trumpets. At this juncture they are commanded by God to take the city and burn it down, but they are forbidden to take any booty or any object belonging to the former inhabitants.[40]

They do just that, but unbeknownst to the others, one person, Achan, steals some items.

The Israelites move on to the next city they had been commanded to conquer, the city of Ai, and meet there with a terrible defeat with many of their number killed. Traumatized by the experience, they plead to know why God had abandoned them and quickly learn the terrible truth. Once Achan's crime is uncovered—and he is sentenced to death for it—the rest of the conquest proceeds smoothly.[41]

The fascinating point here is that the Bible seems to be saying that obedience to God's commands is paramount and that in God's mind—at least as far as the Jews are concerned—it is all for one and one for all.

As an outgrowth of that lesson, Judaism teaches[42] collective responsibility as well as individual responsibility—no person is an island, and each person exists as part of the whole and is responsible for the actions of others as well as his or her own.[43]

Despite many difficulties the Israelites do finally lay claim to the Promised Land, but their life there is far from calm. The Bible relates that they had only themselves to blame:

> *And the children of Israel did that which was evil in the eyes of the Lord . . . and the anger of the Lord was kindled against Israel and he delivered them into the hands of spoilers . . . and he gave them over into the hands of their enemies.*[44]

The highly self-critical nature of the above description is typical of other passages that make the Hebrew Bible a unique document—a holy book of a people, but also one that relates the sinful history of this people. It has been said that if the Hebrew Bible had not been written by God, it surely would have been written by anti-Semites. As Sivan observes:

> *Biblical heroes and heroines . . . are depicted as they are, with their virtues and their human failings. . . . This ethically uncom-promising aspect of the scriptural narrative particularly impressed the Anglo-Jewish writer Israel Zangwill: "The Bible is an anti-Semitic book. Israel is the villain not the hero in his own story." Alone among epics, it is out for truth, not high heroics.*[45]

During this period when the Israelites are trying to hold onto the Promised Land, they have no central government. Basically, every individual has taken upon himself or herself the responsibility for correct ethical behavior as spelled out by the Torah, and when the need arises and the nation faces an external threat, judges are appointed to lead the people through the crisis. This is why this time in Jewish history is known as the Period of Judges:

*And the Lord raised up judges and they saved them [the Israelites]
from the hands of those who had spoiled them.*[46]

One of the first of those judges was Deborah (previously mentioned in
Part II). She was famous for sitting under a palm tree where anyone
could seek her advice, and she could issue battle orders. Barak, Israel's
top warrior during that time, refused to go into battle without her.
Together they led the troops against the much larger Canaanite force that
was backed up by nine hundred iron chariots, while Israel had none.
Barak was doubtful that Israel's warriors could ever beat such a strong
opponent, but Deborah stood firm. Suddenly, an unexpected storm was
unleashed in the heavens, the resulting downpour turned the ground to
mud, the iron chariots got stuck and the Canaanites panicked. Deborah's
prophecy that "This is the day on which the Lord will deliver Sisera into
your hands" was thus fulfilled.[47]

Some other famous judges were:

- Gideon, who led the Israelites to victory over Midianite invaders in
  an impossible fight that pitted the huge Midianite force against a
  miniscule group of Israelites.[48]
- Samson, famous for his superhero strength, who led the struggle
  against Israel's archenemy, the Philistines, before being snared by
  Delilah, a scheming Philistine woman who cut off his hair after
  learning that it was the secret of his strength.[49]
- Samuel, the prophet and the last of the judges, who is also famous
  for anointing the first two kings of Israel, Saul and David.[50]

After Samuel ceased to function as a judge, and his sons took over for
him, the Israelites became dissatisfied with the system. In the ninth

century B.C.E., they decided that it was time they too had strong central leadership, so they entered a period of monarchy—although, as noted earlier, it was a much more complicated system of checks and balances involving the king, the high priest and the Sanhedrin, the supreme court (not to mention a few dynamic and charismatic prophets who appeared on the scene to add spice to the mixture).[51]

Saul, the first king, was an able warrior, but his reign was marred by his inability to stand up to his subjects, who, it must be remembered, did not have a tradition of relating to kings as if they were gods. Saul was followed by David, who was considered one of the greatest personalities in Jewish history.

It was David who—after slaying Goliath in the famous story—finally completed the conquest of the Promised Land by capturing the last remaining non-Jewish city. The year was circa 1000 B.C.E. and the city was, of course, Jerusalem—the city of peace—which David made the capital of the land.

There, on a hill overlooking the city, the site on which Abraham had offered to sacrifice his son Isaac, David's son, King Solomon, built the famed Temple, a magnificent structure admired all over the world. (Today, this is the site of Islam's Dome of the Rock.)

David and Solomon are both viewed as ideal examples of leadership—wise, humble, just and pious. And it is during their reigns, but particularly that of Solomon, that the Jewish people came the closest to achieving their goal of a model civilization. For forty years, peace and prosperity reigned, and kings and scholars came to Israel from around the world to hear "the wisdom of Solomon."[52]

One of those who came on a much-celebrated visit was the Queen of Sheba,[53] who wished to test the king with her most difficult questions.

What was she so curious about? The oral tradition[54] relates that she had come armed with sexually provocative riddles, one of which went like this: "A woman said to her son, 'Your father is my father, your grandfather is my husband, you are my son, and I am your sister, who am I?'" King Solomon promptly answered, "A daughter of Lot." (Lot's daughter slept with her father in order to repopulate the world after the destruction of Sodom and Gomorrah.) The queen went home highly impressed with the king and his kingdom.[55]

But this utopia would not last.

In King Solomon's day, we already see the first problems creeping up with the many wives (some say seven hundred) of Solomon who begin to worship idols. The Bible ends Solomon's story by relating that God was angry with him and told him:

> *Since you are guilty of this, and you have not kept My covenant and My laws . . . I will tear the kingdom away from you. . . . But I will not do this in your time, for the sake of your father David. Instead, I will tear it away from your son. . . . I will give your son one tribe for the sake of My servant David, and for the sake of Jerusalem, which I have chosen.*[56]

After Solomon's death, his son Rehoboam proved to be a weak leader whose poor decisions contributed to the disastrous split of ten tribes away from the nation. Thus in the year 933 B.C.E., the country was divided into two states—the Ten Tribes in the north (Israel) and the rest in the south around Jerusalem (Judea).

The northern state quickly began to lapse into idolatry. One of the stories that the Bible relates from this time is the sad tale of King Ahab and his pagan wife, Jezebel, the daughter of the Phoenician king of

Sidon: "There never was anyone like Ahab, who committed himself to doing what was displeasing to the Lord, at the instigation of his wife, Jezebel."[57]

Ahab covets the beautiful vineyard of his neighbor Navot, but as a Jewish king he cannot just take what he wants. So, to help him obtain it, Jezebel volunteers to frame poor Navot for treason. After the neighbor is unjustly accused and executed, Ahab gets the land, by then having violated the commandments against bearing false witness, stealing and murder.

Next, Jezebel brings into Israel hundreds of pagan priests, institutes worship to the god Baal and tries by various other means to outlaw Judaism. At this juncture, she confronts the prophet Elijah, who through an amazing miracle—where fire comes down from heaven and consumes not only a sacrificial offering but the stone altar as well—demonstrates the power of the one God.[58]

The prophet's efforts are not enough, however, and although the people momentarily repent, it is too little, too late. The northern state survives only until 722 B.C.E., when it is attacked and destroyed by invading Assyrians. The Ten Tribes are exiled by the invaders and scattered to other parts of the world, hence historians and Bible scholars speak of the Ten Lost Tribes of Israel. No record remains as to what happened to them, although it is likely that most were assimilated into other cultures.[59]

The southern state, despite the woeful leadership of Rehoboam, did better, retaining a greater loyalty to God's law. Although it was small and the overpowering presence of Assyria certainly gave cause for alarm, nevertheless Judea managed to attain a period of prosperity during the reign of King Hezekiah (716–687 B.C.E.). Stressing return to obedience of God's law, Hezekiah also beefed up the country's defenses, reinforced the walls of Jerusalem and had a tunnel dug to provide a protected water source to the city. (The hand-hewn tunnel has been preserved to this day and is a tourist attraction in Jerusalem.) When the Assyrians attacked, he was ready. He refused to surrender the city to the mighty empire that had just swallowed up the Ten Tribes, believing that God would protect his people. Indeed, the Assyrians laying siege were smitten by a sudden plague and fled home in panic.[60]

One of the more fascinating personalities of this time was the prophet Isaiah, who has probably been quoted more often than other Jewish prophets largely because of his messianic visions. In one of them he saw God's presence fill the Earth, while six-winged angels proclaimed "Holy, holy, holy! The Lord of Hosts!"[61] In another, he described a time when "nation shall not lift up sword against nation, neither shall they know war anymore."[62] He also predicted that the Jews will be "a light unto the nations"[63] and that in this role they will be a suffering and despised "servant of God."[64]

Following Hezekiah and Isaiah, Judea's fortune changed for the worse in large measure due to the efforts of the next monarch, Manasseh, the son of Hezekiah, who seemingly set out to undo the good work of his father. The Bible describes him as an evil man: "Manasseh put so many innocent persons to death that he filled Jerusalem [with blood] from end to end."[65] He rebuilt pagan temples and even put an idol in the Temple of Jerusalem. Under his banner, the people began to slip into idolatry. Although the next king, Josiah, tried to bring them back to the worship of the one God, his reforms did not have a lasting effect.

The people of Judea were clearly straying from the path of righteousness, and proof of God's growing wrath comes in 586 B.C.E.

when King Nebuchadnezzar (famous for building "the Hanging Gardens of Babylon") attacked Jerusalem and—on the ninth day of the Hebrew month of Av—destroyed Solomon's beautiful Temple and with it the Jews' visible connection to their God.[66]

Thus begins the first Jewish exile from the Promised Land—known as the Babylonian exile—a painful period in Jewish history that gave rise to this famous Psalm:

> *By the rivers of Babylon,*
> *there we sat and wept*
> *when we remembered Zion. . . .*
> *For there our captors demanded of us words of song,*
> *and our tormentors asked of us with mirth:*
> *"Sing to us from the song of Zion."*
> *How shall we sing the song of Adonai on alien soil?*
> *If I ever forget you, Jerusalem,*
> *May my right hand wither.*[67]

Under any normal circumstances, the destruction of a country and the exile of the population would spell the end of any nation.[68] But one of the most fascinating aspects of Jewish history is the Jewish people's seemingly supernatural ability to beat all the odds and out-survive everyone, even the great empires that conquered them. Many historians have remarked on this phenomenon, and even Mark Twain puzzled about it:

> *If the statistics are right, the Jews constitute but one quarter of one percent of the human race. It suggests a nebulous dim puff of star dust lost in the blaze of the Milky Way. Properly, the Jew ought hardly to be heard of; but he is heard of, has always been heard of.*

He is as prominent on the planet as any other people, and his importance is extravagantly out of proportion to the smallness of his bulk. . . . He has made a marvelous fight in this world in all ages; and has done it with his hands tied behind him. He could be vain of himself and be excused for it. The Egyptians, the Babylonians and the Persians rose, filled the planet with sound and splendour; then faded to dream-stuff and passed away; the Greeks and the Romans followed and made a vast noise, and they are gone; other peoples have sprung up and held their torch high for a time but it burned out, and they sit in twilight now, or have vanished. The Jew saw them all, survived them all, and is now what he always was, exhibiting no decadence, no infirmities of age; no weakening of his parts, no slowing of his energies, no dulling of his alert and aggressive mind. All things are mortal but the Jew; all other forces pass, but he remains. What is the secret of his immortality?[69]

Part of the secret of Jewish survival is that when the Jewish people arrived en masse in Babylon, rather than assimilating into the conqueror's culture, they established a strong community of their own, maintaining their customs, their traditions and, most importantly, their religion. Not long after, in 539 B.C.E., the Babylonians were themselves conquered by the Persians. The Persian king Cyrus offered the Jews an opportunity to return to their homeland. But, surprisingly, only about forty thousand took up his offer. The rest, having settled comfortably in Babylon, preferred to wait out the tumultuous times to see what would happen next.

But that proved to be a mistake. After the death of Cyrus, an army coup placed a dubious monarch on the throne of Persia, a certain

Ahasuerus, who promptly murdered his wife and selected his new queen through a beauty contest.

This, of course, is the famous story of the Biblical Book of Esther, which tells how a Jewish girl living incognito became the queen of Persia and saved her people from annihilation. The drama began when the king's minister, Haman, decided to exterminate the Jews living in Persia. A descendant of the Amalekites, who had been the archenemies of the Jews since Sinai,[70] Haman wanted revenge because one of the leaders of the Jewish community in Babylon, a certain Mordechai, wounded his pride by refusing to bow to him. Soon enough, a royal decree ordering the genocide of the Jews was issued. Mordechai, who unbeknownst to anyone was Esther's uncle, learned of the plot and told his niece that, as the queen, she must do something to stop it. But anything she did might reveal that she was Jewish and get her killed as well. Nevertheless, Mordechai beseeched Esther with this odd plea: "If you keep silent in this crisis, relief and deliverance will come to the Jews from another quarter."[71]

From this we can discern the Jewish view of the interaction of fate and free will. Judaism holds that there is a divine plan and a divine order to how the world is run. God had promised the Jews an eternal covenant, and he will always deliver. But within the great drama of life, human beings have free will to choose their roles—whether to play the part of the hero, the villain, the bystander or the victim.

Esther, of course, chose to play the part of the hero, and the story has a happy ending—Haman was hanged for his evil plot and the Jews were saved.[72] Not surprisingly, the near catastrophe motivates more Jews to return to the land of Israel, where the rebuilding of the Temple has not been very successful due to the interference of the neighboring

Samaritans. However, as in the time of judges, there arose a charismatic prophet, this one named Ezra,[73] under whose ironfisted leadership an Israelite nation again began to take shape.

Among the most dramatic events of the period under Ezra's leadership was a mass gathering on Rosh Hashana, the Jewish New Year, when the Torah was read. Shockingly, the holy word had to be translated into Aramaic since so many of the exiles could no longer understand Hebrew. As Ezra read, the people wept, realizing how much of God's law they had forgotten and violated.[74] However, the day ended in celebration as they recommitted to obey all the commandments and to establish a nation dedicated to the mission their ancestors undertook at Mount Sinai. Little did they know how soon their commitment would be put to the test.

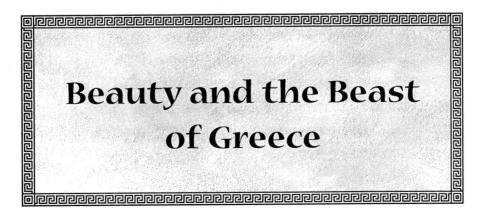

Beauty and the Beast of Greece

By the year 516 B.C.E.,[75] the rebuilding of the destroyed Temple in Jerusalem was finished. It was not as magnificent as the Temple of Solomon, but its completion was a major moment in Jewish history, the dawning of Israel's Second Commonwealth.

All this was possible, in large part, because Darius, the Persian king who followed Ahasuerus, pursued a policy of multicultural tolerance, allowing the Jews to observe their odd religion in relative peace.[76] Jewish historian Berel Wein writes of the Persian attitude in *Echoes of Glory:*

> *The Persians normally were not interested in building a "melting pot" empire. They saw themselves as rulers of a vast and universal empire that would politically and economically unite the world under their hegemony, yet allow individuals freedom of person and belief, and enable cultures to maintain their own societal norms. In this, they presaged many important ideas of the modern, democratic world.[77]*

But the Jews were not to be left alone for long. By 334 B.C.E., Alexander the Great had begun his campaign of world conquest and within two years arrived in the Middle East on his way to destroy his archenemies, the Persians. He peacefully absorbed the recently reestablished nation of Israel into his ever-expanding Greek empire and proceeded into the heart of the Persian empire and beyond.

In his wake came a culture invasion, probably unsurpassed in human history, as Greek colonists poured into the newly acquired lands, bringing their worldview and their philosophical ideas with them. As it happened, Hellenism conquered minds much more effectively than Alexander or any invader could conquer lands. Its influence would continue to be felt long after the breakup of the Greek Empire and its absorption into the Roman Empire.

For the Jews, the arrival of the Greeks represented a major turning point in Jewish history. For the first time in their existence, the Jews came face to face with a non-Semitic culture unlike any they had ever seen before—a culture that dazzled. (We could compare the influence of Hellenism to the influence of American pop culture, which also has dazzled—or as some might say, invaded—the world, most recently even mainland China and Japan, with its movies and rock music, clothes and fast food.)

There is no doubt that the Greeks intrigued the Jews. And it is easy to see why. The Greeks spoke an intricate, precise language that sounded beautiful to Hebrew ears. (Greek is spoken of highly by many rabbis who decreed it to be the only language, other than Hebrew, in which a Torah scroll could be written.[78]) They were intellectual, literate and creative. More importantly, the Greeks, like the Hebrews, had a strong philosophical tradition that valued knowledge and sought to understand the essence of existence. Yet despite these and other superficial similarities, there were many more points of profound ideological difference between the Greek and the Jewish worldviews:

- To the Greeks what was beautiful was holy; to the Jews what was holy was beautiful.
- The Greek envisioned their gods in the image of man. The Jews believed the reverse—man had been created in the image of God.
- The Greeks, being polytheists, had their own pantheon of gods and were open to including others. The Jews demanded exclusive worship of the one God.
- At the most basic level, the Greeks put man first. The Jews, by the very nature of their existence, put God first.

Greek morality was based on the rational perceptions of the human mind, and as such was subjective and malleable. Furthermore, Greek morality had nothing to do with religion; the gods of Greek mythology were not concerned with moral issues, such as what was good or what was evil.

Jewish morality was seen as emanating from a supernatural source beyond the world of man and as such was objective and unchangeable; adaptations to new conditions had to be in total agreement with the Torah, the law as laid down by God.

To the Greek mind, this made no sense.

Writing of the Jewish idea of the one God, Aristotle sounds totally puzzled: "It would sound odd for a man to say that he loved a god." [79]

Plato, his mentor, had declared his misgivings earlier: "The maker and father of all, it is difficult to discover and when found, it is impossible to declare him to all men." [80]

It is not that the Jewish God was outside the realm of Greek comprehension, but rather that the Jewish concept of God ran contrary to

Greeks' very understanding of the nature of the universe. The Greeks believed[81] strongly in the concept that perfection was found in those objects and ideas that were permanent, static and immutable. To them, the ideas of movement and change were signs of imperfection and therefore weakness and inferiority. It was not the concept of one Infinite Being that bothered the Greeks, but rather the fact that this perfect Being created an imperfect world and continually interacted with it.

These key differences in philosophical outlook almost immediately pitted the Jews against the Greeks, though outright hostility was not evident at first. There was considerable trade and exchange of creative dialogue between the two groups. (Indeed, Ptolemy II, who ruled in the third century B.C.E., was so curious about the Torah, he insisted it be translated into Greek; it was the very first translation to be commissioned from the original Hebrew, and it has come down today as the *Septuagint,* named so after the legendary seventy scholars who created it.[82]) But, for the most part, the distinct nature of Jewish belief and practice set up barriers that made friendship and socializing difficult and engendered other problems as well.

Jewish dietary laws held that only certain animals and fishes were permitted as food. Further, animals whose meat was to be consumed had to be slaughtered in a proscribed, painless fashion. And, if that wasn't enough, meat and dairy foods had to be separated, cooked in separate vessels and served with separate utensils, all of which generally prevented the Jews from eating with foreigners; drinking wine with non-Jews was completely forbidden.[83]

But there was more. Jewish Sabbath observance required the total cessation of all work for one day, which was to be dedicated to prayer and contemplation.

The food laws seemed to the Greeks like arrogance, the idea of a Sabbath like laziness. (No one had heard of a weekend back then.) Furthermore, the Greeks revered the perfection of the human body and saw the Jewish practice of circumcision as barbaric mutilation. Greek social and cultural life revolved around the gymnasium and theater, which the Jews for the most part viewed as centers of immorality and decadence. This Jewish rejection of the basic Greek institutions was seen as an unforgivable slap in the face.

In the final analysis, the Jews and their lifestyle were so bizarre, so different from anything the Greeks had encountered previously, as to arouse suspicion, anger and eventual hatred.

Be that as it may, the Greeks penetrated deeply into Jewish social structure. Greek colonists settled in Israel, and their influence was strongly felt in many areas of life. As envoys of the ruling regime, they ran the show. To do business with them, you had to meet them at least halfway. And many Jews did. Soon, Greek was widely spoken among the Jewish population, and Greek philosophy, culture and aesthetics were making a mark on the local inhabitants. Some Jews, mostly from the upper strata of society, even became Hellenized and assimilated into Greek culture. These Jews adopted Greek names and dress, dropped the Sabbath observance and dietary restrictions, and involved themselves in Greek culture and sports, some even undergoing operations to reverse their circumcisions.

The Hellenization/assimilation phenomenon led to a societal division in Israel. The majority of the population was loyal to Judaism and Jewish observance and backed the rabbis. A Hellenized minority sided with the gentile population of Greeks and other foreigners.

Inner conflict among Jews did not help to improve Greek and Jewish relations overall. Rather, it drove traditional Jews to reject Hellenistic influences even more vehemently. And rejection was something the Greeks could not abide.

The Greeks had a strong sense of destiny and believed that their culture was ordained to become the universal culture of humanity. The Jews had a different vision. The Jews believed that a world united in the belief in one God and ascribing to one absolute standard of moral values was the ultimate future of the human race. This Jewish ideology was wedded to an extreme, uncompromising exclusivity of worship (as demanded by the belief in one God) and a complete intolerance of polytheistic religious beliefs or practices. There was only one God and so only one God could be worshipped—end of story.

Unlike other cultures that had been easily absorbed into the Hellenistic world, Judaism, with its intractable beliefs and bizarre practices, stood as an open challenge to the concept of Hellenistic world supremacy. For the generally tolerant Greeks, this challenge became more and more intolerable.[84] It was only a matter of time before open conflict occurred.

The initial period of the Greek occupation of Israel was for the most part stable and peaceful. The Greek authorities preserved the rights of the local Jewish population and did not attempt to interfere with Jewish religious practice. The Jews continued to flourish as a separate and distinct entity for 165 years—a rare phenomenon in the Hellenistic world. The vast majority of the peoples conquered by Alexander the Greek had willingly allowed themselves to be Hellenized. The fact that the Jews—with the exception of a small minority—rejected Hellenism was a strong testament to that ever-present Jewish drive and sense of mission. Grant, in his *From Alexander to Cleopatra,* explains:

The Jews proved not only unassimilated, but unassimilable, and
. . . the demonstration that this was so proved one of the most sig-
nificant turning-points in Greek history, owing to the gigantic
influence exerted throughout subsequent ages by their religion,
which not only survived intact, but subsequently gave birth to
Christianity as well.[85]

The period of relative calm and stability ended around 170 B.C.E., during the reign of the Antiochus Epiphanes. At this time, the Greek Empire
was split into three: Seleucid (Syrian Greece, where Antiochus ruled);
Ptolemaic (Egyptian Greece); and Macedonia (which also largely controlled Greece proper, the independent city-states). Each segment vied
for supreme power. Seeing his throne threatened by both the Ptolemies
and the emerging Roman power, Antiochus sought to solidify his control
over the Greek Empire by accelerating the pace of Hellenization of the
local populations. Israel, which represented the southern buffer between
his territory and Egypt, became a major priority in the campaign of
forced conversion to the Greek way of life. Antiochus, no doubt, found
the continued Jewish rejection of Greek culture to be not only insulting,
but worrisome—the Jews could easily prove a subversive element in the
event of war.

Between 169 and 167 B.C.E., Antiochus took deliberate steps to
Hellenize the Jews of Israel by attempting to destroy Judaism. In this, he
was aided by Hellenized Jews, foremost among them a man named
Menelaus whom he appointed as high priest, but whom he did not wholly
trust.[86] Therefore, Apollonius, a Syrian general, was dispatched to
Jerusalem with a large army to make sure the job got done.

Decrees were posted announcing that all Jewish laws were henceforth banned, and observance of the Sabbath, Jewish festivals, dietary laws and even the practice of circumcision were punishable by death. Study of Torah was forbidden, and all Biblical scrolls sacred to the Jews were to be collected and burned; Antiochus even sacrificed swine over sacred Jewish books.[87] Indeed, Antiochus seemed obsessed by swine, knowing that this animal was particularly repugnant to the Jews; he forced the high priest to institute swine sacrifices in the Holy Temple in Jerusalem and also to allow worship there of a whole array of Greek gods.

Jews resisted, of course, so Apollonius and Menelaus went about driving the point home in a crude and cruel fashion. Wein relates how the unholy duo went about it:

> *Women who allowed their sons to be circumcised were killed with their sons tied around their necks. The scholars of Israel were hounded, hunted down and killed. Jews who refused to eat pork or sacrifice hogs were tortured to death. . . . Even the smallest hamlet in Judah was not safe from the oppression of the Hellenists. The altars to Zeus and other pagan deities were erected in every village, and Jews of every area were forced to participate in the sacrificial services.*[88]

All this was nothing less than a declaration of war, and war is what Antiochus got.

That the Hellenized Jews supported such acts against their fellows was particularly painful to the mainstream Jews who saw that armed resistance was the only way—not only to throw off the yoke of the oppressor, but also to save the weaker members of Jewish society from the corrupting pagan influence.

Resistance formed around the leadership of the priest Mattathias and his five sons, who later became known as the Hasmoneans or Maccabees, meaning "hammers" in Greek.[89] Echoing the cry of Moses when he saw some Jews worshipping the golden calf at the foot of Mount Sinai— "Whoever is for God, let him come to me!"—Mattathias rallied around himself a guerilla army estimated at six thousand to ten thousand men. This small but fierce group, short on weapons but armed with plenty of raw valor, took on the technologically superior, elephant-equipped Greek force of forty thousand men and—unbelievably—won.[90]

In a series of battles over a period of three years, the Greeks were defeated and driven out of much of the country. On the twenty-fourth of the Hebrew month of Kislev in 165 B.C.E., Jerusalem was recaptured, the Temple purified and rededicated to the one God of the Jews. Today, the holiday of Hanukkah commemorates the victory of the Maccabees, which for the Jews was not so much a military as a spiritual triumph of Judaism over pagan Greek culture.

The Maccabean revolt proved to be far more than a war of mutual liberation—it became a major event in the history of monotheism. Not only was the religious nature of the conflict unique—indeed, this war between the Greeks and the Jews was the first purely religious/ideological war in recorded history—it also marked a turning point in the relationship between the Jews and the rest of the world.

Nearly seventeen hundred years had passed since the time of Abraham. Over the years, the Jews and their strange belief in the One God were largely ignored by the polytheistic cultures around them. While Israel experienced attacks by the Philistines, Babylonians and Assyrians, none of the invaders tried to annihilate the Jews *because* of their faith. It is true, of course, that the Jews had been the objects of mistrust, even scorn, but their religion was never the target of open attack. Not until Antiochus.

With the Greek declaration of war on Judaism, polytheism crossed a line that it had never crossed before and set the precedent for other such attacks on Judaism in the future. (It is interesting to note that during the period of the Maccabean revolt, we see the emergence of the first anti-Semitic propaganda. Vicious lies against Jews were circulated by the Greeks, including that the Jews were expelled from Egypt because they were lepers; that they worshipped a donkey's head in their Temple; and that they fattened up Gentiles and ate them. This anti-Semitic propaganda was later disseminated throughout the Roman empire.[91])

Henry Bamford Parkes, writing in *Gods and Men: The Origins of Western Culture,* sees as the cause of this precedent-setting war on Judaism the stubborn Jewish attachment to their faith in one God:

> *Polytheism is in general regarded as naturally tolerant and it is a fact that Antiochus did not resort to religious compulsion in respect to other nations in his kingdom . . . with the exception of the Jewish religion, which he persecuted mercilessly. . . . Apparently, the long-lasting tension in Judea made the king realize that the Jewish religion with its militant monotheism lay behind the stubborn resistance of the Jews to the innovations that he wished to introduce.[92]*

It was precisely their "militant monotheism" that enabled the Jewish people to survive. But it also kept them at odds with the rest of humanity for many years to come. Even when millions of people began to finally accept the concept of monotheism, the persecution of the Jews would not only continue, but it would intensify.

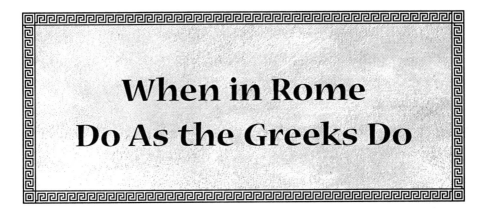

CHAPTER 20

When in Rome
Do As the Greeks Do

At the same time that the Maccabees were waging—and winning—their fight against Greece, the power of Rome was rising on the horizon.

Over the next century, the Greeks lost their domination of the world. And with the destruction of Carthage in 146 B.C.E., Rome became the undisputed master of the Mediterranean. But while Rome conquered Greece militarily, it did not conquer Greece culturally. If anything, the Romans became Hellenized in the process and began to act as disseminators of the Greek values to an even wider world population. This cultural phenomenon would affect the Jews in the short and long run.

The Jews and the Romans were not strangers. Since the time of the Babylonian exile, the Jews had been dispersed all over the Middle East and were a significant presence in Egypt, Syria and Babylonia; they came to interact with the Romans as the Jewish communities of the Diaspora were absorbed into the Empire. Furthermore, as the Empire continued to expand, Jews migrated into the various Roman provinces in Europe. Two thousand years ago, there were already Jewish communities in Spain, southern France, Germany and Italy.

Historians estimate that of the fifty million people who lived within the Roman Empire then, as many as six to seven million—or about 14 percent—were Jews.[93]

Such a significant number of people was bound to leave its mark. Indeed, while the monotheistic ideas of the Jews were still considered strange and incomprehensible to the Romans, it seems they were far more open to Jewish ideas than peoples of previous cultures. It is clear from the accounts of the chroniclers of the day that Judaism found a receptive ear in the Roman world and that conversions were not uncommon, especially among the upper-class, better-educated Romans.[94] Goldberg reports:

> *In the days before Christianity, the Jews had such a force of Billy Grahams that the Roman satirist Horace alluded to their proselytizing in one of his works. In fact, the zeal of Jews in the Roman empire was so intense—and the number of converts so large—that in 139 B.C.E. and again in 19 B.C.E. Jewish missionaries were exiled from Rome . . . one such convert was no less than the Roman Empress Poppaea, the wife of Nero.*[95]

Indeed, Jewish influence was so widespread for a time that it became an irritant, as we learn from Seneca, who, writing early in the first century C.E., bitterly complained, "This abominable nation has succeeded in spreading its customs throughout all lands; the conquered have given their laws to the conquerors."[96]

It was not just Seneca who was upset by the Jewish influence in Rome. Roman historical records[97] reveal several occasions when Jews were expelled from Rome for proselytizing and prominent Roman citizens were sentenced to death in court for converting to Judaism. It is interesting to note that these individuals were charged not with converting to Judaism, but with atheism. This is further testament to how incomprehensible many Romans still found the idea of monotheism. In their minds, belief in one invisible God was akin to belief in no God at all.

In general, however, the Romans followed a policy of "live and let live" toward the Jews, as they did toward the various conquered peoples of their vast empire. As long as a conquered nation remained loyal to Rome and paid its taxes, it was generally allowed to live in peace.

In many ways, the Romans were better to the Jews than the Greeks had been, having less to prove perhaps and being more interested in physical rather than cultural conquest. As a unique, monotheistic faith within the vast polytheistic world of Rome, Jews often enjoyed exemptions from various Roman laws and state religious practices, if these were deemed by the Romans to violate Jewish religious sensibilities. This tolerance was, however, erratic, varying from emperor to emperor, and a special tax—*fiscus Judaicus*—was levied on the Jews for these privileges.

There is no doubt that the privileges granted to the Jews were not granted out of any kind of special love or respect on the part of the Romans towards the Jews. The main interest of Rome was the stability and preservation of the Empire. The Jews were a large minority, and it seemed like common sense to the Romans not to ruffle their feathers. As the Greeks had seen, the Jews were capable of making much trouble if deeply offended. Therefore, the Romans felt it was in their best interest to ensure their passivity.

That policy worked well enough as far as the Diaspora Jews were concerned.[98] But the Jews of Israel proved to be another story.

In Israel, the Maccabees and their Hasmonean dynasty ruled a country in which internal strife ebbed and flowed, in no small measure due to the fact that the Maccabees did not come from the royal line of King David and therefore had no real claim to the monarchy in the eyes of Jewish law. It also didn't help that some of the later Maccabee rulers assumed functions of both king and high priest in direct violation of the explicit dictates of Jewish law, which called for a delicate system of checks and balances and condemned absolute power vested in any one human being. (Furthermore, in time the descendants of the very Maccabees who had so fiercely fought against Hellenization of Israel became Hellenized themselves.)

Nevertheless, while Romans were establishing themselves as a world power, the Maccabees proceeded to reestablish (or redefine) the Biblical borders of Israel. In so doing, they conquered the Idumeans, a pagan tribe in the southern part of their kingdom, and forced them to convert to Judaism. This is the only known instance of forced conversion to Judaism in history, and it proved to be a very serious mistake.[99]

After the death of Alexander Yannai, the Hasmonean great-grandson of Mattathias, and his queen Salome, a civil war erupted between their two Hellenized sons, Hyrcanus and Aristobulus, over who would be the next king. In 63 B.C.E. the two brothers turned to the Roman General Pompey, who was at the time campaigning in Asia Minor, to mediate this dispute. Pompey was more than willing to help and claim Israel for the empire in the process. He entered Jerusalem with his legions and promptly took control after a massacre of twelve thousand defenders on the Temple Mount.[100]

The Roman-Jewish historian Flavius Josephus records that when Pompey entered the Holy of Holies, he had expected to find some huge idol, a grotesque representation of a mighty and monstrous deity. Instead, he was astonished to find what the Jews had laid down their lives for—an empty room, a sanctuary dedicated to an invisible God.[101]

Naively, the brothers attempted to bribe the Roman general to win the kingship of Israel, but after taking money from both, Pompey decided to listen to the counsel of an Idumean leader named Antipater. Antipater, who was advising Hyrcanus at the same time, argued on behalf of the weaker of the two brothers, seeing him as the vehicle through which he himself could wield power.

Thus Roman intervention in Israel had effectively ended Jewish independence and ushered in one of the bleakest periods of Jewish history. Rome ruled, not Hyrcanus, or any Jew for that matter. (The Sanhedrin's authority was effectively abolished by Roman decree six years after Pompey's conquest[102]; the supreme Jewish court continued to sit until the fourth century, but with its powers truncated and restructured.)

The independent state of Israel ceased to exist and became the Roman province of Judea. Pompey split up much of the land, giving large chunks to his soldiers as a reward for their prowess in battle. Gaza, Jaffa, Ashdod and other Jewish cities were now a part of the map of the Roman Empire. Hyrcanus, though he might have called himself king, got only Jerusalem, along with a few pieces north and south, but even this small area he could not govern without checking first with the Roman proconsul in Damascus.

Antipater continued to guide Hyrcanus and—when in 49 B.C.E., Pompey and Julius Caesar became engaged in internal struggle—helped him choose the winning side. Soon, Antipater was the man in power. The

Romans judged correctly that this forcibly converted Jew did not identify with Jewish values or nationalism, and that, with him in power, "militant monotheism" would not again rear its dangerous head.

While Antipater did not go down in history as a household name, his son (who took after his father and then some) did. He was Herod the Great (not to be confused with Herod Antipas of New Testament fame), who ruled from 37 B.C.E. until 4 B.C.E. as a Roman puppet king.

During Herod's reign, Hellenism dominated Judea. A significant number of Greeks, as well as other Gentiles who adopted the Greek lifestyle, had lived there since the days of the Greek empire, and now, encouraged by the Romans, more Hellenist outsiders came to settle the land. Additionally, the Jewish upper classes, though a minority, subscribed to this "higher" culture. Most importantly, the king was an avowed Hellenist. Seeing himself as an enlightened leader who would bring his backward people into the modern world, Herod did what he saw necessary to accomplish his "idealistic" end. This included the persecution and murder of numerous rabbis whom he viewed not only as threats to his authority, but as obstacles to the mass Hellenization of the Jews.

Thus, the struggle between Hellenistic polytheism and Judaism continued.

Herod's megalomaniacal vision also played itself out in his many grandiose building projects. He distinguished himself as a relentless builder of cities, palaces and fortresses, some of which still stand—the fortresses at Masada, Antonia and Herodium, the port of Caesarea, the huge edifice at the top of the Cave of the Patriarchs in Hebron, and the Citadel at the entrance to the Old City of Jerusalem, to name but a few.

But one of his most ambitious projects was the rebuilding of the Temple, which was almost certainly an attempt to gain popularity among his subjects who, he knew, held him in contempt. Here, he outdid himself, and even the Talmud acknowledges that the end result was spectacular. The Holy of Holies was covered in gold; the walls and columns of the other buildings were of white marble; the floors were of Carrara marble, its blue tinge giving the impression of a moving sea of water;[103] the curtains were tapestries of blue, white, scarlet and purple thread, depicting, according to Josephus, "the whole vista of the heavens."

Josephus waxes ecstatic as he describes what has been called one of the wonders of the classical world:

> *Viewed from without, the Sanctuary had everything that could amaze either mind or eyes. Overlaid all round with stout plates of gold, the first rays of the sun it reflected so fierce a blaze of fire that those who endeavored to look at it were forced to turn away as if they had looked straight at the sun. To strangers as they approached it seemed in the distance like a mountain covered with snow; for any part not covered with gold was dazzling white.*[104]

Herod saw fit, however, to place at the main entrance a huge Roman eagle, which the pious Jews saw as a sacrilege. A group of Torah students promptly smashed this emblem of idolatry and oppression, but Herod had them hunted down and dragged in chains to his residence in Jericho, where they were burned alive.[105]

Having built the Temple, Herod took pains to make sure it would be run without future problems of this kind. He appointed his own high priest, having, by then, put to death forty-six leading members of the Sanhedrin, the rabbinical court, along with his Hasmonean (Jewish) wife and virtually all the members of his own family who had Hasmonean blood, including his brother-in-law, his mother-in-law and his two sons.[106]

As a result of Herod's interference and the ever-spreading Hellenistic influences among the Jewish upper classes, the Temple hierarchy became totally corrupt. The Sadducees, a religious group of the wealthy who collaborated with the Romans in order to keep their power base, now controlled the Temple, much to the chagrin of the more traditional majority, the Pharisees, and of the extreme religious minority, the Zealots.

The cauldron was boiling and soon it would explode.

Soon after Herod's death in 4 B.C.E., Judea reverted to direct Roman rule and the administrative center of Israel was moved from Jerusalem to Caesarea, the grand city on the Mediterranean built by Herod in honor of Augustus Caesar. Caesarea, one of the largest and most important ports in the Roman Empire, was—with the exception of the Jewish minority—totally pagan and totally Hellenized. In the mind of the traditional majority of the Jews, Caesarea was the antithesis of Jerusalem and, therefore, everything Jewish.

The Talmud gives us much insight into the extent to which the Jews viewed the struggle between Israel and Rome as a continuation of the ideological struggle between Judaism and Hellenism:

> *Caesarea and Jerusalem: If someone will tell you, "both are destroyed," do not believe it; if someone will tell you, "both are settled," do not believe it. But if someone will tell you, "Caesarea is destroyed and Jerusalem is settled," or "Jerusalem is destroyed and Caesarea is settled" that you can believe."* [107]

Clearly, the rabbis were not speaking about the physical cities—both of which, in point of fact, were settled and thriving at the same time. Rather, they were making the point that the ideologies the two cities represented could not exist at the same time: One would have to be destroyed for the other to flourish. The strong language indicates just how high the stakes were for the Jews.

Adding fuel to the ideological fire was the way the Romans tried to extract money—by taxation and sometimes outright looting—from the local population. This was especially true of several of the governors (procurators) of Judea who were exceptionally cruel and avaricious.

Christian historian Paul Johnson in his *History of the Jews* explains why this proved a particularly incendiary element in the conflict:

> *The Hellenized gentiles . . . [who] constituted the local civil service and the tax collectors . . . were notorious in their anti-Semitism. . . . Foolishly, Rome insisted on drawing its Judaean procurators from Greek-speaking gentile areas—the last and most insensitive of them, Gessius Florus came from Greek Asia Minor."* [108]

Florus persuaded Nero to strip the Jews of Caesarea of their citizenship, effectively making them aliens in the city and totally at the mercy of the Greco-Roman population. The Jews revolted, and their protest was viciously put down with many people killed and synagogues desecrated. The pogrom spread to other cities where the Hellenized population seized the opportunity to get rid of the Jews—Jewish homes were invaded, looted and burned down.

Jewish refugees, vowing vengeance, began to stream into Jerusalem. Florus escalated the conflict, first by giving Roman soldiers free rein to massacre more than thirty-six hundred Jews who had jeered him, and then by arresting Jewish elders, having them publicly flogged and crucified. [109]

Now there was no turning back. The Jews took up arms.

To go up against the might of the Roman Empire was nothing short of suicidal, and indeed, the Jewish War would end in great tragedy. But when it began in 66 C.E., it had some astonishing successes, with Florus fleeing for his life and the Roman garrison isolated and overwhelmed.

But such insults to its might Rome could not abide. Wein relates graphically what happened next:

> *The success of the Jews in driving Rome from Jerusalem sent shock waves throughout the Roman Empire. It also unleashed a wave of bloody pogroms against Jews, especially in Caesarea, Alexandria and Damascus. Thousands of Jews were slaughtered in these riots, and thousands more were sold into the slave markets of Rome.*[110]

The sages and rabbis advised a reconciliation with the Romans, seeing that, if irritated any further, Rome would retaliate with even greater force and surely destroy the whole country and decimate the Jewish people. Considering that the Sadducees were already pro-Rome and the Pharisees held generally moderate views, their wisdom might have prevailed. But the Zealot extremists would have none of it.

Vowing to fight to the death, they went up against a new Roman contingent making its way toward Jerusalem and slayed six thousand Roman soldiers.[111] Coincidentally, the victory was won on the very same spot where the Maccabees had vanquished the Greeks, and the Zealots, seeing a divine hand helping them, were encouraged further.

The Roman answer was to dispatch four legions under the Empire's most experienced commander, Vespasian.[112] His strategy was to subdue conflict throughout the region first and leave Jerusalem for last. One by one, the various Jewish enclaves of resistance fell, and in 69 C.E.,

Vespasian turned to take the final prize.

Meanwhile, Jerusalem was rife with internal conflict. The city was divided between the moderates (made up of the Sadducees and Pharisees) and the Zealot extremists. When it appeared that the moderate faction would win, the Zealots brought in Idumean mercenaries who slaughtered the moderate forces and pillaged the city. With their opposition murdered, the fanatical Zealots continued their reign of terror, even destroying Jerusalem's vast warehouses of food so the residents would have no choice but to fight the Romans or starve.

Here it must be said that in their actions the Jews were betraying the basic tenets of their religion. "Love thy neighbor" was replaced by baseless hatred, and Jew was pitted against Jew. Had the Jews been united in their strategy, they might have succeeded in, at least, saving Jerusalem. In the early years of the Jewish War, Rome was at its weakest—69 C.E. saw the throne of Rome changing hands four times after the death of Nero. Confusion and fear reigned; the Empire was in danger of disintegrating. Given the chance to save face, Rome might have grabbed it, and Vespasian might have returned home to tend to more pressing matters. But, having instigated a fight to the death, determined never to back down, the Jewish Zealots were daring Rome to take them on.

Realizing that for the Jews the end was near and that Jerusalem would shortly fall, the leader of the Pharisees, Rabban Yochanan ben Zakkai, came up with a scheme to preserve the soul of Judaism from extinction. The Talmud relates that he had himself smuggled out of the city in a coffin and managed to gain a hearing from Vespasian, flattering the commander and predicting he would be the next emperor. Miraculously, a messenger arrived at that very moment to inform the commander that Nero was dead and he was in line to be emperor. The happy Roman magnanimously agreed to spare the center of Torah learning at Yavneh along with the lives of numerous Jewish scholars.[113]

With Vespasian off to Rome to secure the imperial throne, the job of finishing off Jerusalem fell to his son Titus.[114]

By then the defenders were weakened from hunger and perhaps even more so from internal strife. Titus attacked just after Passover in the year 70 C.E., battering the city with his catapults, which propelled a rain of stone, iron and fire onto the population. Jerusalem began to burn.

Even so, it took Titus two months of intense fighting before he was able to overrun the city and yet another month of even fiercer fighting before he was able to breach the walls of the Temple Mount. Now a duel to the death ensued, and finally, four months after he had begun his attack—on the ninth day of the Jewish month of Av—Titus ordered the Temple razed to the ground.[115]

All of the neighboring countryside, including the Mount of Olives, was denuded of trees to create the siege-works and the giant bonfire that would burn the buildings of the Temple to the ground. The intense heat from the fire caused the moisture in the limestone to expand, and it exploded like popcorn, causing a chain reaction of destruction. In a day's time, the magnificent Temple was nothing but rubble.

The Romans sacked all of Jerusalem, bringing the priceless artifacts from the Temple to Rome in a triumphant march, which is memorialized in engravings of the Arch of Titus, still standing in Rome today. Congratulating themselves on asserting the Roman might against the defiant Jews, they minted coins proclaiming *Judea Capta,* "Judea is captured."

But was it?

The land was no longer under Jewish control, but it had not been since the days of Hasmoneans anyway. True, the Temple, the center of Jewish worship and the symbol of Judaism's special connection to the one God, was gone. But Judaism—along with all its unique value system—was alive and well.

Thanks to the foresight of Rabban Yochanan ben Zakkai, the center of Torah learning at Yavneh thrived. It was here that the rabbis systematically recorded all of the rich oral tradition that was essential to understanding and carrying out the many commandments of the Torah. It was here that the rabbis institutionalized public prayer as a replacement for the Temple service and made the synagogue, formerly a meeting place for Torah study, the center of Jewish communal life. But most importantly, it was here that the rabbis devised a system of transferring all the Temple ceremony—with its inherent symbolism—into the average Jewish home. The Sabbath table became the Temple altar, and the Sabbath meal became ritualized to recall the Temple offerings, as well as the daily prayers. In the coming years, when the Jews would be dispersed the world over—doomed for two thousand years to have no common land, no centralized leadership and, aside from Hebrew scriptures, no common language—they would carry with them their Judaism undiminished.[116]

But that was yet to come.

As the rabbis labored in obscurity, virulent anti-Semitism continued to be generated by the Hellenists who, not happy to leave well enough alone, seemed determined to pour salt into Jewish wounds.

(This same need for overkill would be exhibited by later enemies of the Jews, who, having exterminated entire Jewish communities and having no more Jews left to slaughter, would then desecrate Jewish cemeteries and mutilate Jewish corpses.)

The level of hostility and mistreatment of the Jews escalated throughout the Empire to the point of being unbearable. In response, the Jews revolted several times, each time seeing thousands of their number killed. The final disastrous revolt of the Jews against the Romans occurred during the reign of the Emperor Hadrian, who at first inaugurated an atmosphere of tolerance. He even talked of allowing the Jews to rebuild their Temple, a proposal that was met with virulent opposition from the Hellenists. Why Hadrian changed his attitude to one of outright hostility toward the Jews remains a puzzle, but Johnson speculates that he fell under the influence of the Roman historian Tacitus, who was then busy disseminating Greek smears against the Jews.[117] Tacitus and his circle were part of a group of Roman intellectuals who viewed themselves as inheritors of Greek culture. (Some Roman nobles actually considered themselves the literal descendants of the Greeks, though there is no historical basis for this myth.) It was fashionable among this group to take on all the trappings of Greek culture. Hating the Jews because they represented the antithesis of Hellenism went with the territory.

Thus influenced, Hadrian decided to spin 180 degrees. Instead of letting the Jews rebuild, Hadrian formulated a plan to transform Jerusalem into a pagan city-state on the Greek polis model with a shrine to Jupiter on the site of the Jewish Temple. Furthermore, like Antiochus three hundred years earlier, Hadrian forbade circumcision and Torah study and enacted other decrees to make sure the last vestiges of Judaism were finally wiped out.

Jewish outrage at his actions led to the single greatest revolution of the Roman era. The uprising, which began in full force in 132 C.E., was led by Simon Bar Kosiba, better known as "Bar Kochba," meaning "Son of the Star." Bar Kochba organized a large guerilla army, part of which thought him to be the Messiah[118] and succeeded in actually throwing the

Romans out of Jerusalem and Israel and establishing, albeit for a very brief period, an independent Jewish state. Rome could not let this be. Such boldness had to be crushed and those responsible punished, brutally and finally.

But the Jews were not easily overcome. Hadrian poured more and more troops into Israel to fight the Bar Kochba forces. By the time the revolt was finally crushed—on the ninth of Av of the year 135 C.E.—the Romans had almost half of their entire army, some twelve legions, in Israel.

No people had revolted more or caused the Romans greater human or material losses than the Jews. But, of course, they had done so at a great price to themselves. The Roman historian Deo Cassius writes that over a million Jews died in the fighting.[119] Even if this figure is exaggerated, there is no doubt that hundreds of thousands of Jews died and the country was laid low.

The Jewish challenge to Rome that had begun in 66 C.E. had lasted almost seventy years. How such a comparatively tiny group could take on the might of Rome over and over again and for so long is hard to fathom. But perhaps the answer lies in the reason behind the conflict.

It was not so much a fight over territory or property as it was a fight over the very way of life. Monotheism and the laws of the Torah were so deeply ingrained in the Jews that any attempt to separate the people from the essence of Judaism was seen as death of the soul, a death worse than any death of the body could ever be.

Like a mother who is capable of superhuman feats of strength to defend the life of her child, so too the Jews found reserves in themselves beyond normal human boundaries.

After the revolt, Hadrian leveled Jerusalem and on top of the rubble built the pagan city he had planned, which he named Aelia Capitolina.

Whatever Jews managed to remain in the land were strictly forbidden to enter the city, which—for the first time since King David had made it Israel's capital a thousand years earlier—was empty of Jews. It's ironic that the first city in history to be made intentionally and completely *Juden rein,* "Jew free" (to borrow a term later used by the Nazis), was their very own Jerusalem.

Jerusalem was no more, the Temple was no more, and finally Israel was no more. To further squelch any nationalistic feeling, Hadrian renamed the land Philistia (Palestine) after the Philistines, an extinct people who once occupied the Mediterranean coastal area and who were some of the bitterest of the enemies of the Jews described in the Bible.[120] Stateless, dispersed throughout a vast and often hostile world, the Jews would spend the next two thousand years praying to return home.

For their stubborn commitment to their faith, they had paid a terrible price; yet had they caved in under the pressure of Hellenism, all of human history would have been different. We will soon see that although the Jewish people lost the war for national determination, they won a far greater spiritual and intellectual victory that, within the space of a few hundred years, would bring about one of the greatest revolutions in history.

Writes Yehezkel Kaufman writes in *The Religion of Israel:*

> *It was a long path of suffering . . . and yet Jerusalem prevailed over the conquerors. Throughout the world where the Jewish people were dispersed, paganism was destined to die. One thing is clear: Since the fall of paganism did not come through a political or military collapse, this triumph of Israelite religion can only have been the product of its inner strength.*[121]

CHAPTER 21

Conclusions: Part III

Thus far, we have predominantly addressed how the Greco-Roman culture clashed with Judaism. But this question remains: Was there any positive interaction between the two cultures?

It is impossible for two peoples to live together without influencing each other in many ways. Both the Greeks and the Jews were curious people who loved philosophy and discourse. Their ideas had to rub off on each other somewhat.

As the dominant culture of the time, Hellenism certainly brought the Greek system of linear thinking and rhetoric, the Greek sense of art and beauty, and Greek forms of storytelling and drama into the Jewish consciousness. In return, Judaism could not help but impact the Hellenistic mind with its vast storehouse of literature. (As was mentioned earlier, the Greeks were very curious about the Torah and it was translated from Hebrew into Greek early in the third century B.C.E.) Additionally, the

Jewish idea of a loving, personal God—as opposed to cruel fate randomly stalking man—made an impression, as did the concept of universal vision for humankind.

It must be noted that there were various factors at play that made the superpowers of the world open to outside influences.

For one, the Greek and Roman cultures—for all their vast pantheon of gods and deification of emperors—were considerably less religiously dogmatic than their Mesopotamian and Egyptian predecessors. I do not mean in any way to suggest that they were leaning toward the secular. (Indeed, atheism was a capital offense both in Greece and Rome.) But their loyalty to their religion and to their gods was less intense. This was especially true of the Romans.

Although Rome had an official state religion, it seems that the Roman people were no longer spiritually satisfied by the gods of their ancestors. Many alien religious cults flourished in Rome—in particular the worship of Mithra, the Persian god of light and wisdom, who became identified with Helios, the Greek sun god, as well as Sol, the Roman sun god. This cult came to be so popular that the Romans named a day of the week—Sunday—in honor of Mithra, and celebrated the sun god's birthday on December 25 in conjunction with the Winter Solstice.

Loyalty to the state gods was further weakened by the Roman policy of stealing the gods of conquered peoples. The "captured gods" were then "owned" by Rome and incorporated into the official pantheon. As the empire grew, the number of gods multiplied wildly; by the middle of the first century B.C.E., according to the Roman writer Varro, Rome had in excess of thirty thousand gods and 157 holidays a year.[122] Who could keep them straight or, for that matter, take them seriously?

No wonder the Romans were casting around for something that made order of the universe. (Their spiritual search seems to have a parallel, though for very different reasons, in the Western world of today with the explosion of interest in nontraditional, New Age and Eastern religions.)

Another important factor that made the Romans receptive to Jewish influence was the constant threat of internal rebellion and external invasion with which they lived. The feeling that merciless fate and a cruel death lurked around the corner made one anxious and fearful. (Perhaps all those hours of watching minor criminals butchered at the Coliseum created a subconscious thought of, "There but for the grace of one of the thirty thousand gods go I.") The atmosphere of impending doom was only heightened by all of the murderous intrigue in politics, the general corruption and the apparent state of moral decline—people gorged themselves on delicacies, then vomited so they could consume even more, and endless sex orgies with slaves and prostitutes at the public baths were the way to spend the night. Grant, in *The World of Rome,* sums it up as follows:

> *The Roman age was a time of not only uncontrolled blood lust but pessimism and nerve-failure regarding the powers of man to work his own future. The existence and propaganda of the imperial government claiming support of the old gods did not remove the deep-seated feeling that every man was adrift, and everything hazardous. So the presiding deity of nerve-failure was Fortune. "Throughout the whole world," says Pliny the Elder, "at every place and hour, by every voice, Fortune alone is invoked and her name spoken. . . . We are so much at the mercy of chance that chance is our god."* [123]

In such an atmosphere, the idea that one is *not* lost at sea in a random and hostile universe, but is looked after by one omnipotent and loving God, who orders and runs the world, was likely to get a receptive hearing.

However, conversion to Judaism has always been a long and difficult process, one which has historically required the prospective convert to "prove" his or her sincere desire to join the Jewish people. Jews have never viewed proselytism as a religious obligation; the Talmud contains no pronouncements from the Sages urging the Jews to go out and preach Judaism to the pagan masses, and forced conversions were virtually unheard of.[124] From their inception, the Jews viewed their mission in history to be, in the words of the Prophet Isaiah, "a light to nations"— meaning they were meant to impact humanity by serving as a living example for the rest of the world to emulate.

This does not mean that Jews were not interested in spreading monotheism. Quite the contrary. Jewish theology holds that—because of their special task in the world—only Jews are bound by the many rigorous codes of behavior enumerated in the Torah, therefore conversion to Judaism is only for those who wish to join in the Jewish mission; the rest of humanity, however, is required to live by seven basic laws, called the Noahide laws because they were given by God to Noah after the flood. Foremost among these laws is the acceptance of the idea of one God as the guiding principle of morality and ethics.

All that notwithstanding, there were Jews in the Roman Empire who were quite excited to see interest in their religion, and they warmly encouraged converts. As noted earlier, Roman historical records show us that—until Christianity became the state religion, following conquest by Constantine in the fourth century C.E., and Jewish missionary activity was banned—Judaism seemed to be catching on, especially in major cultural centers such as Rome and Alexandria. The best-known exporter of Jewish ideology was philosopher Philo Judeas, who lived from 20 B.C.E. to 50 C.E. Strongly influenced by Hellenism, he sought to fuse Greek philosophy with Judaism and export this hybrid to the world. Philo was a prolific writer with a considerable non-Jewish following. His writings not only influenced the polytheistic world, but also had a significant impact on early Christianity.[125] Early church fathers seriously studied Philo and translated many of his works into Latin.

It cannot be denied that the message and lifestyle of Judaism were very attractive to many Romans. Historian Howard Sachar, in his *History of Israel,* suggests an explanation for why this was so:

> *The conditions were highly favorable. The old paganism . . . was decaying, and sensitive minds were repelled by it. The clear-cut monotheism and the rational practices of the Hebrews, expounded with charm by the Hellenized Jewish writers, made a deep impression. There were great numbers of converts, if not officially to Judaism, at least to Jewish practices and ideals. Sabbath lights gleamed through the darkness from many cultured Roman homes.*[126]

Just because many citizens of the empire converted and more openly sympathized with the Jews and even kept some of the Jewish commandments, this is not to imply that the religion of Moses was taking Rome by storm. The reason why not was simple: Jewish laws, restrictions and rituals were complicated and difficult. While certain commandments such as Sabbath rest and dietary laws were very popular and relatively easy to observe, other rituals of Judaism—in particular, circumcision for men, and sexual abstinence during a part of each month and ritual baths for women—were seen as too extreme and too difficult.

Additionally, many saw Judaism as a national religion of a specific people—that is, being Jewish meant not only ascribing to a religious faith, but adopting a different national identity. But if you were born in Rome, you surely did not want to appear to be giving up your Roman citizenship. It didn't help matters that Judea was one of the most rebellious and troublesome provinces in the Empire, and Jews in general were often viewed with suspicion and hostility. This no doubt caused many Romans to think twice about joining Jewish ranks.[127]

But even if the Jews did not convert the Empire, they impressed the Roman mind and influenced the Hellenist culture in an important way. For the first time in history, significant numbers of non-Jews were receptive to the Jewish lifestyle—which offered a sense of community and a sense of security in an uncertain world—and to Jewish ideas of one God who wants a relationship with man and who wants man to treat his neighbor with love, justice and equality.

These ideas—though in modified form—would soon play a pivotal role in transforming the world of Rome as a dramatic religious metamorphosis began to unfold.

Part IV

With Sword
and Fire:
The Rise
of Christianity
and Islam

Although Judaism had long owned a worldview flowing from ethical monotheism that embodied groundbreaking human rights and values, that view had stayed largely in-house up to the time of the destruction of the Temple. This was to some degree intentional, as Jews did not believe in proselytizing, convinced that their mission was to teach by example.

Of course, wherever Jews went, curiosity was aroused about them, their odd way of life and their beliefs, and they added some converts to the cause. But large-scale conversions were not heard of. So, how would the polytheistic world—which had fashioned its many gods in its own image and its moral system to suit itself—come to accept one God with some tough rules to follow regarding interactions between man and God, and man and man?

By the year 1 C.E., the prospects of such a thing happening appeared nil. Indeed, any bookie worth his salt placed the odds on the Hellenistic lifestyle winning out. But, as it happened, it was the bookie who lost his toga.

Within a five-hundred-year span, Christianity and Islam would succeed—though more with fire and sword than with friendly discourse and persuasion—in spreading monotheism worldwide. One would think, of course, that part and parcel of monotheism would be the theology of an absolute God-given ethical standard. As logical as it may seem, it didn't work out that way in practicality.

The acceptance of moral values—and a code of behavior flowing from them—was much slower in coming. Why it happened that way, and how it all did finally come about, are the two questions explored in the next chapters.

CHAPTER 22

The Religion
Revolution

As we have seen, it had been a very dark period in Jewish history. Some of the most brilliant of the rabbinical sages had been murdered by Herod. Corruption had crept into the Temple hierarchy. Jews had split three ways: the wealthy Sadducees, who denied the authority of the oral law, pledging allegiance to Rome; the fanatical Zealots, ready to battle Rome to the death in a suicidal war; and the mainstream Pharisee majority, still loyal to Torah and oral law, caught in between.

Out of this time—marked by virulent anti-Semitism and cruel oppression of the Jews—were born a number of splinter sects, whose members believed that the Apocalypse was at hand. Finding a receptive ear among the disenfranchised, these sects preached that the ultimate battle of good versus evil would soon be fought, followed by the messianic redemption of humanity. The group of ascetics known as the Essenes,[1] who became famous in modern times after the discovery of the Dead Sea Scrolls, was one such sect, but there were many others.

The teachings of these sects did not catch on in any significant way among the Jews. In the same way that the Jews usually rejected foreign religions, they also rejected attempts to tamper with the inner workings of Judaism.

Nevertheless, at this tumultuous time, they were more susceptible than ever before. The countryside was alive with charismatic healers and preachers called *hassidim* (not to be confused with modern-day *hassidim*), meaning "holy men," and people flocked to them hoping to hear prophecy that the years of strife and suffering were at an end. The one who would become most legendary was Joshua—or "Jesus" in Greek—later to be called "Christ" after the Greek term for "Messiah."

It is outside the scope of this book to describe the beginnings of early Christianity under Jesus. Currently, there exist approximately twenty-seven hundred books on the subject, many of them written in recent years, discussing the issue of the historical Jesus versus the legendary Jesus, and debating what he said or did not say and what can be said of him with any certainty.[2]

At the very minimum, the Christian world does agree that Jesus was a Jew who was familiar with the Torah, observed the so-called "Law of Moses" and taught many of its precepts, though he also departed from some of them.

One of the most famous of Jesus' teachings consists of two Torah quotations (that were staples of Judaism) and echoes the emphasis of the rabbinic teachings of his era.[3] Asked to name the greatest commandment, Jesus, as cited in the Gospel of Matthew, replies:

Love the Lord your God with all your heart and with all your soul and with all your mind. This is the first and greatest

commandment. And the second is like it. Love your neighbor
as yourself. All the law and the prophets hang on these two
commandments.[4]

There is also reasonable certainty that there existed among the Jews a
group of Jesus followers with adherents in Galilee and Jerusalem. But
after the dispersion of the Jews by the Romans, the sect disappeared
along with the Essenes, the Sadducees and the Zealots. (The Pharisees
survived in part due to the vision of their leader, Rabban Yochanan ben
Zakkai.)

Historical record shows that the teachings of Jesus were transformed
into Christianity as we know it today chiefly by the efforts of Saul, better known as Paul, of Tarsus (a city in Asia Minor, now in Turkey). Paul
was a Jew, who, although he never physically met Jesus, was said to have
conversed with him in visions.[5] Paul took Christianity to Rome as well
as to various parts of the Roman Empire (circa 47 to 60 C.E.), and he
attracted a number of converts to his religion. It preached monotheism
and many Jewish codes of behavior, but then completely separated itself
from Judaism by disavowing Jewish law and ritual and by preaching
immortality through faith in Jesus as god.

Through Paul's efforts and the zeal of his early disciples, Christianity
experienced a meteoric rise in popularity. Its initial successes were all
in places where the non-Jewish inhabitants had had significant exposure
to Jewish ideas. As noted, many non-Jews had been previously attracted to
Judaism but were not willing to "go all the way." Paul's brilliance was
to retain the most appealing parts of Judaism and the close connection
to the Bible, while dropping the "objectionable" components (like

circumcision, for example). Writes John G. Gager in *Kingdom and Community: The Social World of Early Christianity:*

> *Christianity preserved all the advantages of its Jewish heritage but without the only two factors that might otherwise have inhibited its growth: the obligation of the ritual law and the close connection between religion and national identity. By proclaiming that the Christ was "the end of the law" and by presenting itself to the world as "the new spiritual Israel," Hellenistic Christianity was able to reap the political and social fruits that had been sown by three centuries of Hellenistic Judaism.[6]*

By the year 64 C.E.—some thirty years after the accepted date for the crucifixion of Jesus and two years after the death of Paul himself—there were enough Christians living in Rome for them to be blamed for the great fire that demolished the city during the reign of Nero. (Christian biographer A. N. Wilson, in his *Paul: The Mind of the Apostle,* suggests that the Christians were made scapegoats because their numbers were insignificant and, therefore, no one would raise a protest.[7] However, other Christian historians maintain that the reason was quite the opposite—Christianity was catching on and threatening the state religion and, therefore, the stability of the state.)

At any rate, after the fire, Christianity was outlawed in Rome, and the Christians who were caught were regularly fed to the lions in the Coliseum.[8] This might well have ended the interest of the Roman populace. It is not likely that under such heavy prosecutions, the Romans —who thought mere circumcision too difficult—would join in droves.

However in 312 C.E., a remarkable thing happened that led to the formal end of paganism and, within a dozen years, to the elevation of Christianity to the official state religion. On the eve of a battle with his rival for the throne of Rome, Constantine reported that he had a dream of Jesus followed by a vision of a cross superimposed on the sun. Constantine was prone to visions, having claimed a couple years earlier to have seen the sun god Sol in a grove of Apollo in Gaul. The juxtaposition of the two—cross and sun—was an omen for victory and, when Constantine won the battle, he gave the credit to his newfound god and converted to Christianity.

Oxford scholar David L. Edwards, provost of London's Southwark Cathedral and author of *Christianity: The First Two Thousand Years,* openly doubts the sincerity of Constantine's conversion as does Christian historian Paul Johnson.[9]

But such are the quirks of history. Soon Constantine was emperor, and he chose to establish his capital in the east, in Byzantium, which was renamed Constantinople. (Eventually, the Empire would split into two— the Western empire would collapse in the fifth century, but the Eastern empire would survive another thousand years.) Thus, Christianity became the official state religion of the new order: the Byzantine Empire.

Constantine had initiated a unique way of seeing Christianity—by a merging of pagan and Christian symbols (sun and cross). Over the next few hundred years, much more of such synthesis followed. The holidays dedicated to the pagan gods became the holidays of the new religion. A population that previously ascribed many human aspects to its heavenly pantheon easily accepted the ideas of a man as god and of his virgin birth.[10] And the notion of the Trinity seemed to fit with the Roman way of thinking in threes: Had not Jupiter, Juno and Minerva always been linked together?

But it was not as easy as it might seem to institute such a vastly different way of doing things—new gods Rome could adopt overnight, but new values were quite a different matter. People used to creating their own morality weren't going to give up such a convenience overnight.

Constantine, the man who arguably did more to propagate Christianity than any other human being, including Jesus and Paul, changed his behavior not one iota. Writes Johnson:

> *He [Constantine] had no respect for human life, and as emperor he executed his eldest son, his own second wife, his favorite sister's husband and "many others" on doubtful charges. . . . He was much criticized for condemning prisoners of war to mortal combat with wild beasts at Trier and Comar and for wholesale massacres in north Africa.*[11]

It didn't help that there was soon unleashed a bitter struggle for wealth and power that was bound to come with being the only act in town.

Thus the campaign to eradicate paganism proved harsh and bloody. Christian mobs scoured the land of the Empire, smashing idols and burning temples. Writes Johnson: "It [the Church] transformed itself from a suffering and victimized body, begging toleration, into a coercive one, demanding monopoly."[12]

Cynics have charged that once it became a state power, the Church turned the cross into a sword, and its ability to convert the Western world had less to do with its message than its methods. By the late fourth century C.E., the official government efforts at intimidation through laws and decrees—aided by mob terrorism—succeeded in imposing Christianity on the majority of the Empire.

With the disappearance of paganism, Judaism began to stick out like a sore thumb. As always, it was strange and separate, and it wouldn't compromise. The stubborn Jews, as they had done with every other religion that had previously assaulted their belief system, were obstinately refusing to bow to the new order.

This presented a special problem, as William Nicholls explains in *Christian Antisemitism: A History of Hate:*

> *The very presence of the Jewish people in the world, continuing to believe in the faithfulness of God to the original covenant . . . puts a great question against Christian belief in a new covenant made through Christ. The presence of this question, often buried deep in the Christian mind, could not fail to cause profound and gnawing anxiety. Anxiety usually leads to hostility.*[13]

Within a short time, Jews living in the Empire had lost most of their civil rights. For a Jew to marry a Christian was an offense punishable by death. Sermons against the Jews, often inciting violence, were routinely preached, and the idea of presenting Jews as the killers of Jesus originated at this time, though it was not popularized until several hundred years later.[14]

By the early seventh century when the Byzantine might began to wobble—facing attacks from the Persians who swallowed up chunks of the territory and even took Jerusalem—the Jews living in the Empire were in a very precarious position. Anti-Jewish legislation, heavy taxes, and outbreaks of violence and forced conversions all had taken their toll on the population. Hoping to find a respite from the Christians, some fled home to safety. But when the Byzantine Emperor Heraclius reclaimed Jerusalem in 629 C.E., the poor Jews there were brutally massacred.[15]

What had happened to the Jewish ideas that had inspired Christianity in the first place—the ideas of love of neighbor, peace and harmony, and justice for all?

If, in its quest for world domination, Christianity had temporarily forgotten them, it would soon be reminded. That reminder would come from an unexpected place: the Arabian peninsula. There in Mecca, a place that had long been the center of worship of the famed Black Stone of Kaaba, an unusual man was preaching an unusual message.

CHAPTER 23

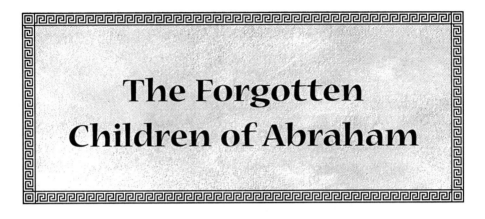

The Forgotten Children of Abraham

During the years that the Jews of Israel were battling the Greeks, the Jews of the Diaspora, who had never returned home after the Babylonian exile, were doing much better among their Arab neighbors.

Although the rulers in Mesopotamia changed—the Babylonians being displaced by a succession of Persians, Parthians and Sassanids—the Jewish population generally lived free of persecution and enjoyed a great deal of autonomy. When Greek and Roman persecutions of the Jews in Israel intensified, many Jews from Israel came to join their Diaspora brethren in relatively more tolerant territories, such as the Arabian peninsula.

With time, the Jews outside the control of Rome swelled to exceed more than one million and founded many towns and villages, including the city of Yathrib in Arabia, which is today known as Medina and is considered Islam's second holiest city (after Mecca). Free from being stigmatized by the anti-Semitic smears of the Hellenists, the local Jews attracted significant numbers of converts to their way of life and many more admirers.[16] Goldberg, in *The Jewish Connection,* sums up the story:

> *Jewish missionary work flourished in the East until the advent of Mohammed in the 600s. In Arabia, whole tribes converted to Judaism, including two kinds of the Himyarites. French Bible critic Ernest Renan remarked that "only a hair's breadth prevented all Arabia from becoming Jewish."*[17]

One of those impressed by the Jews' uncompromising devotion to monotheism was a pensive young trader whose giving and gentle disposition had, early on, earned him the title of *Al-Amin,* "the trusted one." The world would come to know him as the prophet Mohammed.

Although his travels had exposed him to Christianity and he was clearly influenced by it, he found aspects of it troublesome—in particular, the doctrine of the Trinity did not seem strictly monotheistic in his eyes.[18] He is recorded as having said:

> *Unbelievers are those that say, "Allah is the Messiah, the son of Mary." . . . Unbelievers are those that say, "Allah is one of three." There is but one God. If they do not desist from so saying, those of them that disbelieve shall be sternly punished.*[19]

However, there is no doubt that in the early stages of his spiritual awakening, Mohammed came to be greatly impressed by the Jews. Writes S. D. Goiten in *Jews and Arabs: Their Contacts Through the Ages:*

> *The intrinsic values of the belief in one God, the creator of the world, the God of justice and mercy, before whom everyone high*

and low bears personal responsibility, came to Muhammad—as he never ceased to emphasize—from Israel.[20]

He clearly had some knowledge of the Torah, as later he would quote Moses more than one hundred times in the Koran, the record of his teachings that became the holy book of his newfound religion.[21] Of the twenty-five prophets listed in the Koran, nineteen are from Jewish scripture, and many ritual laws of Islam parallel Judaism—circumcision and prohibition against eating pork, for example.

Through his studies, Mohammed concluded that the Arabs were the other children of Abraham—through the line of his son Ishmael by the Egyptian maidservant Hagar—and that they had forgotten the teachings of monotheism they had inherited ages ago. He saw his mission as bringing them back. Johnson explains:

> *What he [Mohammed] seems to have wished to do was to destroy the polytheistic paganism of the oasis culture by giving the Arabs Jewish ethical monotheism in a language they could understand and in terms adapted to their ways. He accepted the Jewish God and their prophets, the idea of fixed law embodied in scripture—the Koran being an Arabic substitute for the Bible—and the addition of an oral law applied in religious courts.*[22]

There is no argument that the Arab world into which Mohammed was born was badly in need of moral values and social reform. The Mecca of his day was a central place of pagan worship. The Arab tribesmen of the region worshipped a pantheon of gods there, including Al-Lat, the sun goddess, and Al-Uzza, a goddess associated with the planet Venus, both of whom were daughters of the chief deity, known as Al-Ilah (Allah) or "the God."[23] The Kaaba, the shrine enclosing the famous black meteorite that was worshipped in Mecca before Mohammed's time, was also undoubtedly a site of an altar where blood sacrifices were offered to these and other gods. The morality of the neighboring tribesmen could, charitably, be described as chaotic. Huston Smith, in his classic *The Religions of Man,* goes so far as to call the Arab society before the advent of Mohammed "barbaric." Tribal loyalties were paramount; other than that, nothing served to mitigate the blood feuds, drunken brawls and sex orgies to which the harsh life of the desert gave sway.[24]

Repelled by the cruel and crude reality around him, the sensitive Mohammed had, by age forty, escaped to a desert cave where, as he later testified, he experienced a series of mystical visions, including revelations from the Angel Gabriel. He returned from the desert imbued with a spiritual mission to transform the pagan society around him.

Preaching an end to licentiousness and the need for peace, justice and social responsibility, Mohammed advocated improving the lot of slaves, orphans, women and the poor, and replacing tribal loyalties with the fellowship of a new monotheistic faith—which he called "Islam," meaning "surrender to God."

Initially, he attracted very few followers. Like the Romans who, while accepting the Christian god were not immediately sold on Paul's moral message, the Arabs of Mecca weren't about to give up gambling, alcohol and sex just because this strange man told them he had had a vision. After three years, Mohammed had barely forty converts.[25] But, imbued with a passion that has been the hallmark of the truly great visionaries of the world, Mohammed would not give up. And, little by little, he built a steady following of committed loyalists.

The more followers he attracted, the more attention he got, and with it, the more hostility. The merchants of Mecca, whose livelihood depended on the pagan sites and rites of the city, weren't going to be easily displaced. A murder plot was hatched, but Mohammed escaped just in the nick of time.

While persecution of the Muslims was mounting in Mecca, the city of Yathrib was experiencing problems of internal strife, and a delegation decided that the fiery preacher from Mecca would be the man to bring order to chaos. After winning the pledge of city representatives to worship only Allah, Mohammed agreed to migrate—his journey there in the year 622 C.E., the year 1 of the Islamic calendar, was immortalized as the *Hijrah*.

Thus his life was saved and a new horizon opened for his teachings. It was in Yathrib, henceforth to be known as Medina, "the City of the Prophet," that Islam took hold in a major way.

Why it did so seems to have a great deal to do with virtues and values that Mohammed exemplified, taught and enacted into law there. Writes Smith:

> *Tradition depicts his administration as an ideal blend of justice and mercy. As the chief of state and trustee of the life and liberty of his people, he exercised the justice necessary for order, unflinchingly meting out punishment to those who were guilty. When the injury was toward himself, on the other hand, he was gentle and merciful even to his enemies. In all, the Medinese found him a master whom it was as difficult not to love as not to obey.*[26]

Once he had made Medina his stronghold, Mohammed mobilized an army of ten thousand men and, in 630 C.E., moved against Mecca, intending to purify the Kaaba and turn it into a center of worship of the one God, Allah. His success is legendary. Two years later, when he died, all of Arabia was under Muslim control. The religion of Islam—the belief in one God and one moral standard—now united all tribesmen who had previously been ready to kill each other.

The one problem Mohammed had faced in Medina (and elsewhere) was the Jews, who were not prepared to accept his Arab version of Judaism. In the same way they had previously rejected Christianity, so too did they reject Islam.

There was agreement, to be sure, that Abraham was the father of both the Jews (through his son Isaac) and the Arabs (through his son Ishmael). This made the two peoples half-brothers. Disagreement arose regarding the issues of whether Mohammed was indeed the last of the prophets to be sent by God and that his word was the final revelation. The Jews found the idea unthinkable.[27]

Their rejection was painful to Mohammed, who reacted with uncharacteristic hostility toward the Jews and took great pains to pointedly separate Islam from its Jewish roots. The Sabbath was changed to Friday; direction of prayers was changed from Jerusalem to Mecca; most of the Jewish dietary laws were excised from Islam with the exception of the slaughter rituals, prohibition on pork and consumption of blood. Further, Mohammed maintained that the Jews had distorted their own Bible: Abraham did not attempt to sacrifice Isaac to God at Mount Moriah, one of the hills of Jerusalem; rather, Abraham took Ishmael to Mecca, where he offered to sacrifice him to Allah on the Black Stone of Kaaba.[28]

If Jews had previously rebuffed Mohammed's claims to prophecy, they now openly sneered at what they considered a complete fabrication. This only made things worse. Mohammed's anger and curses against the Jews are recorded in the Koran:

- "And humiliation and wretchedness were stamped upon them, and they were visited with wrath from God." [29]
- "Of all men you will certainly find the Jews . . . to be the most intense in hatred of those who believe." [30]
- "Vendors are they of error and are desirous that you go astray from the way. . . . But God has cursed them for their unbelief." [31]

Some of his followers would interpret such statements as license to purge the world of the Jews. Other Muslims would concentrate more on the commonality of heritage and belief that Mohammed had also emphasized, and they would treat the Jews as *ahl al-dhimma,* "the protected people," or *ahl al-kitab,* "the people of the Book," which in practicality turned out not to be as nice as it sounds, but at least they weren't being slaughtered.[32] Writes Robert S. Wistrich in *Anti-Semitism: The Longest Hatred:*

> *Admittedly, under Muslim rule, Jews before the modern era usually found greater toleration than under Christianity and were spared the regular massacres and frequent expulsion which were their curse in Christendom.*[33]

At the time of Mohammed's death, Arabia was united and poised for *jihad,* the "holy war" or "holy struggle," to bring the world to Allah. Shortly, it moved with a fearsome power against the Byzantine and Persian Empires. Commanded by Khalid ibn al-Walid, known as the "Sword of Allah," the Arab armies were victorious wherever they set foot.

The first big Islamic victory at the River of Yarmuk in 636 C.E. was due to twelve thousand Christian Arabs going over to the Muslims.[34] Vast numbers of people oppressed by the Byzantines were more than happy to welcome the new invaders with open arms.

Byzantine Egypt and Byzantine Palestine, including Jerusalem, fell between 638 and 642 C.E., as did Syria and Persia. From there came conquests of North Africa and Spain. A few years later, the Muslim Moors had crossed the Pyrenees and sacked Bordeaux, and were advancing northward toward Tours when, in 732 C.E., their rapid march was halted by the Franks at the battle of Poitiers. It would take several hundred years to get them out of Europe.[35]

The Muslims had managed such spectacular victories even while coping with intense internecine warfare over the direction of Islam and succession—specifically, who would assume the top title of caliph, i.e., become successor to the Prophet Mohammed. Things began to go from bad to worse starting in 656 C.E. when Caliph Uthman was hacked to death by Muslim rebels while sitting at home studying the Koran. Then Caliph Ali, the prophet's son-in-law, died after being stabbed with a poisoned sword as he was leaving prayers at the mosque in Kufa. Next, Caliph Al-Husayn, the prophet's grandson, was killed in a struggle for power with his rival Caliph Yazid. And finally, Caliph Abu'l-Abbas, also known as Al-Saffah, "Shedder of Blood," showed who was caliph by inviting the remaining members of the rival Umayyad dynasty to dinner, having them massacred before the first course and then enjoying a feast over their corpses.[36]

Like the Christians, who seemingly forgot the message of love they initially preached and went on to convert by intimidation and force, so too the Muslims reverted to tribalistic behavior, seemingly forgetting the spirit of brotherhood and unity that had brought them together under Mohammed's banner.

However, there were some key differences between the Christian conquerors and the Muslim ones.

Most importantly, the Muslims generally treated their new subjects well.[37] They did not (at least initially[38]) force conversions to Islam; instead, they offered tax incentives. All non-Muslims paid a tax; all Muslims did not. Needless to say, new believers signed up in droves.[39] Those monotheists who chose not to convert were merely required to acknowledge the Koran as divine teaching and to learn Arabic. (Nonmonotheists had a less attractive range of choices: convert, become a slave, or die.)

The Muslim empire continued to grow. Within a century, it occupied a vast swath of land from Spain across Central Asia all the way to India, becoming larger than the Roman Empire ever was.[40]

As noted, the Muslims were not mere barbaric conquerors. Wherever they went they absorbed the cultures of the people in the lands they conquered and commingled them with Islamic culture, which then was experiencing its Golden Age. They also played a significant role in the preservation of the classical knowledge of the Greeks and Romans, which during the Dark Ages was largely lost in Europe. In addition to their great contributions to art, architecture and philosophy, Arab scientists and thinkers changed the face of the sciences:

- In astronomy, the Muslims made the invaluable contribution in the ninth and tenth centuries, thanks to their great observatories in Baghdad and Damascus. They compiled new star catalogs and also developed the first tables of planetary motion.
- In mathematics, they gave the world a system they called "the science of restoration and balancing." The Arabic word for "restoration" is *al-jabr,* or "algebra."[41] In the ninth century, the Arab mathematician

Al-Khwarizmi developed the first theory of equations, with both examples and proofs, and the Egyptian mathematician Abu Kamil explained the basic laws of algebra and solved such complicated problems as finding x, y and z.

- In medicine, Avicenna (Abu Ali al-Husayn ibn Abd Allah ibn Sina), an eleventh-century Arab philosopher and doctor, produced *The Canon of Medicine* used throughout the Middle East and in Europe as a medical and pharmaceutical textbook. Avicenna also wrote the classic philosophical work known as *The Book of Healing,* a collection of treatises on Aristotelian logic, metaphysics, psychology, the natural sciences and other subjects.

- In biology, Abu Ali al-Hasam Ibn al-Haytham, an eleventh-century optician, introduced the world to the revolutionary idea of empirical proof. Before his time, various theories of science were arrived at through philosophical speculation. Ibn al-Haytham conducted an experiment and proved empirically that light started outside the eye and reflected into it, not the other way around. He also invented the first primitive camera obscura.[42]

The many other contributions of Muslim thinkers would take another book to list. But it is their efforts in the field of religion that interest us more here.

Without a doubt, the Muslims deserve great credit for introducing a significant portion of the world's population to monotheism. However, they cannot be given the credit for bequeathing to the Western world the values that we today hold so dear.

Perhaps they might have, but their influence was stopped dead in its tracks before they could have begun. The brakes were first put on in the eleventh century when the flowering of Islam was interrupted by the Crusades, by Muslim wars over Spain and by the concurrent attempts at reconquest of Spain by the Christians.

These various inter-Muslim and Muslim–Christian conflicts not only drove the Muslims out of Europe, but stunted the economic, political and cultural development of the Islamic world. It is a sad fact of history that since that time—for the last thousand years—progress in the area of the world to which Islam retreated has remained fairly static, the one notable exception being the fiery rise of the Ottoman Empire in the sixteenth century. Most of the Islamic world has neither industrialized nor democratized and, as a result, has lost its ability to influence the world at large.[43]

Once the Muslims left Europe, they left for good, leaving Christianity—and the West—to develop on its own course. They had played out their role in the largest religious revolution in world history.

It was an impressive revolution. By the middle of the eighth century, tens of millions of people had been converted—whether by Christianity or by Islam, whether they wanted to be or not—from a belief in many gods to a belief in one God.

And thus the concept of monotheism—which had seemed for so long to be a strange and incomprehensible idea limited exclusively to the Jews—became a religious prerequisite to the majority of the world's population.

CHAPTER 24

Gloomy Ages

Now that a large percentage of the world believed in one God, it would seem that it was only a matter of time before the values of ethical monotheism—reverence for life, justice and equality, peace and harmony—would bring about a universal utopia.

Soon the lion would lie down with the lamb and the world would beat its swords into plowshares.

As we know, it hasn't happened yet. And why it hasn't may have a lot to do with how the Christian Church went about spreading the message. (As previously stated, Islam had left the picture as far as its influence over the West was concerned.)

From the time of Constantine, when it came to power, the early Church was beset by bitter disputes and controversies concerning its theology, hierarchy and succession. Accusations of heresy, conspiracy, greed, immorality and consorting with the devil flew fast and loose as various bishops (some of whom were elected before being baptized or ordained to the priesthood) vied for territory.[44] In *A History of Christianity,* Paul Johnson relates that:

> *The venom employed in these endemic controversies reflects the fundamental instability of Christian belief during the early centuries, before a canon of New Testament writing had been established, credal formulations evolved to epitomize them, and a regular ecclesiastical structure built up to protect and propagate such agreed beliefs.*[45]

Christian theology was finalized in a series of councils at Nicea (in 325 C.E.), Constantinople (in 381 C.E.) and Chalcedon (in 451 C.E.). The key controversies concerning the divinity versus humanity of Jesus and the concept of the Trinity were settled. But others remained, especially whether supreme authority rested in the bishop of Rome (who claimed succession from the chief apostle Peter[46]) and whether the bishop of Rome and bishop of Constantinople were equal in power and rank.

As long as the seat of the empire was in Constantinople, the balance of power between East and West was maintained. However, once chunks of the Byzantine Empire began to fall to the Muslims, and once the bishop of Rome (called "Pope" after the Latin *papa* or "father") shored up his power base by allying himself with the Frankish emperors, the latter eclipsed the bishop of Constantinople.

The primary factor that helped establish the authority of the popes was the collapse of the Western Roman Empire. The disappearance of the economic, administrative and legal infrastructure led to a state of chaos.

The Church stepped in to restore order. Consciously modeling its bureaucratic framework on the model of the now-defunct Roman Empire, the Church created titles and administrative positions that people were used to—it's not by accident that the Pope was called "Pontiff" (from *pontifex maximus* or "chief priest"), a title previously reserved for the Roman emperor. With its well-organized bureaucracy, the Church found itself assuming a position of paramount importance in the evolution of feudal European society.

Explaining how the power of the church swelled, Johnson assigns the blame to Ambrose, bishop of Milan from 373 to 397 C.E., as the one who set the precedent:

> *"Power" was a word constantly on Ambrose's lips—in his mind, the degree of power the Church exercised reflected its spiritual authority and claims, which ultimately must be limitless. . . . Ambrose was thus instrumental in hastening the process which aligned imperial authority completely behind the orthodox Catholic Church, and also the Church completely behind imperial authority.*[47]

Today we remember the period when the Church ruled Western Europe with an iron hand as the "Dark Ages," although more charitable historians will call it the "Middle Ages." But there is a reason it deserves to be called dark—it was a period of repression, oppression and depression. The light of monotheism remained but a tiny spark that was almost extinguished by the doom and gloom of the period.

This black time began in the late fifth century C.E. when various Germanic tribes, barbarians all, overthrew the Romans. First came the Goths, who conquered Rome (in 410 C.E.) and most of the western territories.[48] Then came the Franks, who took the northern territories and eventually overran the Goths as well. (With time, the land of the West

Franks would become France, and the land of the East Franks would become Germany.) Tough customers, the Franks nevertheless accepted Christianity and were the first to challenge the Islamic Empire in its northward advance. No fool, Pope Stephen II made an alliance with them by which both sides benefited—the Franks gained legitimacy, the Pope gained land and security. The Frankish king, Pepin the Short, gave the Pope dominion over the city of Rome and all surrounding land, no small chunk of territory, to which successive popes added considerably.

The next and greatest of the Frankish kings, Charles the Great, better known as Charlemagne, took on the pagan Saxons, Italians, Bavarians and Slavs and, once victorious, gave them a simple choice—accept Jesus or die. He thus swelled the Christian fold by thousands and as a reward, on Christmas Day in 800 C.E., was officially crowned "Emperor of Rome" by Pope Leo III who, by then, felt powerful enough to bestow such a title. According to his biographer, Einhard, Charlemagne was surprised by the coronation, which happened during Christmas mass in Rome. He felt that he had won the crown by his conquests, and that he didn't need the Pope to "give" it to him.[49] But the Pope was purposely sending the message that Charlemagne should not forget where the real power lay.

All the warring of the Franks, first done by infantry, eventually necessitated a cavalry, which required long and expensive training. Furthermore, a cavalry had to have horses, horses had to have pastures, and pastures had to have land.

To support the cavalry, Frankish kings gave their soldiers estates of land farmed by dependent laborers, and thus was feudalism born. It was not a novel idea—the Greeks, the Romans and many other civilizations had practiced it in different forms. But the Frankish kings, with help from the popes, refined the system so that it would last in some parts of Europe (Germany and Russia, to be specific) until the nineteenth century. This is how it worked.

All the land was said to actually belong to the king, who granted fiefs (or holdings) to the lords in return for fealty and military service. The lords then granted fiefs to knights and vassals in return for protection and for performing military services for them. They also invested bishops and abbots with their ecclesiastical titles and the lands that went with these offices. At the bottom of the pyramid, basically all the land had been divided among various noblemen with the majority of the population working as serfs or virtual slaves for somebody else.

Much has been written about the misery and below-subsistence existence that characterized the day-to-day life of the vast majority of the inhabitants of medieval Europe. And a great deal of the blame for it has to be laid at the Church's door.

Far from worrying about injustice and oppression, the Church supported the inequality of the feudal system through its various dogmatic formulations, which strongly implied that God himself wanted things this way. For example:

- God ordained inequality in response to the sinful nature of man.[50]
- Poverty has great spiritual value.[51]
- The king is a divinely ordained human being whose authority cannot be questioned.[52]

Of course, the Church was not a disinterested party in all this. Indeed, the medieval Church was a major player in the feudal game, soon becoming the largest landowner in Europe.[53]

Historically, power and wealth have had a tendency to corrupt, and the popes of the Dark Ages were not immune. In the late ninth and early tenth centuries, the Vatican was rocked by scandal after scandal.[54]

Pope Stephen VI so hated his predecessor, Pope Formosus, that he had the dead pontiff's corpse exhumed, tried, condemned for ecclesiastical errors and then mutilated, stripped of its pontifical vestments and thrown into the Tiber River.

From 896 to 904 C.E.—that is, in the eight short years after the so-called "Cadaver Synod"—Rome saw a quick and bloody succession of seven popes! (One, Leo V, ruled only thirty days before being thrown in jail and executed.)

All that murderous intrigue was followed by a sordid episode that remains one of the most shameful in the history of the Church. Pope Sergius III, who ascended the papal throne in 904 C.E., fathered an illegitimate son by a fifteen-year-old girl named Morazia, daughter of the wealthy Theophylact family, which aided and abetted papal power plays. Then, Sergius's successor, Pope John X, had an affair with Morazia's daughter, for which Morazia had him killed (suffocated), thus ensuring that her bastard son by Sergius would become the next pope, John XI.[55]

With so much going on in Rome, the popes had little time to worry about the status of the serfs. But another and more important reason might be that as the largest landowner, the Church also collected huge amounts of taxes from the hapless peasants, whose lot there was no motivation to improve.

It is here that we see the great schizophrenia in the Church's relationship to its adherents. On the one hand, the Church touted a New Testament that proclaimed, "There is no such thing as Jew, Greek, slave, freeman, male and female; for you are all one person in Christ Jesus."[56] On the other hand, the Church actively supported a social and economic feudal structure that was inherently unequal and cruelly oppressive.

The early Christians took from the Jews the values and ideals of brotherhood, justice and social responsibility, but the all-powerful Church fathers practiced very little of what their Bible preached. It was easy to see why. For the Church to live by the beautiful and lofty teachings of the Bible would mean that it would have had to relinquish much of its wealth and power; submission to an absolute God-given standard of morality would have demanded it. But the Church was not there yet.

Henry Phelps-Brown in *Egalitarianism and the Generation of Inequality* suggests that the Church, while it embodied monotheism, had yet to rid itself of the old Hellenistic pagan tendencies:

> *Thus Christianity itself, and the views on wealth and power that came down from it, did not challenge the inequality of the secular world. They rather upheld it. . . . In this way they followed the main drift of the pagan philosophies. The inequality of human capacity was obvious, the need for subordination inescapable.*[57]

It is not hard to understand why the Church sought to keep the Dark Ages dark. The lamp of knowledge would have gone a long way to illuminate and change the unjust social structure that benefited the rich while exploiting the poor. If the masses could read, if the masses were allowed access to the Scriptures, they would quickly see the moral hypocrisy of Church behavior.

God forbid that a serf should get hold of a Bible[58] and find out what it actually said about the obligations of every person (even "His Lordship" and "His Eminence") to love his neighbor and treat him with equality since *all* human beings are created in the image of God.

It is precisely for this reason that the Church refrained from translating the Bible from Latin (which few people knew) to the vernacular. Access to the Bible, even by priests who could read Latin, was severely restricted. Writes Phelps-Brown:

> *Despite its anxiety to save man's souls from the perdition of earthly pursuits in order to preserve them for the salvation of the life after death, the medieval Church insulated pupils from the dangerous contamination of Scriptures. Only those entering holy orders were allowed to study theology and delve into Holy Writ. Unsupervised, independent exploration of the Bible was tantamount to heresy, and only clerics in good standing were permitted to expound Scripture from a Latin text incomprehensible to the Christian masses.*[59]

This situation persisted for a thousand years.

As the Church's empire grew in size, so did its need for more money to support it. The Crusades were launched in part to curb the growth of the Islamic Empire, but in part also to gain new lands and wealth for the growing population of Europe. They also offered an outlet for the ambitions of land-hungry knights and noblemen.

As such, they succeeded brilliantly with the grand prize—Jerusalem—being wrenched from Muslim control. In the summer of 1099 C.E., the Crusaders took the city and promptly massacred virtually every inhabitant. In the Crusaders' view, the city was thus purified in the blood of the defeated infidels—who included Muslims and a substantial number of Jews. In less than a hundred years the Muslims, under the famed Salah ah-Din, better known as Saladin, reclaimed Jerusalem, although the various Crusades had significantly expanded the power and control of Rome.

Pope Innocent III, who was elected pope before he was ordained as a priest, is given credit for the founding of the Papal empire, which came to be known as the Papal States, in 1197. In a controversy with King John of England over the appointment of the Archbishop of Canterbury, the Pope not only won the dispute but received from the king the whole kingdom as a fief.[60] With time the Papal States would cover a vast area of 16,000 square miles or 41,400 square kilometers.

Rolling in wealth, the Church built great edifices, fielded its own armies, and sank deeper and deeper into decadence and debauchery.

It was well-known that Pope Alexander VI bribed some of the college of cardinals to ensure his election in 1492. Once in office, he brought the papacy to new heights of spiritual laxity. A number of popes before him had abandoned celibacy, but Alexander VI openly flaunted his reputation as a great lover. He had a portrait of his mistress—dressed up like the Virgin Mary—painted over the door in his bedroom, and he publicly acknowledged his illegitimate children, Cesare and Lucrezia Borgia, who became famous in their own right.

The Church could not pretend to be a place of holiness, morality and spirituality while its popes wallowed in the moral gutter. Something had to give sooner or later.

But rather than clean up its own act, the Church decided to use the office of the Inquisition to clean up the heresies presumed common in the countryside. Created in the thirteenth century with the mission of finding and excommunicating heretics, the Inquisition became an instrument of terror, using intricate techniques of torture and putting vast numbers of people to death.

The hypocrisy of this situation was becoming intolerable, but the

Church was so powerful and so vengeful when it met opposition that any defiance was successfully stifled.

Giovanni Boccaccio, the great Italian humanist writer, offers us a humorous insight into the corruption and decadence of the Church of his day, circa 1350. In his classic work, *The Decameron,* a Jew by the name of Abraham is convinced by his Catholic friend to visit Rome in the hope that he will be so impressed by the visit that he will convert to Christianity. Abraham returns disgusted and reports:

> *"I say this for that, if I was able to observe aright, no piety, no devoutness, no good work or example of life or other what did I see there in any who was Churchman: nay lust, covetise, gluttony and the like and worse. . . . And as far as I judge, meseemeth your chief pastor and consequently all others endeavor with all diligence and all their wit and every art to bring to nought and to banish from the world the [values of the] Christian religion."* [61]

Tongue in cheek, Abraham nevertheless agrees to convert, because, despite the excesses of its leadership, Christianity is prospering, which to his mind must mean that God is on its side and not on the side of the persecuted Jews.

This brings us to the question: How bad was the lot of the Jews during this dark time?

Well, as one can imagine, it was not fun to be Jewish. According to early Church theology, the Jews knew that Jesus was the Messiah but they first rejected him, then killed him and now refused to accept him. They were, therefore, a corrupt people.

Initially, as this line of thinking was developing, the Jews were merely shoved into a corner. Politically and economically, they were cut out of medieval society and isolated. Their ability to directly influence the world was, therefore, significantly reduced.

But as the Dark Ages progressed, the picture of the Jews the Church painted grew much worse. Johnson describes it as follows:

> *There were stories that the Jews had concealed tails, suffered from bloody flux, had a peculiar smell—which instantly disappeared when they were baptized. This in turn led to reports that Jews served the devil—which explained everything—and communed with him in secret, vicious ceremonies.*[62]

At the heart of the matter was the Church's view of Judaism as a direct competitor for the soul of humanity. Writings of the early Church fathers (Pope Gregory I the Great, John Crysostom, Gregory of Nyssa) as early as the fourth century and through the seventh century clearly reveal both the competitiveness and hostility felt by the Church toward the Jews.[63]

From John Crysostom we get this:

> *Jews are the most worthless of men—they are lecherous, greedy, rapacious—they are perfidious murderers of Christians, they worship the devil, their religion is a sickness.*[64]

And this:

> *The Jews are the odious assassins of Christ and for killing god there is no expiation, no indulgence, no pardon. Christians may never cease vengeance. The Jews must live in servitude forever. It is incumbent on all Christians to hate the Jews.*[65]

From Gregory of Nyssa we get more of the same:

Slayers of the lord, murderers of the prophets, adversaries of god, haters of god, men who show contempt for the law, foes of grace, enemies of the father's faith, advocates of the devil, brood of vipers, slanderers, scoffers, men whose minds are in darkness, leaven of the Pharisees, assembly of demons, sinners, wicked men, stoners and haters of righteousness.[66]

Official Christian doctrine, as was mentioned earlier, further taught that because the Jews rejected Jesus they were in turn rejected by God. But there was one hitch to that theory. Since they no longer served a function as God's elected nation, the Jews should have ceased to exist. This they stubbornly refused to do.

The very fact that the Jews did not disappear—but insisted on professing and practicing their faith—created a philosophical problem for the Church. In an effort to explain it away, Christian theologians came up with the doctrine of *teste veritatis,* the "witness people"—the very existence of the Jews was living proof of the genuineness of the Old Testament (the Hebrew Bible), which served as the philosophical basis for the New Testament. In the future, the Jews would also come to testify to the validity of Jesus as the Messiah when he returned in the "Second Coming."

Thus the Jews were dismissed from the Christian map. It must have given them some satisfaction, therefore, to watch from the sidelines as a corrupt Church was brought to its knees from the inside out.

It began in the fourteenth century with challenges to Church doctrine and attempts at translating the Bible into other languages. Those responsible for these "illegal" translations were, of course, persecuted.[67]

Oxford scholar John Wycliffe, who first translated the Bible into English, was branded a heretic and dismissed from his position; when he died shortly thereafter, his body was disinterred and burned. (Incidentally, the preface to Wycliffe's Bible read, "The Bible is for the government of the people, by the people and for the people." He also believed serfdom and warfare were un-Christian.)[68]

Another challenger and reformer, John Hus of Bohemia, was branded a heretic and burned at the stake.[69]

Such efforts, while planting a seed of protest, did not however make a real dent.

Not until the sixteenth century, when Martin Luther came on the scene, did the Earth begin to shake. The young Augustinian friar accused the Church of decadence and internal rot, and this time he and his protesters would not be silenced by threats of excommunication or by the rattling of pontifical sabers.

Once unleashed, the Reformation would make a grand sweep of Christendom and, in so doing, play a vital role in the process of spreading Jewish ethical ideas into Western consciousness.

CHAPTER 25

A Spark in the Dark

In 1506, the Church of Rome undertook one of its grandest and most expensive projects: the building of a new St. Peter's Basilica as the centerpiece of the Vatican. The Church was to be so lavish and so huge that, when completed one hundred and fifty years later, it was the largest church ever built and remained so until 1989.

Such an astronomical project would take an astronomical sum of money, and, as a source of fund-raising, the Church turned to—or more accurately, turned up—the sale of indulgences.

The practice of granting indulgences—remission of punishment for sins through the intercession of the Church—already had a long history. Early on, indulgences were granted when a sinner performed some hazardous duty for the Church—like going on a crusade. (A crusade to the Holy Land got you forgiveness for all sins ever committed.) Later, it became possible to buy indulgences on your deathbed. (Thus you

ensured that you would enter heaven immediately, bypassing purgatory.)
Now, with the Church engaged in a major fund-raising effort, the sale of
indulgences took on new significance.[70]

Pope Sixtus IV's fund-raising campaign touted indulgences that
would free your deceased loved ones suffering in purgatory. Engaging in
emotional extortion, Church envoys resorted to imitating the anguished
wailing of parents who, in the throes of holy purification fires, pleaded
with their children to buy an indulgence and ease their torment.
Auctioning of indulgences to the highest bidder—on the basis of "buy
now, pay nothing later"—was another favorite tactic.[71]

The state of affairs was so shocking that in 1512, Johann Geiler, the
famed preacher from Strasburg, predicted that God himself would see to
the much needed house-cleaning:

> Since neither pope, nor emperor, kings nor bishops will reform
> our life, God will send a man for the purpose. I hope to see the day
> . . . but I am too old. Many of you will see it; think, then, I pray you,
> of these words.[72]

The reformer whose coming Geiler foretold was none other than
Martin Luther.

Born in 1483 to a wealthy German mining family (with roots in the
peasantry, as is much stressed in his biographies), Luther was brought up
in an atmosphere of piety and discipline. He attended a Latin school run
by a medieval lay group dedicated to the study of the Bible and gradu-
ated from the University of Erfurt, where he reportedly studied the
Biblical commentaries of Nicholas de Lyra, a Christian scholar who
heavily borrowed from Rashi, the famed Jewish scholar of the eleventh
century. Much affected by his Bible studies, Luther decided, despite the

anguish of his father, to enter an Augustinian monastery. His father apparently wanted his son to become a lawyer.

The facts of his life are important, because here the pattern is set. Once an Augustinian monk, Luther, a big and tough but simple man, involved himself in a movement to revive stricter discipline in the order. As a representative of a like-minded group, he traveled to Rome in 1510 and, once there, was shocked to discover the laxity and worldliness of the Vatican clergy. Needless to say, his petition was denied.

Luther returned and was plunged into a crisis of faith. As he would later write:

> *I did not love, indeed I hated this just God, if not with open blasphemy, at least with a huge murmuring, for I was indignant against Him, saying, "as if it were really not enough for God that miserable sinners should be eternally lost through original sin, and oppressed with all kind of calamities through the law of the ten commandments. . . ." Thus I raged with a fierce and most agitated conscience.*[73]

He resolved his dilemma by coming up with the theory of grace. As he explained, "At last I began to understand the justice of God as that by which the just man lives by the gift of God, that is to say, by faith."[74]

It would later become part of the Protestant theology that salvation came by God's grace or God's indulgence, so to speak. A gift from God could clearly not be sold by the Church. This difference of viewpoint was what caused Luther to break with the Roman Catholic Church.

By then, the sale of indulgences had reached a fever pitch. A Dominican monk named Johann Tetzel was plying the land preaching, "As soon as the coin in the coffer rings, the soul from purgatory springs."[75]

Full of youthful idealistic zeal (he was only thirty-four at the time), Luther reacted by posting his protest—the now famous "Ninety-Five Theses"—on the door of All Saints Church in Wittenberg on October 31, 1517.

The consequence was that his protest reached Rome, and he was asked, in no uncertain terms, to recant. He refused, proclaiming his famous defense, "Here I stand, I cannot do otherwise."[76] He was excommunicated four years later.

But it was too late to silence him, thanks to a remarkable technological advance that would change history forever—the Gutenberg press. Luther's "Ninety-Five Theses"—which, in effect, were an indictment of the Roman Catholic Church—was printed and widely distributed.

It is important to understand how this came to be.

A mere fifty years earlier, Johann Gutenberg had perfected a system of making metal letters in moulds, setting them in rows and using the templates thus formed to print multiple copies of a document in minutes, which previously would have had to be copied tediously by hand over many hours. (The Gutenberg Bible was printed, in Latin, sometime between 1450 and 1456.)

This incredible printing machine was applied to Luther's protest, and what might have been a local dispute with the protestant muzzled by his excommunication became a public controversy that spread far and wide.

Luther went on to translate the Old Testament from the original Hebrew into German vernacular and the New Testament from the original Greek, also into common German. This act of rebellion followed from his belief that the Church did not hold a monopoly on interpreting the Bible.

With the proliferation of Gutenberg's presses, all the world would soon know what the Bible said and would use that knowledge to indict and curtail the powers of the corrupt Church.

Naturally, Luther thought that the Jews would be on his side. Luther saw that the Catholic Church had treated the Jews shamefully until then, and he had a different plan. He wrote:

> *For they [Catholic clergy] have dealt with the Jews as if they were dogs and not human beings. They have done nothing for them but curse them and seize their wealth. . . . I hope that if the Jews are treated friendly and instructed kindly enough through the Bible, many of them will become real Christians and come back to the ancestral faith of the prophets and patriarchs.*[77]

Alas, the Jews rejected Luther (as they had rejected similar offers in the past), and Luther did not take the rebuff kindly:

> *What then shall we do with this damned rejected race of Jews? . . . Let me give you my honest advice. First, their synagogues or churches should be set on fire. . . . Secondly, their homes should like-wise be broken down and destroyed. . . . Thirdly, they should be deprived of their prayer-books and Talmuds. . . . Fourthly, their rabbis must be forbidden under threat of death to teach anyone.*[78]

And he goes on and on like that. (Four hundred years later, Hitler and the Nazis would use much of Luther's writings in their anti-Jewish propaganda.[79])

However, in the big picture that was now forming, the Jews were an insignificant element. The Reformation was imminent, but before it could be unleashed on Europe, one more historical event had to take place.

The political reality of medieval Europe was that the Church policies routinely undermined the authority and treasuries of the various monarchs. Of course, the Church, preoccupied as it was with its own greed, did not realize that the additional financial burdens it imposed—the vast sums it collected through its land holdings, taxes and selling of religious appointments—would prove its own undoing.

All the European monarchs were chafing under the yoke of the Church and were dying to be free of it. King Henry VIII of England—propelled by his overactive libido—proved to be the man of the hour who dared to make the break.

The eighteen-year-old monarch ascended to the throne in 1509 and, having secured a special papal dispensation, married the significantly older widow of his brother, Catherine of Aragon. After eight years, the good-looking and virile king grew tired of his bride, who had failed to produce a male heir. In addition, Henry was in love with Anne Boleyn, a young and beautiful lady-in-waiting to the queen. He asked the papacy to annul the marriage, claiming that the original dispensation allowing him to marry her had been in error.

However, though the Church was known to bend its rules willy-nilly, several obstacles stood in the way of Henry's demand. Chiefly, the Holy Roman Emperor of the day, Charles V, just happened to be related to old Catherine and strongly opposed her being thrown off like a used robe.[80]

Charles was having a hard time of it just then, waging war against the French king, Francis I, who counted Pope Clement VII as his ally. But Charles won, and he promptly put Pope Clement VII in prison for a few months to meditate on the wisdom of making different alliances. This was not a time for Henry to be asking the Pope for a favor that ran counter to the wishes of a monarch in possession of his dungeon keys.

So Henry took matters in his own hands. If Charles V could lord over the Church, so could he. Thus, in 1534, he had himself declared the head of the Church of England and married Anne Boleyn.

He was then excommunicated by Rome, which only solidified his position as the supreme ecclesiastical authority in England. Although some internal objections were raised—most notably from Sir Thomas More, who was executed for his trouble—the English people affirmed Henry's supremacy, as did the nobles who were given Church land in exchange for their support.

After the establishment of the Church of England in 1538, Henry VIII issued a proclamation that a copy of the Bible be placed in every Church.[81] (It is stunning to a Western mind, used to a Gideon Bible in every hotel room, that such a proclamation was needed!)

It just so happened that William Tyndale had, a short while earlier, completed a translation of the Bible into English, for which the poor man—in keeping with Church policy of that time—had been burned at the stake in 1536. (Tyndale's and Wycliffe's translations would later be commingled and come to be known as the King James Bible.)

Public reading of the Holy Word—in English—became a regular feature of worship. Private ownership of a copy of the Bible became a common phenomenon. In many homes it was the only book in the house and was read from extensively. (This would soon come to have significant impact on the religious and political development of England.)

As for Henry, he got tired of Anne Boleyn just as he got tired of Catherine and went on to marry a total of six times. But never mind. His role in the Reformation had been played out. He had defied the Church and lived to tell about it.

If Henry VIII could dismiss the power of the Church to excommunicate and condemn him to eternal damnation, other monarchs would soon follow. They had much to gain—the Church was the biggest landlord in medieval Europe, collecting more money through taxes than the Crown.

If the power of the Church could be broken, then not only would the monarchy have absolute authority, it would also vastly increase its wealth.

As freedom from oppression and repression of the Church spread, it carried with it the spirit of the Renaissance, a "rebirth" of classical (ancient Greek and Roman) literature, philosophy and the arts. So although today we think of the Renaissance as "renewal," in fact, it began as a return to ideas that the Church had trashed.

The thinkers of the Renaissance encouraged a new humanism and intellectual curiosity, which refocused the center of scholarship away from the religious to the temporal and forever weakened the Church's hold on the minds of its Christian subjects. The major intellectual core of the Renaissance was based on the renewed interest in Hellenistic texts (though Galileo challenged some of Aristotle's most important conclusions regarding physical laws and overturned the Ptolemaic system in favor of the Copernican system of viewing the heavens). But most importantly, the Renaissance introduced the world to the philosophy of humanism.

Humanism was a human-centered (as opposed to Church-centered or God-centered) worldview, which stressed human values, exalting human free will and human superiority to the rest of nature. The primary intellectual focus of humanist scholars was on the study of the "humanities": philosophy, science, mathematics, history, languages and poetry.

The Church's persecution of Galileo in the early 1600s only empowered these scholars all the more and showed the Church's vulnerability and ignorance. Believing Galileo's teachings—that the Earth moved around the sun instead of standing still—to be somehow contradictory of the Bible's teaching,[82] the Inquisition took steps to silence the famed scientist. It accused him of heresy and sentenced him to life imprisonment (later commuted to lifetime house arrest), condemned his teachings and ordered his books burned. Yet by then too many knew better and ridiculed the Church's position, seeing it as a desperate attempt to cling to power through suppression of knowledge.

All of that weakened the Church's hold everywhere, including on the politics of Europe. The pre-Renaissance continent was structured around rural feudalism with monasteries acting as the cultural and administrative centers for societies. But with the Renaissance came the growth of large cities, as well as the rise of strong lay leadership. It was this newly centralized authority that ultimately overpowered the authority of the Church, and it was in these cities that a new and better-informed middle class grew and became a major cultural and political force in the development of modern European society.

The shape of new things to come would be dictated by these people— reformers, defenders of new ideas, and, surprisingly, most of all, by the lovers and disseminators of long-suppressed Biblical values and concepts.

CHAPTER 26

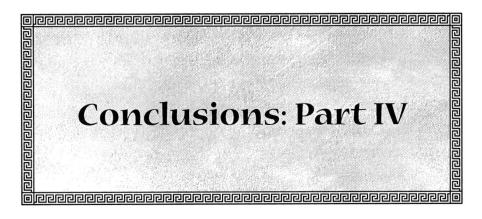

Conclusions: Part IV

Thus the landscape of the world was undergoing irrevocable change. For our purposes, what is significant in this giant slice of history is that the Protestant reformers of the fourteenth, fifteenth, and sixteenth centuries all shared the viewpoint that the Roman Catholic Church had betrayed the spirit of Christianity as portrayed in the Bible. It had placed itself between God and his creation, robbed the individual of responsibility to control his own destiny, and cut humanity off from the absolute standard of right and wrong that only God can impose.

To restore that balance, the reformers advocated Bible reading and Bible study. It is important to note than when we speak about the Christian world reading the Bible, we are not talking just about the New Testament but, even more importantly, also about the Old Testament, or the Hebrew Bible. Historian Barbara Tuchman offers this analysis of what that meant in *The Bible and the Sword:*

*With the translation of the Bible into English and its adaptation
as the highest authority for an autonomous English Church, the history, traditions and moral code of the Hebrew nation became part
of the English culture; became for a period of three centuries the
most powerful single influence on that culture.*[83]

Why the stress on the Hebrew Bible?

Protestant reformers wanted to return Christianity to its pure roots—
that is, to before the Catholic Church corrupted Christianity as they saw
it. In their minds, the roots of Christianity were not in Rome, but Israel.
As a consequence, understanding of the Jewish roots of Christianity
became a primary task of Reformation Bible study.[84]

Protestant thinkers also realized that the spiritual and moral origins of
Christianity and virtually all the beautiful ideas of the New Testament
had their source in the Old Testament.[85] Study of the Hebrew Bible,
therefore, was a fundamental component of Protestantism, and in many
cases was viewed as even more important than later Christian texts.

From the sixteenth century onward, the Bible became the most influential book, not only in England, but in all of Europe, and especially in
those areas effected by the Protestant Reformation. The idea, adopted by
the Protestants, of using the Bible not only as a religious guidebook, but
also as the blueprint for society and government, played a very significant role in the political and social evolution of Western society.

Thus the popularization of the Bible presents another major step forward in the transmission of Jewish ideas into Western consciousness.
These ideas would be played out in the modern democracies soon to take
shape.

Part V

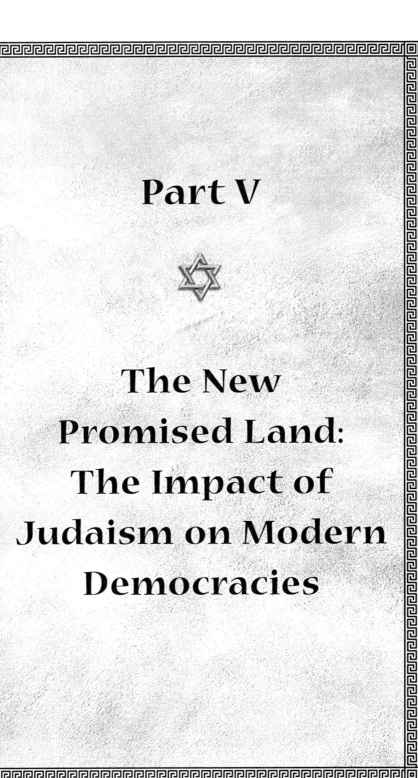

The New
Promised Land:
The Impact of
Judaism on Modern
Democracies

This twelve-hundred-year period—from the fourth century, when Christianity became the state religion of the Byzantine Empire, through the seventh century, when the Islamic Empire established itself in North Africa, the Middle East and Asia Minor, to the sixteenth century, when Martin Luther posted his protest and began the Reformation—saw a dramatic change in the concept of humanity's relationship to God.

Monotheism—the idea of one God, which until the beginning of this period had been the sole doctrine of a tiny band of Jews—had become the major religious tenet of millions. But up to the Reformation, humanity's view of its obligation to others changed very little. Inequality and injustice had been the order of the day in both the Muslim and Christian worlds.

Beginning with the sixteenth century, we start seeing the stirrings of what will become the great social revolution of modern history: the birth and growth of democracy.

Jewish ideas, spread primarily through the Bible, played a key role in this next great period of political and social transformation, which finally established the ethical system of the Torah as the values of the Western world.

CHAPTER 27

The Puritans
Are Coming

Everybody was reading the Bible.

As a consequence of the Reformation—and the tidal wave of Bible translation, Bible distribution and Bible study—the mindset of Europe was undergoing slow but progressive change. The impact on society and government was not immediately felt, but the Bible—and the Jewish values and ideals it contained—served as one of the main catalysts for the sweeping changes of what would soon follow.

Beginning in the seventeenth century, the Bible's influence was felt far more than in just the sphere of religion. Once the power of the Church was broken, Europe was far freer to develop governmentally, socially, religiously and philosophically. Gabriel Sivan, in *The Bible and Civilization,* explains:

In the wake of the reformation, independent thinkers turned their attention to the legislative and social organization of ancient Israel and also came to appreciate the Biblical concept of justice and morality as expounded by the Rabbis after the time of Jesus. The Old Testament thus became the model for the concepts and ideals of a world feeling its way toward democratic government.[1]

Some of the first to send out such feelers were the Puritans.

Who they were and how they came to define early democratic society can only be understood properly in the historic context.

Let us return to the court of England, where the health of the monarchs had not been holding up too well. Following the death of King Henry VIII (at age fifty-six), his son Edward VI (the son of Henry's third wife) ascended to the throne, but six years later died of tuberculosis (at age twenty-four). After some confusion, Henry's first daughter by the hapless Catherine of Aragon became queen; she was Mary I, though we've come to know her by her nickname—"Bloody Mary."

In his short reign, Edward did much to carry on the work his father started of divorcing England from the Roman Catholic Church. He favored the principles of the Reformation and did much to establish Protestantism in England; he was also responsible for introducing his countrymen to the first *Book of Common Prayer.*

But Mary was a staunch Catholic. She was eighteen years old when the Church of England was founded by her father and would not easily forget the unholy intrigue when Henry broke with the Pope in order to cast aside her mother. Mary felt duty-bound to avenge that insult and set things right. Her efforts at reinstating Catholicism in England—by fierce religious persecution, which included burning some three hundred

Protestants at the stake—earned her her nickname. But her reign lasted only five years (she also died early, at age forty-two), and much of what Mary started was undone by her half-sister and successor Elizabeth I.[2]

Trying to be a peacemaker, Elizabeth returned England to Protestantism, but some would say that her religious settlement, known as the "Elizabethan Compromise," did not go far enough and failed to purify the Church of England of the remnants of Roman Catholic "popery."

Those who wanted to complete the process of purification came to be known as the Puritans and their social activism as the Purification Movement, later the Puritan Revolution.[3]

The movement began in earnest with a controversy over—of all things—clothes and titles.

Elizabeth had retained the Catholic hierarchy of archbishops and bishops, but many felt that a "presbyterian" church governed by local councils of clergy and laity would be more in keeping with the new thinking of the day.[4] After all, had not the Catholic Church—in its obsession with direct succession and centralized power—betrayed Christianity by injecting itself between man and God?

Elizabeth had also insisted that the Church of England preachers wear uniform vestments and conduct services according to a uniform liturgy; unfortunately, she had the order issued after many had already done away with clothes and practices they felt smacked of the Catholic Church, thus Elizabeth's decree sent the wrong message.

But even though the movement seemingly started over robe styles, it would be unfair to suggest that the concerns of the Puritans were trivial. In fact, these people came to be known for their intense commitment to a morality, a form of worship and a civil society strictly conforming to God's commandments as set forth in the Bible.

Fearful that the Anglican Church would become just another version of the Roman Catholic Church, the Puritans viewed with suspicion Elizabeth's decrees that seemed only to establish the supremacy of a monarchy over a Church that could be easily corrupted by corruptible kings and queens.

They refused to acknowledge any authority other than the Bible. And the Bible said that only God—and that meant no human being, not a king, not a queen, not a pope nor a bishop—was the supreme and sole source of religious standards.[5]

To Puritan eyes, the picture worsened in the early 1600s when King James I came to the throne and forced conformity in ecclesiastical matters left hanging by Elizabeth.[6] Then, to add insult to injury, he mandated the reading—in church, on Sunday, no less!—of his *Book of Sports,* which enumerated recreations permissible on that day. The Puritans, of course, believed in strict adherence to the Biblical definition of the Sabbath: a day of rest from all earthly pursuits and dedicated to prayerful preoccupation with spiritual matters only. To say they were horrified by this would be an understatement.

Seeing that no good would come of the monarchs' meddling in ecclesiastical matters, some one hundred Puritans boarded the *Mayflower* in 1620, intent on establishing a community in the New World that would abide by God's laws and not be forced into indignities of this kind. Upon landing on Plymouth Rock, they signed the Mayflower Compact, forming the first American political democracy.[7] A few years later, another Puritan ship, *John of London,* landed on the same spot, its passengers taking the Oath of a Freeman and conspicuously leaving out any mention of the king or loyalty to the crown; they swore loyalty only to God and their conscience.

Meanwhile, back in England, Charles I ascended to the throne and, in a political alliance, married the Catholic princess Henrietta Marie of France. It didn't help that Charles also saw fit to assert the divine right of kings and dissolved Parliament, or that his spiritual advisor, William Laud, the new archbishop of Canterbury, turned out to be an avowed anti-Puritan.

When Laud tried to introduce a new liturgy, riots broke out in Scotland, and Charles—unable to raise funds to quell the uprising—had to reinstate Parliament. Religion played a key role in parliamentary elections and, suddenly, the Puritans wielded uncommon influence in politics.

The first two acts of the new Parliament when it convened in 1640 were to set aside a day for "fasting and humiliation" and to appoint house preachers, whose sermons urged the nation to renew its covenant with God so England could become "our Jerusalem, a praise in the midst of the Earth."[8]

It goes without saying that any king would be threatened by a Parliament whose members had nothing but disdain for the temporal power of the monarchy and strongly believed that the sole legal–moral authority came from God via their interpretation of the Bible.

Sensing that confrontation was inevitable, Charles marshaled the heavily anti-Puritan Royalist forces. Meanwhile, Parliament also got ready, recruiting the New Model Army, a force of twenty-two thousand men under Oliver Cromwell.

Civil war—which came to be known as the English Revolution or the Puritan Revolution—had started.

At issue was whether England should be ruled by Parliament or by a monarch claiming supreme authority by virtue of the divine right of kings.

It took eight years, but Parliament won. In January of 1649, Charles was tried and beheaded. Now Parliament—with Cromwell at its head as Lord Protector of the Commonwealth—governed supreme.

The English Revolution was a watershed event in European history, and it shook the foundations of European nobility. For the first time a monarch was not only dethroned by the masses, but also executed. (This revolution would be followed by several others—in America, in France and eventually in Russia.)

It wouldn't have happened without the Bible. The Puritans were obsessed with it, and in it they found the model for a just society under God.[9]

The Puritan political agenda—which led to the revolution—was overwhelmingly a product of their religious beliefs, which stressed the right of every man to interpret God's law, as embodied in the Bible, and to appeal to that law above any other authority.

Furthermore, the Puritans viewed their struggle as a mirror image of the struggle of the ancient Hebrews against the pharaoh of Egypt or the wicked king of Babylon. Because they identified so strongly with ancient Israel, they also chose overwhelming to identify with the Torah and the other books of the Hebrew Bible. They gave their children Old Testament names, studied Hebrew and modeled their day of rest after the Jewish Sabbath. Cromwell's New Model Army marched into battle singing Psalms and carrying banners embroidered with the Lion of Judea; their battle cry was "The Lord God of Hosts."[10]

So intense was Puritan identification with the Jews that some of the extremists among them advocated transforming England into a theocracy based on Jewish Biblical law. Some even went so far as to reject the divinity of Jesus.

One has merely to read the writings of the great Puritan poet John

Milton to appreciate the all-pervasive influence of the Hebrew Bible on the Puritan worldview. For example:

> *There are no songs comparable to the song of Zion; no oration equal to those of the prophets; and no politics like those which Scripture teach.*[11]

All that obsession with teaching and studying Scripture had a significant side-benefit. To read the Bible you had to learn *to read.*

Throughout history, the powers-that-be have realized that it is far easier to control an illiterate population than a literate one. Knowledge empowers the individual, and an empowered individual is a potential revolutionary. (If anything, the Puritan Revolution was proof of that; it wouldn't have come about if its instigators had not read the Bible.)

This widespread idea of controlling literacy was one of the major reasons literacy rates had been so low throughout history, even among the most advanced societies of the ancient world, such as Greece and Rome.

As we now know, the Catholic Church also followed this policy of limiting both literacy and knowledge. In medieval Europe (with the notable exception of the Jews, who always maintained an unusually high rate of literacy due to the requirement of knowing God's law), the Church had a virtual monopoly on literacy. The only literate people were monks and upper-level clergy, and virtually all major libraries were contained within monasteries.

The way it looked to the Church, a literate peasant reading the Bible by the light of the hearth fire in the wee hours of the night was the most dangerous picture imaginable.[12] Soon, his fellow peasants would be sitting about discussing what they had read and figuring that maybe God, sin, hell and the rest of it were not exactly like the Church would have them believe. Once the Church's power to intimidate and inspire fear of damnation on behalf of God was shaken, its comfy spot at the top of the medieval world could be undermined as well.

In contrast to the Church's attitude, Protestantism found literacy essential. Its fundamental doctrine held that the individual is obliged to create a direct relationship with God, using the Bible as the moral–spiritual guidebook to find the correct path.[13] The Puritans, even more than other Protestants, put tremendous stress on literacy as necessary to Bible education.

As a result of this outlook, by the end of the seventeenth century and certainly by the beginning of the eighteenth century, about 40 percent of the adult male population of Protestant Europe could read. To us today, 40 percent may seem low, but compared to the abysmal literacy rates of Greco-Roman times or to the Dark Ages when Catholic clergy kept books under lock and key, 40 percent seems like a tremendously significant leap forward.[14]

Another significant leap forward came in the area of religious tolerance. Having had their right to worship denied by the decrees mandating uniform liturgy, the Puritans were anxious to make sure no human being ever held that power over the conscience of others. In the words of Puritan preacher Roger Williams (later the founder of Rhode Island):

> *It is the will and command of God that conscience and worship be granted to all men in all nations and countries. . . . An enforced uniformity of religion denies the principles of Christianity.*[15]

It is this attitude that the Puritans applied to the Jews wherever they encountered them, though it must be made clear that the Puritan love of the ancient Jews of the Bible didn't exactly translate to the Jews of their day.

Still, in 1653, the Puritans permitted the return of the Jews who had been thrown out of England some four hundred years before when Edward I found expulsion the most efficient way of seizing Jewish assets. The reasons for the reversal were twofold. First, the Puritans (erroneously) assumed that since their beliefs and practices were so close to those of the ancient Hebrews, converting the Jews to the Puritan version of Christianity would be a snap. Second, they believed that the messianic redemption would not come about until the Biblical prophecy concerning the Jews was fulfilled. The particular prophecy that became the center of Puritan focus was a verse from the Book of Deuteronomy, which speaks of the Jews being scattered "from one end of the Earth to the other." [16] It just so happened that the medieval Hebrew name for England was *Ketzeh Ha-Eretz,* literally meaning "end of the Earth." Therefore, the Puritans reasoned, without Jews coming to England there could not be a Second Coming of Jesus.

The Jews did return to England but (as was generally their pattern through history) they did not convert to yet another people's version of their religion. However, the Puritans, staying true to their principles of religious tolerance, let the Jews worship in peace.

It must be said that, while the Puritans are worthy of admiration in this and many other respects, they did not always act in keeping with the beliefs they professed. For example, even though the revolution was waged against the absolute power of the monarchy, when Oliver Cromwell came into office, he ruled as a virtual dictator and was constantly at odds with Parliament until his death in 1658.

Cromwell's constituency could also behave in a manner that could charitably be described as bellicose, if not downright oppressive. This is why even today the term "Puritan" usually has a pejorative connotation.

Yet the impact of these people on the values of today's democracy should never be underestimated. Tuchman stresses this point:

> *Because the Puritans were not likeable, few have done them jus-*
> *tice. As targets for ridicule they are as a barn door to a marksman.*
> *Nevertheless they gave permanent underpinning to two principles*
> *that are the basis of democratic society: for one thing, the security*
> *of parliamentary government; for another, the right of nonconfor-*
> *mity or freedom of worship, as we call it today. The principle of*
> *toleration . . . brought the Pilgrim Fathers to America and formed*
> *the moral basis of a new society in a New World.*[17]

When Cromwell died, the Puritan domination of England died with him. By 1660, there was a shift back in favor of the monarchy, and a new king, Charles II, was crowned. The Puritans once again found themselves the persecuted minority.

But Europe after the Puritans was not the same.

The Puritans had left a lasting legacy of political reform not only in England, but the rest of the continent as well, even as they packed their bags and fled for the safety of America.

On their heels came the Enlightenment—or the Age of Reason—the proponents of which took advantage of the weakened Roman Catholic Church and did their best to attack and undermine its power even further. The philosophers of the Enlightenment put the human mind above all else, seeing reason and the tools of scientific observation as the key vehicles for the discovery of truth. Thus, they accused the Church of the crime of holding the human mind hostage to its convoluted theology that only encouraged ignorance and superstition.

Yet, while they attacked the church, it is important to stress that the thinkers of the Enlightenment—particularly the English and American ones—did not reject God, opting instead for Deism, a belief in the existence of God minus Christian theology.

A key figure of the time, Sir Isaac Newton, the English mathematician and physicist who is considered by many the greatest scientist of all time, was a staunch believer in God. He wrote in *Mathematical Principles of Natural Philosophy:*

> *As a blind man has no idea of colors, so have we no idea of the manner by which the all-wise God perceives and understands all things. . . . We know him only by his most wise and excellent contrivances of things, and final causes; we admire him for his perfections; but we reverence and adore him on account of his dominion. . . . Blind metaphysical necessity, which is certainly the same always and everywhere, could produce no variety of things.*[18]

Most importantly, the thinkers of the Enlightenment stressed—just like the Hebrews of the Bible—that the mission of human beings needs to be focused on fixing and improving the human lot down here on Earth, rather than in some heavenly hereafter.[19]

Their ideas would soon be married to the ideas of democracy and to the Puritan love of Biblical law in the New World. There, the Puritans and other Protestant splinter sects would play a crucial role in the political and religious formation of the United States, which is the next link in the chain of the spread of Jewish values to humanity.

CHAPTER 28

America the Beautiful

The creation of the United States of America represented a unique event in world history. Unlike other countries where democracy evolved over a period of hundreds of years, the United States was the first country to be created, from its inception, as a democracy. (While the Founding Fathers actually called the United States government a "republic" [according to *Merriam-Webster's Collegiate Dictionary, Tenth Edition*, "a government having a chief of state who is not a monarch and who . . . is usu. a president" and "a government in which supreme power resides in a body of citizens entitled to vote and is exercised by elected officers and representatives responsible to them and governing according to law"], it clearly embodied the central principles of a "democracy" ["government by the people; esp: rule of the majority" and "a government in which the supreme power is vested in the people"].) And the Bible played a major role in this process.

As we already saw with the Puritans' Massachusetts Bay Colony at Plymouth Rock, many of the earliest "pilgrims" who settled the "New England" of America in the early seventeenth century were refugees escaping religious persecutions in Europe.

Over the next century, America continued to be not only the land of opportunity for many people seeking a better life but also the land of religious tolerance. By the middle 1700s, the east coast of America was settled by a virtual who's who of Christian splinter sects from all over Europe. Among them were:

- Puritans
- Quakers, an extremist Puritan sect who did not believe in ministers and for whom a Society of Friends meeting together was good enough to bring down the Holy Spirit
- Calvinists, who early on had challenged the Catholic belief that the bread and wine became the body and blood of Jesus in the celebration of the Mass
- Huguenots, or French Calvinists
- Moravians, followers of John Hus, the Protestant martyr from Bohemia
- Mennonites, a Swiss sect of Anabaptists who rejected infant baptism
- Amish, the most stringent of the Mennonites

These were just some of the numerous groups who arrived in America in search of religious freedom.

The majority of the earliest settlers were, of course, Puritans. Beginning with the *Mayflower,* over the next twenty years, sixteen thousand Puritans migrated to the Massachusetts Bay Colony, and many more settled in Connecticut and Rhode Island. Like their cousins back in England, these American Puritans strongly identified with both the historical traditions and customs of the ancient Hebrews of the Old

Testament. They viewed their emigration from England as a virtual re-enactment of the Jewish exodus from Egypt. To them, England was Egypt, the king was Pharaoh, the Atlantic Ocean was the Red Sea, America was the Land of Israel and the Indians were the ancient Canaanites. They were the new Israelites, entering into a new covenant with God in a new Promised Land. Thanksgiving—first celebrated in 1621, a year after the *Mayflower* landed—was initially conceived as a day parallel to the Jewish Day of Atonement, Yom Kippur; it was to be a day of fasting, introspection and prayer. Sivan observes:

> *No Christian community in history identified more with the People of the Book than did the early settlers of the Massachusetts Bay Colony, who believed their own lives to be a literal reenactment of the Biblical drama of the Hebrew nation. They themselves were the children of Israel; America was their Promised Land; the Atlantic Ocean their Red Sea; the Kings of England were the Egyptian pharaohs; the American Indians the Canaanites (or the Lost Ten Tribes of Israel); the pact of the Plymouth Rock was God's holy Covenant; and the ordinances by which they lived were the Divine Law. Like the Huguenots and other Protestant victims of Old World oppression, these émigré Puritans dramatized their own situation as the righteous remnant of the Church corrupted by the "Babylonian woe," and saw themselves as instruments of Divine Providence, a people chosen to build their new commonwealth on the Covenant entered into at Mount Sinai.*[20]

As previously stated, in England, the Puritan identification with the Bible was so strong that some Puritan extremists sought to replace English common law with the Biblical laws of the Old Testament, but were prevented from doing so. In America, however, there was far more freedom to experiment with the use of Biblical law in the legal codes of the colonies, and this was exactly what these early colonists set out to do.

The earliest legislation of the colonies of New England was determined by Scripture. At the first assembly of New Haven in 1639, John Davenport clearly stated the primacy of the Bible as the legal and moral foundation of the colony:

> *Scriptures do hold forth a perfect rule for the direction and gov-ernment of all men in all duties which they are to perform to God and men as well as in the government of families and common-wealth as in matters of the Church . . . the Word of God shall be the only rule to be attended unto in organizing the affairs of govern-ment in this plantation.*[21]

Subsequently, the New Haven legislators adopted a legal code—the Code of 1655—which contained some seventy-nine statutes, half of which contained Biblical references, virtually all from the Hebrew Bible.[22] The Plymouth Colony had a similar law code, as did the Massachusetts assembly, which, in 1641—after an exhortation by Reverend John Cotton, who presented the legislators with a copy of *Moses, His Judicials*—adopted the so-called "Capitall Lawes of New England" based almost entirely on Mosaic law.[23]

A very significant political evolution was taking place in the New World. Unlike the Puritans in England who, of necessity, lived under English common law and were ruled by a king and Parliament, the Puritans of America had no central authority or national governing body. Yet they did not lapse into anarchy. Instead, they created communities governed by elected councils of elders similar to the "presbyters" of

England. Their communities were both stable and prosperous, with mandatory school systems modeled after the Jewish ones.

This unique political evolution goes a long way toward explaining the strong sense of independence shared by the colonies and the early success of democracy in America. The Puritans felt that God was watching them, and their fear of heaven was a thousand times stronger than fear of the crown.

It almost seems as if these early settlers had recreated the Biblical period of the Judges, when, following the conquest of Jericho and settlement of Canaan, Israel had no king or central authority and "every man did what was right in his own eyes."[24]

What was right in Puritan eyes, of course, was what the Bible said. But what did it say exactly? So much of it could be subject to the interpretation of the reader.

In the absence of Jewish oral tradition, which helped the Jews understand the Bible, the Puritans were left to their own devices and tended toward a literal interpretation. This sometimes led to a stricter, more fundamentalist observance than Judaism had ever seen. For example, the Jewish Sabbath is a day of refraining from work as the Bible mandates. However, "work"—in Hebrew *melacha*—is defined by Jewish oral tradition as cessation of all creative activity that was in progress when the Tabernacle was being built and which, the Bible states, ceased on the Sabbath.[25] But the Puritans took the commandment to cease work as unconditional. And their prohibitions were actually more restrictive than what the Jews had themselves practiced. Even household chores such as sweeping floors, making beds or feeding animals were not allowed for the twenty-four hours of the day of rest. Adherence was enforced by fines and public floggings.

While we stress the importance of the Hebrew Bible to the early

American settlers, it is important to note that, of course, the gospels of Jesus were revered as well. However, the Hebrew Bible—the Old Testament—was seen as the original and pure source of Christian values, and also as a legalistic and ritualistic guide, something which the New Testament was not.

In addition, there was a political agenda involved in this special focus in the Old over the New Testament. Many New Englanders viewed the New Testament as an instrument of justification, used by powers-that-be in Europe to preserve the existing order, as Paul had written in his letter to the Romans:

> *Every person must submit to the authorities in power, for all authority comes from God, and the existing authorities are instituted by him. It follows that anyone who rebels against authority is resisting a divine institution, and those who resist have themselves to thank for the punishment they receive.*[26]

That sure smacked of the divine right of kings and condemnation of the rebels of the Puritan revolution. No wonder that the Hebrew Bible, with its message of obedience to God alone, of personal responsibility and of freedom from tyranny, was far more in tune with the mind-set of these Protestant splinter sects of America.

Focusing even further on the issue of individual responsibility, the Massachusetts Bay Colony enacted legislation requiring parents to teach their children to read and understand the basic principles of religion and capital laws. All towns in New England with a minimum of fifty households were required by law to establish schools and appoint teachers.

In 1670, British commissioners making a survey of conditions in the American colonies reported that in Connecticut fully one-quarter of the annual revenues were set aside for free public education.[27] Universities were established (the first being Harvard University, founded in 1636 as a training school for Puritan ministers), and many printing presses were imported for the printing and dissemination of books.

In insisting on education for all, the Puritans were following Jewish law. (The twelfth-century Jewish philosopher Maimonides had admonished, "Appoint teachers for the children in every country, province and city. In any city that does not have a school excommunicate the people of the city until they get teachers for the children."[28])

Education for all thus became a hallmark of early America and not just New England. In addition to Harvard, many other colleges and universities were established under the auspices of various Protestant sects: Yale, William and Mary, Rutgers, Princeton, Brown, Kings College (later to be known as Columbia), Johns Hopkins, Dartmouth, etc. The Bible played a central role in the curriculum of all of these institutions of higher learning, with both Hebrew and Bible studies offered as required courses.[29]

Many of these colleges even adopted some Hebrew word or phrase as part of their official emblem or seal. Beneath the banner containing the Latin *Lux et Veritas,* the Yale seal shows an open book with the Hebrew *Urim V'tumim,* which was a part of the ceremonial breastplate of the high priest in the days of the Temple. The Columbia seal has the Hebrew name for God at the top center, with the Hebrew name for one of the angels on a banner toward the middle. Dartmouth uses Hebrew words meaning "God Almighty" in a triangle in the upper center of its seal.

So popular was the Hebrew language in the late sixteenth and early seventeenth centuries that several students at Yale delivered their commencement orations in Hebrew. Harvard, Yale, Columbia, Brown, Princeton, Johns Hopkins and the University of Pennsylvania taught courses in Hebrew—all the more remarkable because no university in England at the time offered it.[30]

Many, including a significant number of the Founding Fathers of America, were products of these American universities—for example, Thomas Jefferson attended William and Mary, James Madison went to Princeton and Alexander Hamilton attended Kings College (Columbia). Thus, we can be sure that a majority of these political leaders were not only well acquainted with the contents of both the New and Old Testaments but also had some working knowledge of Hebrew.[31] Notes Abraham Katsh in *The Biblical Heritage of American Democracy:*

> *At the time of the American Revolution, the interest in the knowledge of Hebrew was so widespread as to allow the circulation of the story that "certain members of Congress proposed that the use of English be formally prohibited in the United States, and Hebrew substituted for it."* [32]

Their Biblical education colored the American founders' attitude toward not only religion and ethics, but most significantly, politics. We see them adopting the Biblical motifs of the Puritans for political reasons. For example, the struggle of the ancient Hebrews against the wicked Pharaoh came to embody the struggle of the colonists against English tyranny.

Numerous examples can be found that clearly illustrate to what a significant extent the political struggles of the colonies were identified with the ancient Hebrews. The first design for the official seal of the United States, recommended by Benjamin Franklin, John Adams and Thomas Jefferson in 1776, depicts the Jews crossing the Red Sea. The motto around the seal read, "Resistance to Tyrants Is Obedience to

God."[33] The inscription on the Liberty Bell at Independence Hall in Philadelphia is a direct quote from Leviticus: "Proclaim liberty throughout the land unto all the inhabitants thereof."[34] Patriotic speeches and publications during the period of the struggle for independence were often infused with Biblical motifs and quotations. For example, Benjamin Rush, in his editorials denouncing the Tea Act, drew inspiration from the Hebrew Bible:

What did not Moses forsake and suffer for his countrymen! What shining examples of patriotism do we behold in Joshua, Samuel, Maccabees and all the illustrious princes, captains and prophets among the Jews.[35]

Likewise, Thomas Paine's antimonarchical pamphlet *Common Sense* cited the Hebrew Bible and words of the prophet Samuel, concluding:

These portions of the Scriptures . . . admit no equivocal construction. That the Almighty hath here entered his protest against monarchial government is true, or the Scriptures are false.[36]

Even the basic framework of America clearly reflects the influence of the Bible and power of Jewish ideas in shaping the political development of America. Nowhere is this more evident than in the opening sentences of the Declaration of Independence:

We hold these truths to be self-evident that all men are created equal, that they are endowed by their Creator with certain unalienable rights, that among them are life, liberty and the pursuit of happiness.

Whereas, these words echo the Enlightenment's—specifically John Locke's—idea of "the inalienable rights of man," without a doubt, the concept that these rights come from God is of Biblical origin.[37]

This and the other documents of early America make it clear that the concept of a God-given standard of morality is a central pillar of American democracy.[38] U.S. President Woodrow Wilson in *The State* acknowledges the obvious:

> *It would be a mistake . . . to ascribe to Roman legal conceptions an undivided sway over the development of law and institutions during the Middle Ages. . . . The Laws of Moses as well as the laws of Rome contributed suggestions and impulse to the men and institutions which were to prepare the modern world; and if we could have but eyes to see . . . we should readily discover how very much besides religion we owe to the Jew.*[39]

Thus we see that it is with the birth of American democracy that we have the next milestone in the process of the spread of Jewish ideas in civilization. For the first time in history, Jewish ethical ideas were legally enshrined into the laws of a non-Jewish nation. That country, the United States, would, in turn, become a powerful model to be emulated by numerous countries around the world.

Aside from the early formative influence on American democracy, the Bible continued to play a significant cultural and ethical role in American society throughout the eighteenth century. Even in the darkest hours of American history, it has shone forth as the major inspiration to the American people. In 1863, after the Battle of Gettysburg during the American Civil War, President Abraham Lincoln gave one of the most stirring speeches in American history. Lincoln concluded his Gettysburg Address with an almost word-for-word repetition of John Wycliffe's fourteenth-century dedication to his English translation of the Bible: "This nation, under God, shall have a new birth of freedom; and that government of the people, by the people, for the people, shall not perish from the Earth." [40]

At the same time that Lincoln was making his speech, the slaves of the American South were singing "Rock My Soul in the Bosom of Abraham," "Joshua Fought the Battle of Jericho," and "Swing Low, Sweet Chariot"—black spirituals that related their plight to the stories of the Hebrew Bible:

> *I looked over Jordan and what did I see?*
> *Comin' for to carry me home . . .*
> *A band of angels coming after me*
> *Comin' for to carry me home.*

Some one hundred years later, Martin Luther King Jr., the leader of the black civil rights movement, would demonstrate how the Hebrew Bible continues to inspire all Americans. The day before his assassination, he compared himself to Moses, in the last days of the prophet's life, standing on Mount Nebo and looking out over the Jordan River and the land of Israel spread before him:

> *We've got some difficult days ahead. But it doesn't matter with me now. Because I've been to the mountaintop. . . . And I've looked over. And I've seen the Promised Land. I may not get there with you. But I want you to know tonight, that we, as a people, will get to the Promised Land.* [41]

But possibly the best testament to the centrality of the Bible in American life was stated by President Franklin D. Roosevelt in a 1935 fireside chat:

We cannot read the history of our rise and development as a nation, without reckoning with the place the Bible has occupied in shaping the advances of the Republic . . . where we have been truest and most consistent in obeying its precepts, we have attained the greatest measure of contentment and prosperity. . . . The ancient Greeks evolved their concept of demokratia, *popular or majority government, through the conclusions of their philosophers; the Hebrews were imbued with the idea that the common people were party to social and political contract deriving from God's covenant with the Patriarchs and with Moses and the congregation of Israel. . . . Democracy in its modern sense thus owes its origin both to the Greeks and to the Hebrews.*[42]

CHAPTER 29

Fanning the Flames of Freedom

It is a historical fact that the American Revolution inspired the French Revolution, which came a mere thirteen years after the American Declaration of Independence. But the underlying aims and course of the French uprising proved markedly different, largely because the Bible did not play the same significant part.

For one thing, the Protestant Reformation, along with its obsession with the Bible and Biblical morality, seemed not to touch down in France as elsewhere in Europe. While the country did have a significant Protestant minority of Calvinists and Huguenots, the majority of the French remained staunchly Catholic.

However, the balance was tipped by the Enlightenment, which truly blossomed here; indeed, some of the most important thinkers of the Age of Reason—François Voltaire, Jean Jacques Rousseau, Charles de Montesquieu—were Frenchmen. In a country chafing under the thumb of the Church, secular–humanist values (such as the "natural rights" of the individual) found a ready ear and incited a rebellion of the overtaxed bourgeoisie and the abused masses against feudal oppression by the nobility and clergy.[43]

Energized by the American Revolution, the opposition to the monarchy —the so-called "Third Estate," made up of middle-class and land-owning peasants—formed a National Assembly and, on August 16, 1789, adopted the Declaration of the Rights of Man and Citizen.[44] It was the key philosophical document of the French Revolution and reflected the French Enlightenment's rejection of the rule of absolute monarchy in favor of natural rights of equality, self-determination and personal liberty. Its author was the Marquis de Lafayette, a soldier and statesman who fought on the side of the colonists during the American Revolution.

Of course, Lafayette's primary source of inspiration was the American Declaration of Independence, whose chief author he consulted while drafting his own manifesto. Indeed, Thomas Jefferson reviewed all of Lafayette's drafts before the creation of the final document.

Despite Jefferson's contributions, the basic tenets of American democracy—Biblical ethics and the idea of one nation under God—were, by and large, absent in the French declaration and in the ideology of the French leadership. Their absence may explain why the French Revolution proved less stable and far more violent than the American one.

Although France had the ethics of the Enlightenment, their impact proved weak. The key difference between Biblical ethics and other ethical codes that specified rights and privileges of human beings has been the same from the earliest times, as far back as the Code of Hammurabi. Basically, Biblical ethics are thought to be absolute and God-given, whereas ethics formulated by people are subject to custom, convenience and sometimes just their whims.

This might explain how a key figure of the French Enlightenment, Jean Jacques Rousseau—the author of *The Social Contract* who espoused that human beings are equal in the state of nature—could have impregnated his twenty-three-year-old laundress five times and forced her to drop each of the newborns on the doorstep of the Hôpital des Enfants-Trouves; this orphanage he himself had written about, noting that two-thirds of the babies there die within a year, one out of fourteen survive to age seven, and of these only five survive to maturity, mostly becoming beggars and vagabonds.[45] (His lofty ideas did not prevent him from practicing a more modern version of infanticide.)

Likewise, all the talk of the equality of man did not stop François Voltaire from spewing out vicious anti-Semitic diatribes and singling out the Jews as "the most abominable people in the world," as "a totally ignorant nation," and as "our enemies . . . whom we detest."[46]

Voltaire was a Deist, a believer in God who held that simple faith (without religion or its rules) was sufficient motivation for human beings to behave morally; he particularly detested the Jews, it seems, because of their insistence that the only moral code that counts is an absolute moral code as revealed by God in the Bible.[47]

Having no absolute rules to rely on, the French reformers were soon at each other's throats. Lafayette, seen as too moderate, was quickly drummed out of the National Guard and had to flee for his life a mere three years later. At least he saved his head. The king and many others were not so lucky. In 1793, after foolishly refusing to abolish feudalism, Louis XVI and his wife, Marie Antoinette, were guillotined, their deaths unleashing the Reign of Terror, during which time twenty-five "counter-revolutionaries" were executed in a similarly bloody manner.[48]

The Reign of Terror for all practical purposes brought to an end the Age of Reason. The bloody brutality of the masses shocked the world and severely tested the Enlightenment's belief that man could govern himself. A period of general unrest followed in France, marked by corruption and runaway inflation. All of it crashed when Napoleon Bonaparte came to power in the coup d'etat of 1804. But even though France now once again had a monarch (who called himself an emperor, no less), the medieval structures were gone and pathways were opened to liberalism and eventual democracy modeled on the American style.

The contrast between the relatively civil American Revolution, inspired by the Bible, and the bloody French Revolution, inspired by secular philosophy, leads us to an inescapable conclusion—people act differently (albeit not perfectly) when they are guided by a God-given standard.[49]

It is an interesting fact of history that since the establishment of modern democracy, no democracy has ever gone to war with another democracy.

But that is getting ahead of the story.

By our last count, democracy, married to the ideals of the Bible, had been established only in America. In retrospect, it seems that there is a direct correlation between the influence of the Bible and the spread of democracy: The greater the influence of the Bible on a given culture, the greater the influence and spread of democracy. America, which was more deeply and overwhelmingly influenced by the Bible than any other nation, adopted democracy more rapidly and decisively than any other country.

England in the seventeenth century was also strongly impacted by the Bible, but the return of the monarchy in 1660 slowed down the process of democratization. The Puritan Revolution, however, legally cemented the power of Parliament and the development of democracy continued throughout the next century without any major violent upheavals. The statements of numerous eighteenth-century British parliamentarians and thinkers clearly illustrate the continued centrality of the Bible in British legal and ethical consciousness. In 1794, the English statesman and philosopher Edmund Burke declared, "There is but one law for all, namely, the law which governs all law, the law of our Creator, the law of humanity, justice, equality—the law of nature and of nations."[50]

In France, at the conclusion of the Franco–Prussian War that France lost, the monarchy was again dissolved and a new democratic government came into being.

By the end of the eighteenth century, there were three democratic countries in the world—the United States, France and Switzerland. By the end of the nineteenth century, there were thirteen. All were Christian (and most of them Protestant) states of Western Europe.

When these nations adopted democracy with its ideals, they were without a doubt influenced by the Bible, even if perhaps unconsciously. Writes Sivan:

> The conceptions of 1642 [Puritan Revolution] and 1776 [American Revolution] inspired the rise of parliamentary government in many countries throughout the 19th century. . . . In the world of today, those who enjoy the blessing of democracy . . . do so only because their political systems honor that ancient "covenant with the people" and "proclaim liberty throughout the land unto all the inhabitants thereof."[51]

Concurrent with the political revolution of the last two hundred years came a major social revolution. Here, too, Jewish ethics played a formative role in the creation of the modern concept of social welfare and government responsibility—ideals that are today fundamental components of any modern democratic system.

Publicly funded social welfare programs, which today we take for granted, are a recent innovation in history. Since the dawn of civilization, nations have created laws to force the individual to conform to the rules of society. But the idea that nations should take responsibility for the welfare and needs of the individual did not begin to take hold in a serious or practical way until the Enlightenment, which, like the Bible, stressed humanity's obligation to improve, and hopefully perfect, the world.

Public health programs, free public education, social security benefits, shelters for the homeless, soup kitchens, etc., were virtually unheard of in antiquity—even in the most advanced and well-organized ancient civilizations. Two thousand years ago, Rome—the largest city on Earth at the time—did not have one public hospital, asylum or shelter.[52] Indeed, two hundred years ago Paris was not a whole lot better[53]—no wonder that Victor Hugo was moved to write *Les Misérables*. What existed was there by the benevolence of one monastic order or another.[54] Nearly all the government-sponsored social welfare programs we are familiar with in the West came into being in the last few hundred years. This social revolution is, to a very significant extent, a direct outgrowth of Biblical ethics and their embrace within democracy.[55]

Along with modern democracy's acceptance of the Biblical concept of the rights of the individual came the concept that the value of the individual supersedes the rights of society. It is, therefore, the primary responsibility of government to concern itself with the welfare of the individual, and a government's right to rule is based on the fulfillment of this basic responsibility.

In order to better understand the nature of this Jewish idea and its impact on the social revolution of the West, we must look at its basis within Jewish philosophy itself. As noted in Part II, a fundamental tenet of Judaism is the concept that every human being is created in the image of God and imbued with a soul, a spark of the infinite. It is the soul that sets human beings apart from animals, that makes each individual unique and that gives each human life its immeasurable value.

From this fundamental tenet flow numerous Jewish laws and principles emphasizing the preciousness of every human life—as in, "If you save one life, it's as if you saved the whole world."[56] From this fundamental tenet also flow numerous Jewish laws and principles emphasizing the responsibilities of every human being, who, having been created in the image of God, is duty bound to act in a godly manner, to emulate the Almighty—"Just as He is merciful and kind, so too shall you be merciful and kind."[57]

Such statements are more than just noble ideas; in the Jewish worldview, they are legally binding obligations. For example, charity in Jewish law is more than an act of kindness; it is a fundamental legal requirement. The Hebrew word for "charity" is *tzedakah,* which actually means "justice." *Tzedakah* requires that both the individual and society as a whole take care of those in need: the poor, the sick, the stranger, the widow, the orphan, even the animals. These concepts, repeated over and over again in the text of the Hebrew Bible, were ultimately incorporated into the Western vision of social responsibility, as numerous historians and thinkers have noted. Thomas Huxley (quoted earlier) wrote, "The Bible has been the Magna Carta of the poor and the oppressed."[58] And the French political economist Pierre Joseph Proudhon also expressed the same sentiment: "The whole Bible is a hymn to justice—that is, in the Hebrew style, to charity, to kindness to the weak on the part of the strong, to voluntary renunciation of the privilege of power." [59]

During the nineteenth century, many governments—not necessarily all democratic, but all Christian/Protestant—made the first serious efforts to create state-sponsored social welfare programs.[60] But by the early part of the twentieth century, these programs were a regular feature of virtually every democracy in the Western world.

The ancient ethical vision of the Bible was thus transformed into the modern Western social and political revolution.[61]

But we have not yet arrived at the door of utopia. As with Christianity and Islam, modern democracy can be viewed as a further stepping-stone in the process. These two monotheistic faiths, which were spiritual offshoots of Judaism, had served to awaken the soul of humanity to awareness of one God; now, the development of modern democracy, as an ethical offspring of the Bible, has awakened humanity's conscience, and thus brought us that much closer to realizing our universal vision of a perfect world.

CHAPTER 30

The Best of the Rest

Up to this point I have addressed the influence of Jewish values on the West and have neglected to discuss Judaism's impact on the Far East. This has been a conscious omission on my part. While a small Jewish population has been scattered throughout Asia since the early Middle Ages, its influence has been negligible. In addition, whereas the West and Near East, through Christianity and Islam, underwent the dramatic spiritual and ethical transformation to monotheism, no such parallel event took place farther East, particularly in eastern and southern Asia. (Some exceptions are a few places, such as Malaysia or Pakistan, which became predominantly Muslim.) For the most part, that part of the world has remained polytheistic, despite cultural inroads made by Western nations.

Since the Middle Ages, when East and West first began to interact, the West has gone to the Orient, bringing with it Western culture and ideas. While the East supplied the West with silk, spices, gunpowder, the compass, etc., the import of Western culture and values to the East has been far more dominant—that is, until the last thirty years when Buddhist and other Eastern philosophies have caught the interest of Western New Agers. But even so, the influence of the West on Asia has been disproportionate.

Much of the early Western cultural dominance can be explained by Europe's forced colonization of the Orient, but there is more to this phenomenon than colonialism. When Japan, which was never colonized by Europe, decided to modernize itself at the beginning of this century, it embarked on a deliberate policy of economic and cultural emulation of the West. The trend has continued ever since and has now been copied by virtually all the emerging nations of the East.

Western influence on the East continues to far outweigh the East's impact on the West. Economically (free-market, capitalist economies), militarily (Western technology and tactics), culturally (movies, music, fashion, fast food) and politically (liberal democracy), the East has been swamped by the West.[62] I am not arguing that this is a positive evolution, but rather a fact of history.

It is only within this recent transformation of the East that we are beginning to see the slow spread of Jewish values in the region.

For example, Japan, which did not have a tradition of organized philanthropy, has been experimenting with private and corporate charitable foundations. Previously, charity had been limited to family, community and kin, and government-fostered philanthropic organizations have been restricted to aiding development of science and technology. But since 1970, Japanese philanthropy, particularly in the corporate sector, has flourished. Writes Kathleen D. McCarthy in *Philanthropy and Culture:*

Japanese corporations inspired a swelling chorus of criticism during the 1970s for their perceived role in fostering worldwide

trade imbalances, environmental pollution and inflationary trends.
Corporate largesse is one means by which Japanese businessmen
may publicly demonstrate their willingness to shoulder a measure
of responsibility for redressing the domestic and international ills
that have accompanied rapid modernization.[63]

Of course, such ideas are still in their infancy. After ten years of opera-
tion, the Toyota Foundation's grant budget was still so small as to equal
2 percent of the Ford Foundation's grant budget. But considering the
short history of Japan's modernization—its rapid transformation from a
feudal country that viewed its emperor as a god to a modern democracy—that was huge progress indeed.[64]

The last century has seen the rise and fall of many different forms of
government: monarchies, fascism and communism, etc. The only form
of government that has survived intact is liberal democracy. While some
may point out that there are still Communist regimes in the world, the
lesson of the last few decades has shown the political and economic fail-
ure of Communism. The former Soviet Union has disappeared, China is
slowly emerging from its Communist shell into a free-market economy,
and countries such as Cuba and North Korea are on the verge of complete economic collapse.

Liberal democracy, on the other hand, has not only emerged seemingly victorious, but it is by far the fastest spreading political system in
the modern world. It is literally changing the face of the globe. Writes
David Potter in *Democratization:*

Democratization has been a major global phenomenon during the
twentieth century. . . . In 1975, 68 percent of countries throughout

the world were authoritarian; by the end of 1995, only about 26 percent were authoritarian.[65]

By 1997 there were close to seventy democracies in the world. That is a mighty quick climb considering that in 1800 there were only three— the United States, France and Switzerland. Forty new democracies were added to the world list just between 1975 and 1997.

While an occasional democracy (Chile and Argentina, for example) has lapsed into totalitarianism, the trend has been overwhelmingly in favor of political transformation toward modern democracy, not away from it. As we have already seen, modern democracy is largely a product of Jewish ethics, and it is with this rapid and remarkable transformation of much of the world to democracy that the indirect spread of Jewish ethics and values continues even to the farthest reaches of the Earth.

This process of transformation holds more or less true around the world today. Whether in Africa, Asia, or South and Central America, the evolution to free-market, liberal democratic systems continues to be the dominant trend in a world at the beginning of the twenty-first century.

Perhaps the best example of the universal influence of Jewish values is found in the United Nations. Founded in 1920 as the League of Nations and reorganized in 1945 as the United Nations, it is an international organization of the world's states that aims to promote peace and international cooperation. Today, the UN counts as its members 190 of the world's 192 countries. While it has certainly become highly politicized and has sometimes fallen miserably short of its lofty objectives, it still remains a unique institution in human history, dedicated to making the world a better place.

It has been observed that such an organization was anticipated by the

Prophet Isaiah.[66] Indeed, as was mentioned earlier, the famed quotation from Isaiah about beating "swords into plowshares" and making "war no more" is prominently featured on the wall of the plaza in front of the UN building.

Having said that, we must also acknowledge that the Western world has, to a significant extent, become secularized since the Enlightenment, which largely damaged the credibility of religion. Separation of church and state, while safeguarding religious freedom, has taken much of the religious/moral feeling out of society.

As a consequence, we would logically expect to see a decrease in the impact of Jewish values during this modern period of world history. But this has not been the case. Modern political and economic developments have brought Jewish ideas to numerous societies that were not previously influenced by the Bible and Judeo–Christian or Judeo–Muslim ethics.

However, the secularization of Jewish ideas has led not only to their alteration, but even, in some cases, to their perversion. From the traditional Jewish perspective, these are nevertheless important steps in the historical process designed to prepare the world for the ultimate actualization of the Jewish ethical vision of utopia.

Conclusions: Part V

So there we have the intricate historical process whereby a tiny fragment of humanity was able to exert such a formidable influence on the development of world civilization. To understand this process, we've examined the last four thousand years of the religious and political evolution of the West:

- We saw the initial gradual and subtle effects of Abraham's profound discovery of one God that led to the birth of monotheism and Judaism.
- We saw the astonishing and dramatic spread of monotheism worldwide via Christianity and Islam, albeit without the ethics and values of Judaism.
- And we saw these values become part and parcel of modern democracy, which has disseminated the Jewish message and concepts through modern political, social and economic movements.

These three phases dominate our Western history. Without them we would not be the people we are today, who envision utopia embodying the ideals of peace, justice, equality, reverence for life, education, family values and social responsibility.

The first phase—the birth of monotheism in a polytheistic world—spanned the two-thousand-year period from Abraham, or about 1800 B.C.E., until the conversion of the Roman Empire to Christianity in the early fourth century C.E. Abraham's insights led to a tremendous revolution in history—the creation of ethical monotheism and a nation of a people (the nation of Israel) dedicated to living with the idea of one God and teaching this idea to the rest of humanity. During this entire time, the Jews survived in a hostile polytheistic world as the only true monotheists. Under Greek and Roman occupation, attempts were made to destroy Judaism, leading to the first ideological–religious wars in history. The Jewish people suffered terrible physical hardship and national defeat, but survived spiritually and nationally, even in exile. Despite polytheistic hostility, Jewish ideas slowly but steadily seeped their way into the collective polytheistic consciousness of the West, setting the stage for the next major period of change.

In the phase that followed, from the fourth to the sixteenth centuries C.E., we witnessed what is probably the greatest mass philosophical–spiritual change in human history: the monotheistic revolution. Two offshoots of Judaism—Christianity and Islam—converted tens of millions of people to monotheism. But it was not until the Protestant Reformation and the mass publication of the Bible that the social and ethical principles of Judaism began to have a significant impact on the world.

In the third phase, we saw the dramatic political evolution of Europe and America in the seventeenth and eighteenth centuries. Much of this political change was instigated by Protestant fundamentalists, in both England and America, who relied heavily on the Old Testament as the model for creating a just society. Even after the secularization of much of the West in the late eighteenth and early nineteenth centuries, the social and moral ethos of the Bible played a major part in the continued development of democracy and served as an inspiration for many other political and social movements in the modern world.

The question that remains is this: What lies ahead? Modern democracy, which is so much a by-product of Jewish ideas, is the most potent political force in the last one hundred years. The democratic revolution has spread, and continues to spread, Jewish ethical ideas to the remotest parts of the globe. Thus the vision of peace, harmony, brotherhood, equality and justice that began as the dream of a tiny people on a small strip of land in the Middle East has today become a large part of the utopian vision of all humanity.

But our story does not end here.

The Torah, which has brought this vision to humanity, teaches that there is more to come. From its perspective, modern democracy is not the be-all and end-all. While representing a significant stage in the historical process, modern democracy is not the *ultimate* state for humanity.

It took two thousand years, from Abraham to Rome, before the world could accept the concept of one God. It took another thousand years (the Dark or Middle Ages) for this idea to become fully entrenched in the consciousness of the West. During this period, the early Church spread the concept of monotheism, but did not preach or practice the Jewish ethical vision and did little or nothing to alleviate human suffering. The Protestant Reformation, with its stress on the Bible and the importance of the individual, introduced the concept of individual responsibility and social justice to the West. Political and social developments since the seventeenth century have translated these Biblical ideas into state-sponsored social welfare programs and a heightened sense of social responsibility.

But along with this spread of Jewish ethics came other diversions in Western consciousness. For example, modern political and philosophical developments—the Enlightenment, Darwinism and the scientific revolution, separation of church and state—introduced secularization into Western consciousness. Just when it seemed that humanity was about to create a working vision for a just society based on ethical monotheism, the world dropped God (or at least separated him from the legal realities of the state). It is almost as if humanity has suffered a collective case of schizophrenia—the world can live with the idea of one God and it can, to a significant extent, actualize the social and ethical vision of the Bible, but it cannot combine the two into a working model. This seems to be the situation we have arrived at today.

Winston Churchill once observed, "It has been said that democracy is the worst form of government, except all those forms that have been tried from time to time."[67]

As tremendous an invention as modern democracy is, its weaknesses are obvious. The Bill of Rights is not balanced by a Bill of Responsibilities, and the stress on individualism can lead to an "every-man-for-himself" attitude, with the individual putting his or her rights and interests above those of the society as a whole. This is what John F. Kennedy meant when he said in his inaugural address, "Ask not what your country can do for you; ask what you can do for your country."

For all the great things that liberal democracy has done for the modern world, it has failed to bring humanity to its ultimate potential—to actualize the utopian dream. But more serious than the flaws inherent within the democratic system itself are the dangers caused by the loss of values, a phenomenon pervasive throughout the liberal democratic world today.

One of the great lessons of history is that great civilizations fall, not so much because of external threat, but rather through internal moral decay. One merely has to look at the United States today, or for that matter any other modern Western democracy, to see how real the danger is.

The *Congressional Quarterly*'s comparison of urban public school problems of 1940 with those of 1990 is telling proof of the growing problems in America today.[68]

In 1940, these were the top eight problems with which public school systems had to cope:

1. running in the halls
2. chewing gum
3. talking in class
4. making noise
5. wearing improper clothing
6. getting out of line
7. littering
8. smoking in the lavatories

In 1990, the top eight problems were these:

1. pregnancy
2. venereal disease
3. drug abuse
4. suicide

5. rape

6. assault and burglary

7. arson

8. murder/gang warfare

The behavior of children reflects the problems of society at large. Breakdown of the family, the subjectivization of morality, decadence, materialism, crime, violence and so forth—the loss of values—are eating away at the foundations of these societies and threaten the whole future of the world.

So where do we go from here?

Judaism has always believed that history follows a pattern and leads to an ultimate goal—the creation of a world based on the concept of an all-powerful, just and loving Creator of the universe, followed by the dawn of lasting peace and harmony, social responsibility and unity. This will be the Messianic Utopian Era.

Judaism has also always believed that the Jewish people have a key role to play in bringing this vision to fruition. This role is to create a just and moral society based on God-given values that will serve as the model for the rest of humanity to emulate—to be "a light to nations."

Given the general state of the world today and the concurrent fragmentation among the Jewish people, this vision may seem impossibly distant. But at the same time, when we look back on the vast sweep of the last four thousand years, we see how significantly the insignificant little tribe, who by all the laws of history should never have survived, has directly and indirectly affected humanity. The world may be far from a perfect place, but the Jewish vision has become the universal vision. It remains to be seen what further surprises the Jews have yet to offer the world.

As the prophet Isaiah once predicted:

In the days to come,
The Mount of the Lord's House shall stand
Firm above the mountains;
And it shall tower above the hills.
And all the nations shall gaze on it with joy,
And the many peoples shall go and shall say:

Come,
Let us go up to the Mount of the Lord,
To the House of the God of Jacob;
That He may instruct us in His ways,
And that we may walk in His paths.
For instruction shall come forth from Zion,
The word of the Lord from Jerusalem.
Thus He will judge among the many people.
And arbitrate for the multitude of nations.
And they shall beat their swords into plowshares
And their spears into pruning hooks.
Nations shall not take up
Sword against nation;
They shall never again know war.[69]

Notes

INTRODUCTION

[1] *New York Times,* March 7, 1998, pp. 13, 15.

PART I

[1] DeMause, Lloyd, "The Evolution of Childhood," *The History of Childhood,* ed. Lloyd DeMause. New York: Psychohistory Press, 1974, pp. 25–26.

[2] Gallant, Thomas W., *Risk and Survival in Ancient Greece,* Cambridge: Polity Press, 1991, p. 133.

[3] Aristotle, *Politics,* VII.16.

[4] Stager, Lawrence E., "Eroticism and Infanticide at Ashkelon," *Biblical Archeology Review,* July/August 1991, p. 47.

[5] DeMause, p. 26.

[6] Seneca, *Concerning Anger,* I.XV.

[7] Kohl, Martin, ed., *Infanticide and the Value of Life,* Buffalo: Prometheon, 1977, p. 69. Also see: Oldenziel, Ruth, "The Historiography of Infanticide in Antiquity," collected in Blok, Josien, and Mason, Peter, eds., *Sexual Asymmetry: Studies in Ancient Society,* Amsterdam: J. C. Gieben, 1987, p. 88.

[8] Oates, Whitney J., and O'Neill, Eugene, eds., *The Complete Greek Drama,* New York: Random House, 1938, pp. II21–II24.

[9] Seneca, The Elder, *Contraversiae,* Cambridge, Mass.: Harvard University Press, 1974, Vol. II, p. 423.

[10] Langer, William L., *The History of Childhood,* Lloyd DeMause, ed., New York: Psychohistory Press, 1974, p. i.

[11] "Infanticide is a practice present day Westerners record as a cruel and an inhuman custom resorted to by a few desperate and primitive people living in harsh environments. We tend to think of it as an exceptional practice. . . . The truth is quite different. Infanticide has been practiced on every continent and by people on every level of culture complexity, from hunters and gatherers to high civilizations, including our own ancestors. Rather than being an exception, then, it has been the rule." Kohl, p. 60.

[12] Frazer, James George, *The Illustrated Golden Bough: A Study in Magic and Religion,* New York: Simon & Schuster, 1996, pp. 150–151. (Frazer additionally cites examples of human sacrifice of this type from Marseilles, a Greek colony, and the city of Abdera in Thrace.)

[13] Sutherland, A., *The Origin and Growth of the Moral Instinct,* Longmans, 1898, p. 136.

[14] DeMause, p. 27.

[15] Montanelli, Indro, *Romans Without Laurels,* New York: Pantheon, 1959, p. 80.

[16] Grant, Michael, *The World of Rome,* London: Widerfield & Nicolson, 1964, p. 121.

[17] Montanelli, pp. 244–248.

[18] Seneca, *Epistulae Morales,* VII, 2; cf.xc, 45. Quoted in Grant, p. 122.

[19] Caldwell, Wallis, *Hellenic Conceptions of Peace,* New York: Columbia University, 1919, p. 139.

[20] *Julius Caesar* 3.1.77.

[21] Phelps-Brown, Henry, *Egalitarianism and the Generation of Inequality,* Oxford: Oxford University Press, 1980, p. 15.

[22] Aristotle, *Politics,* III.IX.1280, and I.V.1254. Quoted in Phelps-Brown, p. 15.

[23] "In ancient Greece, even artisans, laborers and tradesmen—lacking the protection of the genos (clan)—could be oppressed with impunity and they had no redress before the law. The feudaristocracy of Sparta ruled over an enslaved peasantry. Before Solon reformed the legislation of Athens in the 6th century B.C.E., peasants in that 'birthplace of democracy' were also largely reduced to slavery. Even a century later, in the age of Pericles, Athenian 'democracy' was built on the back of slave population; nor

did Socrates, Plato or Aristotle influence the Greeks against this abuse of their fellow man." Sivan, Gabriel, *The Bible and Civilization,* Jerusalem: Keter Publishing House, 1973, p. 94.

[24] H. O. Lancaster in *Expectations of Life,* New York: Springer Verlag, 1990, p. 7, writes, "In Nero's time, according to an old law over 400 slaves were executed on one occasion because their master had been murdered."

[25] DuBois, Page, *Torture and Truth,* London: Routledge, 1991, p. 37.

[26] Kaufman, Yehezkiel, *The Religion of Israel,* Chicago: University of Chicago Press, 1960, p. 52.

[27] Garnsey, Peter, "Legal Privilege in the Roman Empire," *Studies in Ancient Society,* ed. M. I. Finley, London: Routledge and Kegan Paul, 1974, p. 153.

[28] Cicero, Laws, XIII, 35.

[29] Grant, p. 111.

[30] Diodorus as quoted in Montanelli, p. 125.

[31] Lancaster, p. 7.

[32] Grant, p. 119.

[33] "There was without a doubt a vast diffusion of reading and writing ability in the Greek and Roman worlds. . . . But there was no mass literacy. The classical world, even at its most advanced, was so lacking in the characteristics which produce extensive literacy that we must suppose that the majority of people were always illiterate. In most places, most of the time, there was no incentive for those who controlled the allocation of resources to aim for mass literacy." Harris, William, V., *Ancient Literacy,* Cambridge: Harvard University Press, 1989, p. 13. Also see p. 328 for statistics.

[34] UNESCO; for statistics see the Web site: *unescostat.unesco.org.*

[35] Bonner, Stanley, F., *Education in Ancient Rome,* London: Methuen & Co., 1977, p. 149.

[36] Ibid., p. 329.

[37] Harris, pp. 333–337.

[38] The gymnasium was the center of cultural and athletic life of the ancient Greeks. The root of the word "gymnasium" is derived from the Greek word *gymnos,* which means

"naked." Since all sporting competitions were performed in the nude, there probably was not much of a market for athletic wear in this time period.

[39] Stager, pp. 41–42. Also see: Murstein, Bernard I., *Love, Sex and Marriage Through the Ages,* New York: Springer Publishing Co., 1974, p. 58.

[40] On the other hand, Julius Caesar also violated the macho code and got away with it. The Roman historian Suetonius says of him, "He was every man's woman and every woman's man."

[41] Stager, pp. 42, 45.

[42] Vanggaard, Tharkil, *Phallus: A Symbol and Its History in the Male World,* London: Jonathan Cape, 1969, p. 28.

[43] Brasch, Rudolf, *How Did Sex Begin? The Sense and Nonsense of Custom and Traditions that Have Separated Men and Women Since Adam and Eve,* New York: D. McKay Co., 1973, pp. 134–135.

[44] Vanggaard, p. 37.

[45] Murstein, Bernard I., *Love, Sex and Marriage Through the Ages,* New York: Springer Publishing Co., 1974, p. 57.

[46] Plato, *Symposium,* 178C–D. Cited in Vanggaard, p. 40.

[47] Murstein, p. 58.

[48] Propertius, quoted in Aries, Philippe, and Bejin, Andre, eds., *Western Sexuality— Practice and Precept in Past and Present Times,* Oxford: Basil Blackwell Ltd., 1985, p. 33.

[49] Hesiod, *The Homeric Hymns and Homerica,* translated by Hugh G. Evelyn-White, Cambridge, Mass.: Harvard University Press, 1977, pp. 31–33, 55, 123.

[50] Hesiod, *Works and Days,* pp. 702–705, quoted in Fantham, Elaine; Foley, Helene Peet; Kampen, Natalie Boymel; Pomeroy, Sarah B.; and Shapiro, H. A., *Women in the Classical World,* Oxford: Oxford University Press, 1995, p. 39.

[51] Rouselle, Alice (translated by Pheasant, Felicia), *Porneia: Desire and the Body in Antiquity,* Cambridge, Mass.: Blackwell, 1988, p. 30.

[52] Plato, *Republic,* Book V. Quoted in Hunt, Morton M., *The Natural History of Love,* New York: Knopf, 1959, p. 27.

[53] The law is described in Demosthenes 46 *[Stephanos II]*: "Any citizen . . . shall have

the right to dispose of his property however he wishes if he has no legitimate male offspring, unless he is not of sound mind as a result of one of these things: madness, old age, drugs, disease, the influence of woman, or unless he is constrained by bonds." Quoted in Just, Roger, *Women in Athenian Law and Life,* London: Routledge, 1989, p. 209.

[54] Xenophon, quoted in Fantham, p. 103.

[55] Massey, Michael, *Women in Ancient Greece and Rome,* Cambridge: Cambridge University Press, 1988, p. 1.

[56] Ibid., p. 18.

[57] Plato, *Laws,* 781c. Quoted in Fantham, p. 103.

[58] Fantham, p. 103.

[59] Massey, p. 6.

[60] Fantham, p. 306; also Murstein, p. 79 (quoting Cato).

[61] Quoted in Murstein, p. 64.

[62] Grant, Michael, *From Alexander to Cleopatra: The Hellenistic World,* New York: Charles Scribner & Sons, 1982, p. 205.

[63] Plutarch, *Parallel Lives.* Quoted in Murstein, pp. 60–61.

[64] Massey, p. 21.

[65] McEvedy, Colin, and Jones, Richard, *Atlas of World Population History,* London: Penguin, 1978, p. 21. While verifying the population drop in the Roman Empire, McEvedy and Jones give the cause as overexpansion of the society which necessitated an opposite reaction. Additionally, the drop in population was to some extent created by the collapse of the Empire in 476 C.E., which meant less food, worse sanitation, more disease, etc.

[66] Murstein, p. 61.

[67] British historian Cecil Roth notes that: "In Europe, it was not until the fourth century that the Emperor Constantine—obviously actuated by the Biblical precept—enacted the earliest law for poor relief, which, however, was repealed two centuries later by Justinian. It was thus left to Elizabethan England to initiate such legislation in the modern world, this example being generally followed in other countries only in the nineteenth century." See *The Jewish Contribution to Civilisation,* London: The East and West Library, 1956, p. 249.

[68] Grant, *From Alexander to Cleopatra*, p. 127.

[69] Ibid.

[70] Plutarch, *Morals* 235A. Quoted in Hands, A. R., *Charities and Social Aid in Greece and Rome,* London: Thames & Hudson, 1968, p. 65.

[71] Hands, p. 64.

[72] Brunt, P. A. *"The Roman Mob, Studies in Ancient Society,"* M. I. Finley, ed., London: Routledge and Kegan Paul, 1974, pp. 84–85.

[73] Kohl, p. 68.

[74] Lamson, Herbert Day, *Social Pathology in China,* Shanghai: Commercial Press Ltd., 1935, p. 241.

[75] Sutherland, p. 144.

[76] Sullivan, Lawrence E., *Death, Afterlife and the Soul,* New York: Macmillan Publishing Co., 1987, p. 18.

[77] Ibid., p. 17.

[78] Hassig, Ross, *Aztec Warfare—Imperial Expansion and Political Control,* Norman, Okla.: University of Oklahoma Press, 1988, pp. 114–121. See also: Vaillant, George, *Aztecs of Mexico—Origins, Rise and Fall of the Aztec Nation,* New York: Doubleday and Co., Inc., 1948, pp. 201–206.

[79] Kierman, Frank A., ed., *Chinese Ways in Warfare,* Cambridge, Mass: Rainbow Bridge, 1974, p. 2.

[80] Ibid., p. 5.

[81] Writes Lynn Montross in *War Through the Ages,* New York: Harper & Brothers, 1944, p. 147: "[There is no basis] for confusing the conservatism of an old civilization with a pacifism inspired by humanitarian motives. If anything, the Chinese displayed a unique delight in the study of war—not war in the contemporary Western sense of trading hard blows, but war as an art and science founded on intellectual values."

[82] Jenghiz Khan, quoted in Montross, p. 144.

[83] Critchley, J. S., *Feudalism,* London: George Allen & Unwin, 1978, p. 92.

[84] Mahatma Gandhi, the proponent and leader of the Indian nonviolence movement, gave as his inspiration two sources: the Hindu doctrine of *ahisma* and the influence

of the very Christian writings of Leo Tolstoy, particularly *The Kingdom of God Is Within You.* See: Brown, Judith, *Gandhi: Prisoner of Hope,* New Haven: Yale University Press, 1989, pp. 76–80.

[85] Reynolds, Craig J., "Feudalism as a Trope or Discourse for the Asian Past," in Leach, Edmund, Mukherjee, S. N., and Ward, John, eds., *Feudalism: Comparative Studies,* Sydney: University of Sydney Press, 1984, p. 137.

[86] Critchley, p. 111.

[87] Ibid., pp. 75, 84.

[88] Ibid., p. 153.

[89] Some would argue that Russia holds this record; while Russia abolished serfdom in 1861, it did not totally disappear until the Russian Revolution in 1917. A case can also be made that the system existing in pre-Communist China (until 1949) was still in many ways feudal, since ownership of the land was held by absentee gentry landlords who charged extortionate rents from the tenant farmers.

[90] Goody, Jack, ed., *Literacy in Traditional Societies,* Cambridge: Cambridge University Press, 1968, p. 70.

[91] Lamson, p. 241.

[92] Ibid., p. 562.

[93] Mitamura, Taisuke, *Chinese Eunuchs,* Tokyo: Charles E. Tuttle Co., 1970, pp. 90–91.

[94] Blunt, Edward, *Social Services in India,* London: The Majesty's Stationary Office, 1946, p. 70.

[95] Padfield, J. E., *Hindu at Home,* Delhi: B.R. Publishing Corp., 1907, pp. 204–207.

[96] Sullivan, p. 27.

[97] Winston Davis in *Japanese Religion and Society,* Albany: State University of New York Press, 1992, pp. 178–179, describes the difficulties Japanese Buddhists experienced in responding to the challenge of Protestant charitable institutions during the Meiji period (1852–1912).

[98] This also explains why—despite their strong belief in compassion—Buddhists in India, for example, have turned a cold eye on the country's horrendous problem of abandoned children and terminally ill left to die in the streets, leaving open a wide door for the saintly work of the late Mother Teresa. The Hindus ignore the dying because Hinduism considers them ritually impure. See: Royle, Roger, *Mother Teresa,* San Francisco: HarperCollins, 1992, p. 32.

PART II

[1] John Adams in a letter to F. A. Van der Kemp, as quoted in Gould, Allan, ed., *What Did They Think of the Jews?* New York: Jason Aronson, Inc., 1991, pp. 71–72.

[2] Johnson, Paul, *A History of the Jews,* New York: HarperCollins, 1988, p. 585.

[3] Smith, Huston, *The Religions of Man,* New York: Harper & Row, 1958, p. 255.

[4] Miller, Avigdor, *Behold a People,* New York: Balshon, 1968, p. 27.

[5] The Code of Hammurabi, ascribed to the king of Babylonia who lived circa 1792–1750 B.C.E., is linguistically similar to the Ten Commandments, but there the similarity ends. While the Ten Commandments are contained within a book of laws describing man's responsibilities to God and to his fellow man, the Code of Hammurabi is nearly lost in a recitation of the accomplishments of the king. Secondly, it is a law that presents a double standard, having been formulated to protect the rights of the property-owning nobility against the lower classes. Thirdly, its provisions, for example "an eye for an eye," were carried out literally, whereas under Jewish law they were not, referring to monetary compensation, as in "the value of an eye for an eye."

[6] Deo Cassius, as quoted in Sivan, p. 126.

[7] Genesis 1:26–27.

[8] Kohl, pp. 24, 27.

[9] DeMause, p. 28. The author goes on to quote Philo as follows: "Some of them [the parents] do the deed with their own hands, with monstrous cruelty and barbarity they stifle and throttle the first breath which the infants draw or throw them into a river or into the depths of the sea, after attaching some heavy substance to make them sink more quickly under its weight. Others take them to be exposed in some desert place, hoping they themselves say, that they may be saved, but leaving them in actual truth to suffer the most distressing fate. For all the beasts that feed on human flesh visit the spot and feast unhindered on the infants, a banquet provided by their sole guardians, those who above all others should keep them safe, their fathers and mothers. Carnivorous birds, too, come flying down and gobble up the fragments." (Philo, *Works,* Vol. 7)

[10] Exodus 20:13; Deuteronomy 5:17.

[11] Babylonian Talmud, Makkoth 7a.

[12] Babylonian Talmud, Makkoth 7a.

13 Numbers 35:15.

14 Leviticus 24:17 and Niddah 44b; Leviticus 18:21 and Deuteronomy 18:10.

15 Genesis 22:1–19.

16 Midrash Hagaddah 21:11; also see Weissman, Moshe, *The Midrash Says,* Vol. 1, Brooklyn: Benei Yakov Publications, 1980, p. 200.

17 *The American Heritage Dictionary of the English Language,* Third Edition, New York: Houghton Mifflin Co., 1992.

18 Talmud, Sanhedrin 74a.

19 Mishna, Sanhedrin 4:5.

20 Rapoport, Anatol, *Peace: An Idea Whose Time Has Come,* Ann Arbor, Michigan: University of Michigan Press, 1992, p. 3.

21 According to Simon Weisenthal Center, *New York Times,* August 24, 2001.

22 Isaiah 2:4.

23 Isaiah 11:6.

24 The English word "Messiah" comes from the Hebrew word *mashach,* which means "to anoint." The *Mashiah,* then, is God's "Anointed One." This, for example, is how the Book of Samuel relates the anointing of David as king: "Samuel took the horn of oil and anointed him [David] in the midst of his brothers, and the spirit of God rested on David from that day on." (1 Samuel 16:13) The Jewish definition of Messiah is a Jewish leader (without question, a human being), descended from the line of King David (that is, from the tribe of Judah), who will have the Torah knowledge and the leadership ability to bring all the Jewish people back from exile to the Land of Israel. He will rebuild the Temple, bring world peace, and elevate the entire world to the realization of one God. (For Jewish sources for these points in the order listed above see: Deuteronomy 17:15; Numbers 24:17; Genesis 49:10; 1 Chronicles 17:11; Psalms 89:29–38; Jeremiah 33:17; 2 Samuel 7:12–16; Isaiah 27:12–13; Isaiah 11:12; Micah 4:1; Isaiah 2:4; Isaiah 11:6; Micah 4:3; Isaiah 11:9; Isaiah 40:5; Zephaniah 3:9; Ezekiel 37:24–28.)

25 Maimonides, *Mishnah Torah,* Laws of Repentance, 9:2.

26 Shimon ben Gamliel, *Ethics of the Fathers,* 1:18.

27 Shimon Bar Yochai, quoted in Midrash Rabbah, Leviticus 9:9.

28 Hillel, quoted in *Ethics of the Fathers,* 1:12.

29 Babylonian Talmud, Gittin 59b.

30 The word "peace" appears 240 times in the Hebrew Bible.

31 I Chronicles 22:7–8.

32 I Kings 10:24.

33 It is interesting to note that in virtually every language, a person who protects you is called a "bodyguard." In Hebrew, he is called *shomer rosh,* which literally translates to "headguard"; the choice of words demonstrates what it is that the Jews value—the mind, the seat of wisdom.

34 *Ethics of the Fathers,* 4:1.

35 Ecclesiastes 9:14–15.

36 This explanation is offered by the eleventh-century Jewish philosopher Bachya ibn Pakuda in his *Duties of the Heart* (translated by Yaacov Feldman), Northvale, N.J.: Jason Aronson, Inc., 1996, pp. 246–247. Pakuda also tells a pointed tale of a group of soldiers who are returning home after winning a war, marching and singing, flushed with victory. A pious man meets them on the road and cautions them: "Brothers, you think you have achieved a major victory, but the truth is you merely won a very minor battle. It is only now that you will confront the great war—the war within yourselves, the war against the evil inclination and its troops." (p. 245)

37 Proverbs 14:19.

38 Leviticus 19:15.

39 Writes S. E. Finer in *The History of Government from the Earliest Times,* Vol. II, Cambridge: Oxford University Press, 1997, pp. 862–863: "In the Jewish tradition, it is the Divine Law, the Law of Moses, which overrode custom. . . . This was the very essence of [sic] Jewish theocracy. The very concept . . . [of] constraint under the Divine Law is found in the Jewish kingship. As we have seen, it is to be found nowhere else in the world before ancient Israel. . . . Lord Acton recognized the ancient Jewish kingship as the first example of limited monarchy."

40 Deuteronomy 17:19. Also see: Maimonides, *Mishnah Torah,* Laws of Kings, 3:1.

41 Maimonides, *Mishnah Torah,* Laws of Judges: Sanhedrin, 2.

42 One ancient decision of the Sanhedrin that illustrates the court's wisdom tempered with mercy was that an offender "cannot incriminate himself." Talmud, Sanhedrin 9b

and 37a. Also see: Lew, Myer S., *The Humanity of Jewish Law*, New York: Soncino Press, 1985, pp. 66–68.

43 What kinds of things did Hillel and Shammai argue about? Well, one debate was on the topic of lying—specifically, should one lie and tell a bride she is beautiful on her wedding day, even if she is not? Shammai weighed in on the side of telling the truth at all times. Hillel said no, lie. But, he added, a bride is always beautiful on her wedding day. Hillel's opinion stands—there are times when it is permissible, even necessary to lie.

44 Another type of *aved* was a child who had been sold by a destitute family who could not afford to bring it up, *not* as way of making money, but as a way of ensuring that the child would be properly taken care of. The child was then adopted into the foster family who had to treat him or her as one of their own. If the child was a girl, when she reached a marriageable age, her master could marry her off to one of his sons, but never against her will. See Exodus 21:7–11; Talmud Kiddushin 19a; Maimonides, *Mishnah Torah*, Laws of Slaves, 4:8.

45 Exodus 21:3, Deuteronomy 15:12.

46 Talmud, Kiddushin 20a.

47 Johnson, p. 156.

48 While the Torah mandates that Jews obey all of its 613 commandments, non-Jews are required to obey seven, the so-called Noahide laws, because they are believed to date back to the time of the flood. (See Genesis 9:4–6). They include (1) a prohibition against eating any limb or meat that was cut off from a live animal; (2) a prohibition against blaspheming the name of God; (3) a prohibition against stealing; (4) an obligation to set up a system of law; (5) a prohibition against worshipping idols; (6) a prohibition against adultery; (7) a prohibition against murder. Kahan, A. Y., *Taryag Mitzvos*, Brooklyn: Keser Torah Publications, 1987, p. 349.

49 Amiel, Moshe Avigdor, *Ethics and Legality in Jewish Law*, Nanuet, N.Y.: Philipp Feldheim, 1994, p. 18.

50 Deuteronomy 6:5.

51 States the Talmud, "A search was made from Dan unto Beer Sheba and no ignoramus was found; from Gabbuth unto Antipetris, and no boy or girl, man or woman was found who was not thoroughly versed in [the most difficult] laws" (Sanhedrin 94b). Archeological artifacts from this period further prove just how high literacy was among the common people (tradesmen's tools are inscribed with names of their

owners) and even thieves could read (judging by the signs on tombs "No Gold or Silver Inside.")

[52] Roth, p. 30.

[53] Talmud, Baba Bathra 21a.

[54] Maimonides, *Mishnah Torah* (Laws of Learning Torah), 2:1.

[55] Abelard, Peter, Commentary to Paul's Epistle to the Ephesians, as quoted in Sivan, p. 75.

[56] Rabinovich, Abraham, "Repository of History," *Jerusalem Post Magazine,* January 10, 1997, p. 9.

[57] Goldman, Israel, *Lifelong Learning Among Jews: Adult Education in Judaism from Biblical Times to the Twentieth Century,* New York: Ktav Publishing House, 1975, p. 89.

[58] Roth, p. 30.

[59] Ibid., p. 31.

[60] Ibid.

[61] Heschel, Abraham, *The Earth Is the Lord's,* Woodstock, Vermont: Jewish Lights, 1995, p. 46.

[62] Also see: Goldman, p. xx.

[63] Genesis 1:27.

[64] *Artscroll Siddur,* Brooklyn: Mesorah Publications, 1994, p. 207.

[65] See Leviticus, chapter 18.

[66] Talmud, Ketubot 61b.

[67] Talmud, Ketubot 61b and 62a.

[68] Talmud, Ketubot 62a.

[69] Genesis 21:12.

[70] Antonelli, Judith S., *In the Image of God: A Feminist Commentary on the Torah,* Northvale, N.J.: Jason Aronson, 1995, pp. 167–170.

[71] Ibid., pp. 192–193.

[72] Palladas, quoted in Hunt, Morton M., *The Natural History of Love,* New York: Knopf, 1959, p. 26.

[73] Talmud, Yevamot 62b.

[74] Roth, p. 29.

[75] Guttentag, Marcia, *Too Many Women? The Sex Ratio Question,* Beverly Hills, Calif.: Sage Publications, 1963, pp. 79–80.

[76] Judges, chapters 4–5.

[77] II Kings 22:14–20.

[78] Zohar, Section 3, 19b.

[79] Talmud, Baba Batra 8a, 8b, 9a.

[80] Deuteronomy 14:28. Also see Roth, p. 250.

[81] States the Talmud in Gittin, 61a: "To promote peace, we support the poor of the gentiles, visit their sick and bury their dead, along with the poor, the sick and the dead of Israel."

[82] Leviticus 19:18.

[83] At the outset, chapter 19 of Leviticus sets forth the reason these principles must be followed: "You must be holy, for I, your Lord, am holy." In other words, to treat one's fellow man in a just way is godliness; it is nothing short of emulating God himself.

[84] Leviticus 19:16.

[85] Even today in the United States, there is virtually no law that makes being a bystander a crime; the few examples of such laws that we do find all came into existence in recent years.

[86] Exodus 23:5; Noda B'Yehudah, chapter 10; Deuteronomy 22:10 and Safer HaHinuch, Mitzvah 506; Deuteronomy 20:19–20, and Maimonides, *Laws of Kings,* chapter 6, Halacha 8, 10, and Safer HaHinuch, Mitzvah 529.

[87] Amiel, p. 111.

[88] Quoted in Meier, Levi, *Jewish Values in Jungian Psychology,* New York: University Press of America, 1991, p. 63.

[89] Roth, pp. 249–274.

[90] Gilbert, Martin, *Jewish History Atlas,* Jerusalem: Steimatzky Ltd., 1986, p. 73.

[91] Goldberg, M. Hirsch, *The Jewish Connection,* Landham: Scarborough House, 1993, p. 145.

[92] Roth, p. 251.

[93] Ibid., pp. 4–5.

[94] Huxley, Thomas, *Controverted Questions,* quoted in Sivan, p. 77.

PART III

[1] "Thus we find no clear cut distinction between worshipping of nature and worship of the gods of nature. What began as worship of natural phenomena, developed into the cult of natural gods. Even in the theistic stage, however, the worship of nature itself, as the embodiment of the life processes of the gods, lingers on. In one way or another, sun, moon and stars, waters, fire, etc. were always worshipped, even after the myth makers had created a universe full of gods of whom these were but symbols." Kaufman, Yehezkel, *The Religions of Israel,* Chicago: University of Chicago Press, 1960, p. 35.

[2] Writes Xenophane of Kolophon: "Both Homer and Hesiod have attributed all things to the gods. As many as are shameful and a reproach amongst mankind—thieving and adultery and deceiving each other." Cited in Dillon, Matthew, and Garland, Lynda, *Ancient Greece: Social and Historical Documents from Archaic Times to the Death of Socrates,* New York: Routledge, 1994, p. 355. Also see: Kaufman, pp. 39 and 54.

[3] Kaufman, p. 22.

[4] In Homer's *Iliad,* we see the average Greek's confusion while the gods squabble among themselves. Hektor, realizing that his death is imminent, remarks: "No use. Here at last the gods have summoned me deathward. I thought Deiphobos the hero was here close besides me, but he is behind the wall and it was Athene cheating me, and now evil death is close to me, and no longer far away, and there is no way out. So it must long since have been pleasing to Zeus, and Zeus's son who strikes from afar, this way; though before this they defended me gladly. But now my death is upon me." *The Iliad of Homer* (translated by Richard Lattimore), Chicago: University of Chicago Press, 1967, p. 443.

[5] Bloch, Abraham, *A Book of Jewish Ethical Concepts, Biblical and Post-Biblical,* New York: Ktav Publishing House, 1984, pp. 7–10.

[6] Rose, H. J., *Religion in Greece and Rome,* New York: Harper and Row, 1959, p. 9.

7   Genesis 11:31–25:8.

8   Forte, Maurizio, and Siliotti, Alberto, eds., *Virtual Archaeology—Recreating Ancient Worlds,* New York: Harry N. Abrams, Inc., 1997, p. 92.

9   Midrash Rabbah, Bereshit 38:13.

10 Weissman, Moshe, *The Midrash Says: The Book of Beraishis,* Brooklyn: Benei Yakov Publications, 1980, pp. 116–118.

11 Kaufman, pp. 29, 60.

12 Pritchard, James B., *Ancient Near Eastern Text Relating to the Old Testament,* Princeton: Princeton University Press, 1950, p. 61.

13 Huston Smith in *The Religions of Man,* p. 257: "For the Egyptians, Babylonians, Syrians, and the lesser Mediterranean peoples of the day, each major power of nature was a distinct deity. The storm was the storm-god, the sun the sun-god, the rain the rain-god. When we turn to the Old Testament we find ourselves in a completely different atmosphere. Nature here is an expression of a single Lord of all being."

14 Montanelli, Indro, *Romans Without Laurels,* New York: Pantheon Books, 1959, p. 66.

15 See Nachmonides Commentary on the Torah, Gen. 14:18.

16 Green, Ronald M., *Religion and Moral Reason,* Oxford: Oxford University Press, 1988, pp. 79–80.

17 Genesis, chapters 42–50.

18 Exodus 1:5.

19 Midrash Rabbah, Shmot 15.

20 Exodus 1:1–22.

21 Exodus 2:11–15.

22 Exodus 3:5–6.

23 For a discussion of the problems of finding a sign of the Israelites in the Egyptian archives, see Rohl, David M., *Pharaohs and Kings: A Biblical Quest,* New York: Crown, 1995.

24 Keller, Werner, *The Bible as History,* New York: Bantam, 1981, p. 110. See also pp. 113–114.

25 Numbers 1:46.

[26] Exodus 13:3.

[27] Exodus 20:2–3.

[28] Exodus 23:9.

[29] Leviticus 19:34.

[30] Scherman, Nosson, and Zlotowitz, Meier, eds., *The Family Haggadah,* Brooklyn: Mesorah Publications, 1995, p. 39: "Some wine is removed from the cup in compassion for the Egyptians. Although they oppressed us, we must not rejoice at the suffering of other humans."

[31] Exodus 19:4–8.

[32] Exodus 19:16–18.

[33] Exodus 24:7.

[34] While the world today recognizes the awesome power ethical monotheism has had in shaping human history, these questions are also asked: If monotheism is such a monumental idea, why did God pick such an insignificant group as the Jews to be its messengers? Shouldn't God have chosen the Greeks, Romans or some other great empire or culture? In other words: "How odd of God to choose the Jews?" The traditional Jewish response is, "It wasn't so odd; the Jews chose God."

[35] Isaiah 49:6.

[36] Talmud, Shabbat 133b.

[37] Louis Finkelstein in *The Jews: Their Role in Civilization,* New York: Shocken, 1971, p. 368: "This is the irony of the Jewish existence—devotion to a universalistic faith marks the Jew off as a 'peculiar' people, a 'chosen' people."

[38] Smith, pp. 258–259.

[39] Numbers 14:34.

[40] Book of Joshua, chapters 1–6.

[41] Book of Joshua, chapter 7.

[42] Babylonian Talmud, Shavuot 39a.

[43] The same holds true for the Jewish perspective on other nations. Therefore, it stands to reason that it wasn't just the Nazis who were responsible for the Holocaust, it was the entire German people. (A great deal of evidence on this issue is presented by

Daniel Goldenhagen in his bestselling book *Hitler's Willing Executioners,* New York: Knopf, 1996.) Every German who never killed a Jew or never fought in the army was responsible and accountable if he stayed in Germany and didn't try to stop the Nazis.

[44] Judges 2:8–14.

[45] Sivan, p. 10.

[46] Judges 2:16.

[47] Judges 4:14.

[48] Judges 6–8.

[49] Judges 3–16.

[50] I Samuel 1–16.

[51] One of the more dramatic stories from this period related by the Bible is of the encounter between the prophet Nathan and King David over David's sexual relationship with the beautiful Bathsheba. As a way of teaching the king a lesson, the prophet tells him a tale of injustice in the land perpetrated by an unnamed "rich man." When David rails against the injustice, the prophet lowers the boom: "You are that man!" King David immediately repents. II Samuel, chapter 12.

[52] I Kings 5:9–14.

[53] Today's Ethiopian Jews have a tradition that they are the descendants of the union of King Solomon and the Queen of Sheba.

[54] Yalkot Shimoni Pivrei Hayomim, 1085.

[55] The Bible—in I Kings, 10:3—relates that Solomon "had answers to all her questions; there was nothing that the king did not know."

[56] I Kings 11:9–13.

[57] I Kings 16:29–22:40.

[58] Elijah works many other miracles as well, including multiplying food and bringing the dead to life, both of which were also attributed to Jesus eight hundred years later.

[59] Theories abound where the remnants of the Ten Lost Tribes might still be found today. One of the wilder compares the similarities in Jewish and Native American rituals and posits that American Indians might represent one or more of the Ten Lost Tribes. Another finds such similarities in the Pathans of Afghanistan, a people who keep various Jewish traditions.

[60] II Kings, chapters 19–20.

[61] Isaiah 6:1–2.

[62] Isaiah 2:4.

[63] Isaiah 49:6.

[64] In all, Isaiah refers to the Jewish people as the "servant of God" nine times—41:8, 9; 44:1, 2, 21, 26; 45:4; 48:20; 49:3.

[65] II Kings 21:16. In another passage, II Kings 21:6, the Bible even suggests that he sacrificed his own son to an idol.

[66] II Kings 24–25.

[67] Psalm 137.

[68] The Jews are the only exhilic people in history. See Kaufman, pp. 275, 279.

[69] Twain, Mark, "Concerning the Jews," *Harper's Magazine,* September 1897.

[70] For history of the long-ranging battle between the Jews and Amalekites, see: Exodus 17:8, 16; Deuteronomy 25:17–19; and I Samuel 15:1–33.

[71] Esther 4:14.

[72] The miraculous events surrounding the salvation of the Jewish people from Haman's plot are celebrated today as the Festival of Purim.

[73] Talmud, Sanhedrin 21a, declares: "Had Moses not preceded him, Ezra would have been worthy of receiving the Torah for Israel."

[74] Nehemiah 8:9.

[75] See: James, Peter, *Centuries of Darkness: A Challenge to the Conventional Chronology of Old World Archeology,* Rutgers, N.J.: Rutgers University Press, 1993.

[76] Jewish tradition holds that Darius was the son of the union between Ahasuerus and Esther. While he was especially good to the Jews, the previous Persian monarchs were also very tolerant of Judaism, much more so than other conquerors of Israel.

[77] Wein, Berel, *Echoes of Glory,* Brooklyn: Shaar Press, 1995, p. 12.

[78] Babylonian Talmud, Sota 39b, Baba Kama 83, Midrash Dvarim Rabbah 1:a.

[79] Quoted in Glover, T. R. *The Ancient World: A Beginning,* London: Penguin Books, 1944, p. 186.

80   Glover, p. 186.

81   Especially Plato.

82   *Tanakh,* Philadelphia: The Jewish Publication Society, 1985, p. xv.

83   Maimonides, *Mishnah Torah,* Laws of Forbidden Foods, 11. See also: *Sefer HaChinuch,* Mitzvah III.

84   Johnson, p. 120.

85   Grant, *From Alexander to Cleopatra,* p. 75.

86   Johnson, pp. 102–103.

87   Ibid., p. 134.

88   Wein, p. 63.

89   In Hebrew, it is an acronym for the Biblical phrase "Who is like You among the power, O God."

90   Goldwurm, Hersh, *Chanukah: Its History, Observance and Significance,* Brooklyn: Mesorah Publications Ltd., 1989, pp. 53–55. Also see Wein, pp. 64–66.

91   Johnson, p. 135. Also see: Prager, Dennis, and Telushkin, Joseph, *Why the Jews?* New York: Simon & Schuster, 1983, pp. 84–86.

92   Parkes, Henry Bamford, *Gods and Men: The Origins of Western Culture,* New York: Knopf, 1959, pp. 149–150.

93   Grant, *From Alexander to Cleopatra,* p. 79; also Johnson, p. 112. McEvedy, Colin, and Jones, Richard, in *Atlas of World Population History,* London: Penguin, 1978, p. 21, put the population of Rome at around this time at forty-six million, which would make the percentage of Jews in the empire somewhat higher.

94   Sachar, Howard M., *A History of Israel,* New York: Knopf, 1979, p. 111; also see: Grant, *From Alexander to Cleopatra,* p. 78.

95   Goldberg, p. 33. (These conversations were not sanctioned by the rabbis nor condoned by Judaism.)

96   Seneca, quoted in Sivan, p. 126; also see: Sachar, p. 111.

97   Goldberg, p. 33.

98   There was one huge Jewish revolt in the Diaspora in 115–117 C.E.; it came to be known as Quietus's Revolt.

[99] Bayne, Steven, *Understanding Jewish History,* New York: Ktav Publishing House, 1997, p. 56.

[100] Wein, p. 119.

[101] Josephus, Flavius, *The Jewish War,* London: Penguin Books, 1981, p. 47. During the time of Solomon's Temple, the Holy of Holies contained the Ark of the Covenant, which held the tablets of the Ten Commandments. Around the time of the Babylonian exile, the Ark disappeared, and when the Jews rebuilt the Temple, the Holy of Holies stayed empty.

[102] Wein, pp. 120–121.

[103] Talmud, Baba Bathra 4a.

[104] Josephus, p. 304.

[105] Johnson, p. 118.

[106] Johnson, p. 111. Johnson notes that while Josephus called Herod a man "full of family affection," that affection only extended to his Idumean family, namely father, mother and brother. Augustus said of Herod, "It is better to be Herod's dog than one of his family."

[107] Talmud, Megillah 6:a.

[108] Johnson, p. 136.

[109] Josephus, p. 152.

[110] Wein, p. 155.

[111] Wein, p. 156.

[112] Josephus, p. 290.

[113] Talmud, Gitten 56a, b. Also see: Kitov, Eliyahu, *The Book of Our Heritage,* Vol. 3, Jerusalem: Feldheim Publishers, 1978, pp. 262–264.

[114] For a detailed description of the siege and destruction of Jerusalem, see Josephus, chapters 17–22.

[115] Both the First and Second Temples were destroyed on the same date in the Hebrew calendar. The ninth of Av is also associated with many other disasters in the history of the Jewish people.

[116] Roth, Cecil, *A Short History of the Jewish People,* London: The East and West Library, 1953, pp. 51–52.

[117] Johnson, p. 140.

[118] For Jewish understanding of the Messiah, see Part II.

[119] Johnson, p. 141, citing Deo Cassius.

[120] When the Abbasids conquered Palestine in the seventh century C.E., they renamed it Jund Falastin. In the tenth century C.E., the Abbasids were overrun by the Fatimids, and thereafter—all through the time the land was in the hands of the Crusaders, Mamelukes and Ottomans—the name "Palestine" disappeared from official use; however, it was retained in Christian literature. It officially reappeared only after World War I as the name of the land governed from London under the mandate of the League of Nations. *Jerusalem Post Magazine,* January 29, 1999, p. 26.

[121] Kaufman, p. 450.

[122] Montanelli, p. 67; also see: Grant, *The World of Rome,* p. 128.

[123] Grant, *The World of Rome,* p. 129.

[124] The one exception of the forced conversion of the Idumeans was discussed earlier.

[125] Williamson, Ronald, *The Jews in the Hellenistic World: Philo,* Cambridge: Cambridge University Press, 1989, p. 136.

[126] Sachar, p. 111.

[127] Gager, John G., *Kingdom and Community: The Social World of Early Christianity,* New Jersey: Prentice-Hall, 1977, p. 136.

PART IV

[1] Despite the discovery and translation of the Dead Sea Scrolls, the Essenes remain a mystery. Scholars disagree about who they were exactly, though it is now generally agreed that the term "Essenes" does not denote a single sect but rather a collection of sects, for the most part ascetic, who withdrew from mainstream Jewish society to await the coming of the end of the world, which they apparently thought was imminent.

[2] The award-winning Christian biographer A. N. Wilson sums up the matter this way in his *Jesus: A Life,* New York: W. W. Norton & Co., 1992, pp. 88–89: "Very little documentary evidence about Jesus survives in non-Christian sources. What they have

to say about Jesus could be written on the back of a post-card and does not prove that he actually existed. Tacitus in his *Annals* tells us that the ringleader of the Christians was 'condemned to death in the reign of Tiberius by the procurator Pontius Pilate.' Pliny the Younger wrote to the Emperor Trajan and, while blandly recommending that the Christians should be persecuted, informs his emperor that 'they sing a hymn to Christ as a god.' This hardly proves that Christ existed. The Jewish historian Flavius Josephus (c. 37–c. 100 C.E.) refers to James as the leader of the Jerusalem Church, and says that he is the brother of Jesus who was called the Messiah. In another passage, Josephus speaks of Jesus as 'a wise man . . . a doer of wonderful works, a teacher of such men as receive the truth with pleasure . . . and the race of Christians, so named after him, are not extinct even now.' It has been suggested that this passage was inserted into Josephus by Christians. This is not very likely. No Christian writer of the New Testament period refers to Jesus as a 'wise man.' It is possible that in this tantalizingly brief reference in Josephus we find an authentic near-contemporary record of what the Jews of Jesus's time actually thought of him: not a God, nor a heretic, but a wise man and a doer of wonderful deeds. Apart from such fragmentary glimpses, we have to accept the fact that all the documentary evidence comes to us filtered via Christian witnesses, and that Christians, after their religion became the official creed of the Roman Empire in the reign of Constantine (died 337 C.E.), busily set to work destroying or altering any evidence which might conflict with the Orthodox view of Jesus."

3   The Talmud records similar teachings from the famed Hillel and Rabbi Akiva. Talmud, Shabbat 31a. See also: Rashi on Leviticus 19:18.

4   Matthew 22:37–40. "Love the Lord your God with all your heart and with all your soul and with all your mind" is a quotation from Deuteronomy 6:5. "Love your neighbor as yourself" is from Leviticus 19:18.

5   Wilson, A. N., *Paul: The Mind of the Apostle,* New York: W. W. Norton & Co., 1997, p. 16.

6   Gager, John G., *Kingdom and Community: The Social World of Early Christianity,* Englewood Cliffs, N.J.: Prentice-Hall, 1975, p. 140.

7   Wilson, *Paul: The Mind of the Apostle,* p. 10.

8   It is during this period of persecution that martyrdom becomes both a common occurrence and an identifying feature of early Christianity. Christian martyrs were familiar with the concept of martyrdom from the Jewish history of persecutions, when Jews chose to die terrible torturous deaths rather than violate the precepts of their religion.

9   Edwards, David L., *Christianity: The First Two Thousand Years,* Maryknoll, N.Y.: Orbis Books, 1997, p. 70. Also see: Johnson, Paul, *A History of Christianity,* New York: Simon & Schuster, 1976, p. 68.

10 Frankfort, Henri, *Kingship and the Gods,* Chicago: University of Chicago Press, 1948, pp. 295, 299–300. Johnson in *A History of Christianity* notes that Christian sects that did not buy these beliefs simply died out: "Jewish Christianity with, in effect, its denial of Jesus's divine nature, never successfully progressed beyond Asia Minor." (p. 92)

11 Johnson, *A History of Christianity,* p. 68.

12 Ibid., p. 76.

13 Nicholls, William, *Christian Antisemitism: A History of Hate,* Northvale, N.J.: Jason Aronson Inc., 1995, p. 90. Also see: Prager and Telushkin, pp. 90–109.

14 Ironically, anti-Semitism now switched from hating Jews because their religion was totally alien to hating Jews because their religion was too similar and seen as competition.

15 Johnson, *A History of the Jews,* p. 166.

16 Guillaume, Alfred, *Islam,* Baltimore: Penguin, 1969, pp. 10–12. Also see: Wein, pp. 299–302.

17 Goldberg, p. 33.

18 Johnson, *A History of the Jews,* p. 167. Also see: Guillaume, p. 38.

19 Koran, Sura 5:71–73.

20 Goiten, S. D., *Jews and Arabs: Their Contacts Through the Ages,* New York: Schocken Books, 1964, pp. 58–59.

21 Prager and Telushkin, pp. 110–126. In their discussion of Islamic hatred of the Jews, the authors point out the many errors contained in the Koran when referring to the Hebrew Bible, and that Mohammed's references to the Jewish texts was far from accurate.

22 Johnson, *A History of the Jews,* p. 167. Also see: Sivan, Gabriel, *The Bible and Civilization,* Jerusalem: Keter Publishing House, 1973, pp. 61, 65.

23 Guillaume, p. 7.

24 Smith, p. 219.

[25] Ibid., p. 224.

[26] Ibid., p. 226.

[27] Guillaume, p. 44.

[28] Koran, Sura 2:125.

[29] Koran, Sura 2:58.

[30] Koran, Sura 5:85.

[31] Koran, Sura 4:48–49.

[32] The term *ahl al-dhimma* was granted to both Jews and Christians, who as non-Muslim monotheists were allowed to live in Islamic countries. A whole code of law applied to them, most of it designed to set them apart, humiliate and emphasize their inferior status. While the term implies "protected minority," a better definition in light of the reality would be "abused minority." Polytheists were not afforded this luxury, but were given the choice of converting to Islam or death. It should also be noted that throughout history these laws were not uniformly enforced and there were periods of time when Jews living in Muslim countries were treated very well, and others when they were openly persecuted.

[33] Wistrich, Robert S., *Anti-Semitism: The Longest Hatred,* London: Thames Mandarin, 1992, p. 196.

[34] Johnson, *A History of Christanity,* p. 243.

[35] Although the Muslim Empire started breaking apart in the eleventh century, the Moors (who conquered Spain in 711 C.E.) were not completely driven out until 1492.

[36] Mercer, Derrik ed., *Chronicle of the World,* London: Dorling Kindersley Ltd., 1996, pp. 249, 251, 259.

[37] Guillaume, pp. 78–79.

[38] Early in the twelfth century, a new group of Muslim zealots called the Almohads changed that policy. Although formed to stamp out Islamic corruption, the Almohads turned on the Christians and the Jews, giving even these monotheists a choice of conversion or death. Johnson, *A History of the Jews,* p. 178. Also see: Wistrich, p. 196.

[39] Guillaume, p. 80.

[40] Mercer, p. 255.

[41] Halm, Heinz, *The Fatimids and Their Traditions of Learning,* London: I. B. Tauris & Co. Ltd., 1997, pp. 71–77.

[42] Powers, Richard, "Eyes Wide Open," *New York Times Magazine,* April 18, 1999, p. 82.

[43] Writes David Pryce-Jones in *The Closed Circle* (London: Paladin, 1990, pp. 403–404): "It is as though the Arabs have trapped themselves inside a closed circle from which they sense they must break out for their own good, but within which identity and its supportive values paralyze endeavors of rescue. . . . Until such time as the restraining circle is breached, the Arab approach to the modern world must peter out in inadequacy and frustration." The author further notes that there are no true democracies in the Arab world today, nor are there any industrialized nations. Oil revenue is virtually the only source of significant income for many of these nations, and it is primarily due to this income that several Arab states have been able to modernize. Unfortunately, even this modernization has not been accompanied, for the most part, by political liberalization or significant industrialization.

[44] Edwards, p. 178.

[45] Johnson, *A History of Christianity,* p. 52.

[46] The popes professed to believe that their actions were infallible because Peter, who "literally held the key of entrance to Heaven," acted through them. When the Pope, in 710 C.E., ordered that the eyes of the archbishop of Ravenna be put out as punishment for disobedience, it was said that this was not the pope's decree as much as Peter's. "The belief was, in fact, that while Peter's relics did their work from his tomb, his earthly persona was entrusted to the current Pope, who acted vicariously." Johnson, *A History of Christianity,* pp. 168–169.

[47] Johnson, *A History of Christianity,* p. 104.

[48] Heather, P. J., *Goths and Romans,* Oxford: Clarendon Press, 1991, p. 309.

[49] Mercer, p. 265; Johnson, *A History of Christianity,* pp. 172–173; Edwards, p. 189.

[50] St. Augustine: "Slaves are therefore, not to revolt, but to remain in subjection, not in crafty fear, but faithful love, until all unrighteousness pass away." Quoted in Phelps-Brown, Henry, *Egalitarianism and the Generation of Inequality,* Oxford: Oxford University Press, 1988, p. 33.

[51] Sivan, p. 85.

[52] Dillenberger, John, and Welch, John, *Protestant Christianity: Interpreted Through Its Development,* New York: Charles Scribner and Sons, 1954, p. 9.

[53] The Church's holdings multiplied enormously thanks to the ingenious idea of a "freehold"—that is, ownership of land in perpetual possession. When the popes first got land from the Frankish kings, they insisted it be given them as "freehold." This was a novel idea, and soon noblemen saw the advantage of transferring land to the Church as a tax shelter.

[54] Mercer, p. 279.

[55] McCabe, Joseph, *A History of Popes,* London: Watts & Co., 1939, pp. 215–220; see also: Borg, William, *The Papal Monarchy,* London: T. Fisher Unwin Ltd., 1922, pp. 152–153.

[56] Galatians 3:28.

[57] Phelps-Brown, p. 33.

[58] Assuming he could read, which, of course, he couldn't.

[59] Phelps-Brown, p. 68.

[60] Dillenberger and Welch, p. 11, write that, "In the 13th century, Innocent III was more powerful than any monarch."

[61] Boccaccio, Giovanni, *The Decameron,* Hardmondsworth, Middlesex: Penguin Books, Ltd., 1978, pp. 85–86.

[62] Johnson, *A History of the Jews,* p. 207.

[63] For these and additional sources, see Prager and Telushkin, pp. 93–95.

[64] Gould, Allan, ed., *What Did They Think of the Jews?* Northvale, N.J.: Jason Aronson, Inc., 1991, pp. 24–25.

[65] Ibid.

[66] Ibid.

[67] In 1408, the Archbishop of London went so far as to decree that anyone making or using an unlicensed translation of the Bible was subject to the death penalty. Tuchman, Barbara, *The Bible and the Sword,* New York: New York University Press, 1956, p. 85.

[68] Sivan, p. 174.

[69] Edwards, pp. 266–268; Mercer, p. 360.

[70] Johnson, *A History of Christianity,* p. 233.

[71] Mercer, p. 398.

[72] Quoted in Johnson, *A History of Christianity,* p. 267.

[73] From a celebrated autobiographical fragment that Luther used to preface his complete works published in 1545.

[74] Ibid.

[75] Dillenberger and Welch, p. 15.

[76] *"Hier stehe ich! Ich kann nicht anders. Gott helfe mir! Amen."* Luther's statement before the Diet of Worms, April 18, 1521, which then excommunicated him.

[77] Luther, Martin, "That Jesus Christ Was Born a Jew." Quoted in Marcus, Jacob R., ed., *The Jew in the Medieval World,* New York: Atheneum, 1973, pp. 166–167.

[78] Luther, Martin, "Concerning the Jews and Their Lies." Quoted in Marcus, pp. 167–169.

[79] In fact, Luther outlined a plan for dealing with the Jews that the Nazis adopted. It included: (1) burn all synagogues, (2) destroy Jewish holy books, (3) forbid rabbis to teach, (4) destroy Jewish homes, (5) ban Jews from roads and markets, (6) forbid Jews to make loans, (7) seize Jewish property, (8) force Jews to do hard labor, and (9) expel Jews from Christian towns. Cited by Johnson, *A History of the Jews,* p. 242. Also see: Prager and Telushkin, p. 107.

[80] Mercer, pp. 421, 425.

[81] Tuchman, p. 80.

[82] It should be noted that the Jewish and Catholic interpretations of the Bible in this regard vary hugely. Judaism never had a problem with science. Indeed, Maimonides taught: "As long as you are occupied with the mathematical sciences and the technique of logic, you belong to those who walk around the palace in search of the gate. . . . As soon as you learn the mathematical sciences, you enter the palace and pass through its forecourts. When you complete your study of the natural sciences and get a grasp of the metaphysics, you enter unto the prince [God] into the inner courtyard and have achieved to be in the same house as He." (*Guide to the Perplexed,* chapter 32).

[83] Tuchman, p. 80.

[84] Sivan, pp. 75–76.

[85] "Basically, its [the Old Testament's] appeal was in the two ideas that made it different from any other corpus of mythico-religious literature—the idea of the oneness of God and the ideal of an orderly society based on the rules of social behavior between man and man and between man and God." Tuchman, p. 82.

PART V

[1] Sivan, p. 57.

[2] Mercer, p. 449.

[3] Edwards, p. 326.

[4] Sivan, p. 80.

[5] Many Puritans were Calvinists, followers of the theology of John Calvin, who had rejected papal authority and maintained that the Bible was the sole source of God's law. Calvin had written, "If they [parents] instigate us to any transgression of the law, we must justly consider them not as parents, but as strangers who attempt to seduce us from our real Father. The same observation is applicable to princes, lords and superiors of every description." Calvin, John, Dillenberger, John, and Welch, Claude, *Protestant Christianity: Interpreted Through Its Development,* New York: Charles Scribner and Sons, 1954, p. 55.

[6] King James I was responsible for the King James Bible, first published in 1611, using a combination of translations including those of Wycliffe and Tyndale.

[7] Katsch, Abraham I., *The Biblical Heritage of American Democracy,* New York: Ktav Publishing House, 1977, p. 39.

[8] Dillenberger and Welch, p. 113.

[9] Writes Phelps-Brown, p. 54: "The Reformation thus promoted the principle of the equality of man in two ways. Because the fate of every soul formed part of the divine plan, all people, it was said, were equal in the sight of God and that cast doubt on the justification of the inequalities of this world. Because responsibility was shifted from the priesthood to the believer, the individual enjoyed a new sense of autonomy: but claiming freedom to exercise it obliged him to recognize the equal claim of others."

[10] This phrase they borrowed from the vision of Isaiah.

[11] Sivan, p. 170.

[12]   This is precisely what William Tyndale, one of the early translators of the Bible to English, threatened the Church fathers with when he said, "I will cause a boye that dryveth ye plough shall know more of Scripture than thous doest." Quoted in Tuchman, p. 92.

[13]   Dillenberger and Welch, p. 45: "For Luther and Calvin, God could be known adequately only through the Bible. It was, after all, on the basis of the Bible that the Reformation was launched."

[14]   Graff, Harvey J., ed., *Literacy and Social Development in the West: A Reader,* Cambridge: Cambridge University Press, 1991, p. 113. Also see: Thomas, Hugh, *A History of the World,* New York: Harper & Row, 1979, p. 433.

[15]   Woodhouse, A. S. P., ed., *Puritanism and Liberty,* London: J. M. Dent & Sons, 1938, p. 266.

[16]   Deuteronomy 28:64.

[17]   Tuchman, p. 126.

[18]   Newton, Sir Isaac, *Mathematical Principles of Natural Philosophy.* Quoted in Manuel, Frank E., *A Portrait of Isaac Newton,* Cambridge, Mass.: Belknap/Harvard University Press, 1968, p. 131.

[19]   It must be stressed that the leading thinkers of the Enlightenment in England, Germany and France differed vastly in their approaches. In France, for example, François Voltaire expressed great animosity toward religion absent in the writings of his English counterpart John Locke, who favored religious tolerance. Voltaire and his German colleague Johann Fichte, for all their concerns with human equality, were rabidly anti-Semitic and did not favor extending such rights to Jews. Even Immanuel Kant called for an end to Judaism. See Prager and Telushkin, pp. 127–136.

[20]   Sivan, p. 236.

[21]   Katsch, p. 97.

[22]   Ibid., p. 115.

[23]   It is important to note that the Puritans believed they were following Mosaic law, but because they lacked access to the vast body of Jewish oral tradition, they reached vastly different conclusions regarding the meaning and observance of Biblical commandments. For example, their understanding of what the Bible means by the term *michshefah* (Exodus 22:18), which they translated as "witch," had nothing to do with

the Torah's definition, nor was their extreme application of the law even remotely similar to that mandated by Jewish law.

[24] Judges 21:25.

[25] Mishna, Shabbat 7:2. Talmud, Shabbat 49b.

[26] Romans 13:1–2.

[27] Katsch, p. 120.

[28] Maimonides, *Mishnah Torah: Laws of Learning Torah,* 2:1.

[29] Cremin, Lawrence A., *American Education: The Colonial Experience 1697–1783,* New York: Harper Torchbooks, 1970, p. 16.

[30] Katsch, pp. 67–68.

[31] Ibid., p. 55.

[32] Ibid., p. 70, quoting Mencken, H. L., *The American Language,* Supplement I, New York: Knopf, 1945, pp. 136–138.

[33] Roth, *The Jewish Contribution to Civilization,* pp. 9–10; Katsch, p. 133.

[34] Leviticus 25:10.

[35] Katsch, p. 115.

[36] Ibid., p. 116.

[37] Thomas Jefferson, the author of the Declaration of Independence, had clearly expressed his views on this matter: "Almighty God hath created the mind free . . . all attempts to influence it by temporal punishments, or burthens, or by civil incapacitation, tend only to beget habits of hypocrisy and meanness and are departure from the plan of the holy author of our religion." Quoted in Sheldon, Garrett Ward, *The Political Philosophy of Thomas Jefferson,* Bombay: Popular Prakashan, 1991, p. 108.

[38] In 1864, during the Civil War, the motto "In God We Trust" was added to the currency of the United States; it is still there today.

[39] Gould, p. 283.

[40] The Gettysburg Address was delivered by President Abraham Lincoln on November 19, 1863, at the dedication of the Civil War cemetery at Gettysburg, Pennsylvania.

[41] King, Martin Luther Jr., speech delivered in Memphis, Tennessee, April 3, 1968.

[42] Quoted in Sivan, p. 178.

43   Up until the French Revolution, in many respects France remained a feudal country ruled by the First and Second Estates, comprising the king, nobility and clergy. A major cause for the revolution was the resistance of the wealthy and powerful to any type of reform.

44   One of the first acts of the National Assembly, even before the adoption of the Declaration of the Rights of Man and Citizen, was the abolition of feudalism on August 4, 1789.

45   Johnson, Paul, *Intellectuals,* New York: Harper Perennial, 1988, pp. 21–22.

46   Voltaire, François, *Dictionnaire Philosophique.* Cited in Prager and Telushkin, p. 128.

47   In Voltaire's *Dictionnaire Philosophique,* 30 of 118 articles are devoted to the Jews. See: Prager and Telushkin, pp. 128, 135.

48   Mercer, p. 699.

49   While the American Revolution did last for eight years, it never degenerated into the reign of terror as did the French Revolution. Almost all of the violent overthrows of the last two hundred years (except for Iran) have taken place in countries where the philosophy of the new order was either secular or atheistic—for example, in Communist Russia, Nazi Germany and Communist China. It seems as if the concept of God as the ultimate ethical authority acts as a moral brake on revolutionary violence and mitigates the level of bloodshed. After the revolution is over, the contrast is even more extreme. All atheistic revolutions of the last century have led to the establishment of totalitarian governments that are uniformly oppressive and disregard basic human rights. It is precisely these totalitarian regimes that then embark on major wars of world conquest or undertake acts of violence in order to export their brand of revolution.

50   Quoted in Sivan, p. 177.

51   Sivan, pp. 173–179.

52   Forte and Siliotti, p. 172. Only with the spread of Christianity in the fourth century C.E. did such insitutions first begin to appear in the city.

53   Troyanksy, David G., Cismaru, Alfred, and Andrews, Norwood, eds., *The French Revolution in Culture and Society,* New York: Greenwood Press, 1991, pp. 135–146. Also see: Finzsch, Norbert, and Jutte, Robert, eds., *Institutions of Confinement: Hospitals, Asylums, and Prisons in Western Europe and North America, 1500–1950,* Cambridge: Cambridge University Press, 1966, pp. 73–74.

[54] The monastic orders founded guesthouses, which after Latin word for "guest"—*hospes* or *hospit*—were called "hospices." As the poor souls who flocked there were often so starved as to be dying, the kindly monks began to minister to their bodily as well as spiritual needs and the idea of a hospital as a place for the care of the sick was born.

[55] Some might argue that England's Poor Law of 1601, the first extensive state effort to aid the needy, preceded this by hundreds of years. However, that law in practicality did not attempt to remedy poverty, rather it created "workhouses" where poor people, and especially poor children, were forced to do hard labor. See Sivan, pp. 85–86.

[56] Talmud, Sanhedrin 4:5.

[57] Talmud, Shabbat 123b.

[58] Huxley, Thomas, *Controverted Questions*. Quoted in Sivan, p. 77.

[59] Sivan, p. 86.

[60] Germany was the first, with social security and social health laws passed in the 1880s, followed by Great Britain in 1911 and the United States in 1935.

[61] We have already seen that there exists a close connection between Biblical ethics and the rise of democracy, especially in Protestant countries. It would be wrong, however, to assume that the influence of Jewish ideas has been limited to democratic countries alone. The creation of other political and social movements focused on social justice and equality of man have further spread biblical ethics, albeit in a greatly modified form.

Aside from democracy, the other great political movements of the last one hundred years have been Socialism and Communism. On the surface, it seems illogical that Communism should in any way be connected with the spread of Jewish ideas. Its founder, Karl Marx, a Jewish convert to Christianity who later became an atheist, called religion "the opiate of the masses." Yet the connection is definitely there.

Marx sought to rectify the social and economic injustices of Europe by economically empowering and politically enfranchising the working classes of industrialized society. In so doing, he took for granted the existence of an absolute moral standard and of universal ethics—a concept that was uniquely Jewish. In a sense, his philosophy preserved the social conscience of Judaism while discarding its source, the Hebrew Bible.

This connection between Marx and Judaism is ironically clear. Later Communist leaders—many of whom were Jews, including Lev Kamanev, Grigori Zenoviev and Leon (born Bronstein) Trotsky—would refer to Marx as "the workers' Messiah," and to Marx's *Das Kapital* as "the Bible of the working classes." (See Goldberg, pp. 76–77.)

It would not be fair to compare the influence of Jewish ethics on liberal democratic society with that on the Communist world. For one thing, Jewish ideas have played a positive and central role in the evolution of democracy precisely because they were linked to an absolute standard of morality attributed to one God. But Communism, while it may have preserved some of the ethical and redemptive ideas of Judaism, was an atheistic movement, and as such lacked the allegiance to the absolute standard of morality unalterable by human convention.

The consequences of this key difference have been very apparent in the last century. In theory, Marxism sounds ideal, but in practice, not only has it been an economic disaster, it has also created the harshest totalitarian regime in history.

There is a very powerful historical lesson to be learned from this. Even in a mutated form, Biblical ideas have been a powerful force in human history, but without a connection to monotheism, they not only do not work, they can also be remarkably destructive.

In addition to Communism, during the last century, numerous social, political and economic movements have sprung up—socialism, feminism, liberalism, the labor union movement, the black civil rights movement, the animal rights movement, the environmental protection movement, the antiapartheid protest, etc.—all seeking to rectify some kind of social injustice. If we look more deeply at these various movements, we see that there is an undercurrent of Jewish ethical influence present in all of them—underlying all these movements are the Biblical ideas of social responsibility, equality, justice, and an end to tyranny or oppression.

[62] As previously noted, the Middle East has not been similarly affected. There are no true democracies in the Arab world today, nor any industrialized Arab nations. See *The Closed Circle* by David Pryce-Jones, cited earlier.

[63] McCarthy, Kathleen D., ed., *Philanthropy and Culture,* Philadelphia: Rockefeller Foundation/University of Pennsylvania Press, 1984, p. 87.

[64] Iwamoto, Kazue, "Japanese Philanthropy and the Third World," anthologized in McCarthy, Kathleen D., ed., *Philanthropy and Culture,* pp. 125, 133. (Figures given are for 1979/1980.)

[65] Potter, David; Goldblatt, David; Kiloh, Margaret; and Lewis, Paul, eds., *Democratization,* Cambridge, Mass.: Open University Press, 1997, p. 1.

[66] "I do not know whether you are aware that the League of Nations was first of all the vision of a great Jew—almost 3,000 years ago—the Prophet Isaiah," Jan Christian

Smuts speaking at the inauguration of the League of Nations in 1920. Cited in *21st Century Dictionary of Quotations,* edited by The Princeton Language Institute, New York: Laurel Books, 1993, p. 118.

[67] The Princeton Language Institute, ed., *21st Century Dictionary of Quotations,* New York: Bantam Doubleday Dell Publishing Company, 1993, p. 118.

[68] *Congressional Quarterly* as cited in Bennett, William, *Index of Leading Cultural Indicators,* New York: Simon & Schuster, 1994, p. 83.

[69] Isaiah 2:2–4; also see: Micah 4:1–4.

Bibliography

Amiel, Moshe Avigdor, *Ethics and Legality in Jewish Law,* Nanuet, N.Y.: Philipp Feldheim, 1994.

Antonelli, Judith S., *In the Image of God: A Feminist Commentary on the Torah,* Northvale, N.J.: Jason Aronson, 1995.

Aries, Philippe, and Bejin, Andre, eds., *Western Sexuality,* Oxford: Basil Blackwell Ltd., 1998.

Armstrong, Karen, *A History of God: The 4,000-Year Quest of Judaism, Christianity and Islam,* New York: Ballantine Books, 1993.

Bayne, Steven, *Understanding Jewish History,* New York: Ktav Publishing House, 1997.

Ben-Sasson, H. H., ed., *A History of the Jewish People,* Cambridge: Harvard University Press, 1976.

Bloch, Abraham, *A Book of Jewish Ethical Concepts, Biblical and Post-Biblical,* New York: Ktav Publishing House, Inc., 1984.

Blok, Josien, and Mason, Peter, eds., *Sexual Asymmetry: Studies in Ancient Society,* Amsterdam: J. C. Gieben, 1987.

Blunt, Edward, *Social Services in India,* London: The Majesty's Stationary Office, 1946.

Boccaccio, Giovanni, *The Decameron,* G. H. McWilliam (trans.), Harmondsworth, Middlesex: Penguin Books, Ltd., 1978.

Bonner, Stanley, F., *Education in Ancient Rome,* London: Methuen & Co., 1977.

Borg, William, *The Papal Monarchy,* London: T. Fisher Unwin Ltd., 1922.

313

Bowman, Alan K., and Woolf, Greg, *Literacy and Power in the Ancient World,* Cambridge: Cambridge University Press, 1994.

Brasch, Rudolf, *How Did Sex Begin? The Sense and Nonsense of Custom and Traditions That Have Separated Men and Women Since Adam and Eve,* New York: D. McKay Co., 1973.

Brock, William R., *The Evolution of American Democracy,* New York: The Dial Press, 1970.

Brown, Judith M., *Gandhi: Prisoner of Hope,* New Haven: Yale University Press, 1989.

Brunt, P. A., "The Roman Mob," *Studies in Ancient Society,* ed. M. I. Finley, London: Routledge and Kegan Paul, 1974.

Bryant, Joseph M., *Moral Codes and Social Structure in Ancient Greece,* New York: State University of New York Press, 1996.

Caldwell, Wallis, *Hellenic Conceptions of Peace,* New York: Columbia University, 1919.

Cantonella, Eva, *Bisexuality in the Ancient World,* New Haven, Conn.: Yale University Press, 1992.

Cantor, Norman F., *The Civilization of the Middle Ages,* New York: HarperCollins Publishers, 1993.

Chang, Kwang-Chih, *The Archaeology of Ancient China,* New Haven, Conn.: Yale University Press, 1963.

Cheetham, Nicolas, *The Keepers of the Keys: A History of the Popes from St. Peter to John Paul II,* New York: Charles Scribner, 1983.

Christ, Karl, *The Romans: An Introduction to their History and Civilization,* Berkeley: University of California Press, 1984.

Cipolla, Carla M., *Literacy and Development in the West,* London: Penguin Books, 1969.

Corbett, James A., *The Papacy,* Princeton, N.J.: D. Van Nostrand Company, 1956.

Cremin, Lawrence A., *American Education: The Colonial Experience 1607–1783,* New York: Harper Torchbooks, 1970.

Critchley, J. S., *Feudalism,* London: George Allen & Unwin, 1978.

Davies, Julian, *The Caroline Captivity of the Church—Charles I and the Remoulding of Anglicanism 1625–1641,* Oxford: Clarendon Press, 1992.

Davis, Winston, *Japanese Religion and Society,* Albany: State University of New York Press, 1992.

DeMause, Lloyd, ed., *The History of Childhood,* New York: Psychohistory Press, 1974.

Diamond, Larry, and Plattner, Marc F., eds., *Economic Reform and Democracy,* Baltimore and New York: Johns Hopkins University Press, 1993.

———, *The Global Resurgence of Democracy,* Baltimore and New York: Johns Hopkins University Press, 1993.

Dillenberger, John, and Welch, Claude, *Protestant Christianity: Interpreted Through Its Development,* New York: Charles Scribner and Sons, 1954.

Dillon, Mathew, and Garland, Lynda, *Ancient Greece: Social and Historical Documents from Archaic Times to the Death of Socrates,* New York: Routledge, 1994.

Dover, K. J., *Greek Homosexuality,* London: Duckworth, 1978.

———, *Greek Popular Morality in the Time of Plato and Aristotle,* Berkeley: University of California Press, 1974.

DuBois, Page, *Torture and Truth,* London: Routledge, 1991.

Edwards, David L., *Christianity: The First Two Thousand Years,* Maryknoll, N.Y.: Orbis Books, 1997.

Elshtain, Jean Bethke, *Democracy on Trial,* Ontario: House of Anasi Press Limited, 1993.

Fantham, Elaine; Foley, Helene Peet; Kampen, Natalie Boymel; Pomeroy, Sarah B.; and Shapiro, H. A., *Women in the Classical World,* Oxford: Oxford University Press, 1994.

Finer, S. E., *The History of Government from the Earliest Times,* Vol. II, Cambridge: Oxford University Press, 1997.

Finkelstein, Louis, ed., *The Jews: Their Role in Civilization,* New York: Schocken Books, 1971.

Finley, M. I., ed., *Studies in Ancient Society,* London: Routledge and Kegan Paul, 1974.

———, *The Ancient Greeks,* New York: Penguin Books, 1977.

Finzsch, Norbert, and Jutte, Robert, eds., *Institutions of Confinement: Hospitals, Asylums and Prisons in Western Europe and North America,* 1500–1950, Cambridge: Cambridge University Press, 1966.

Forte, Maurizio, and Siliotti, Alberto, eds., *Virtual Archaeology: Recreating Ancient Worlds,* New York: Harry N. Abrams, Inc., 1997.

Frankfort, Henri, *Kingship and the Gods: A Study in Ancient Near Eastern Religion as the Integration of Society and Nature,* Chicago: University of Chicago Press, 1948.

Frazer, James George, *The Illustrated Golden Bough: A Study in Magic and Religion,* New York: Simon & Schuster, 1996.

Fukuyama, Francis, *The End of History and the Last Man,* New York: The Free Press, 1992.

Gager, John C., *Kingdom and Community: The Social World of Early Christianity,* Englewood Cliffs, N.J.: Prentice-Hall, 1977.

Gallant, Thomas W., *Risk and Survival in Ancient Greece,* Cambridge, Eng.: Polity Press, 1991.

Garnsey, Peter, "Legal Privilege in the Roman Empire," *Studies in Ancient Society,* ed. M. I. Finley, London: Routledge and Kegan Paul, 1974.

Gilbert, Martin, *Jewish History Atlas,* Jerusalem: Steimatzky Ltd., 1986.

Glover, T. R., *The Ancient World: A Beginning,* London: Penguin Books, 1944.

Goiten, S. D., *Jews and Arabs: Their Contacts Through the Ages,* New York: Schocken Books, 1964.

Goldberg, M. Hirsh, *Jewish Connection,* Lanham, Md.: Scarborough House, 1993.

Goldenhagen, Daniel, *Hitler's Willing Executioners,* New York: Knopf, 1996.

Goldman, Israel M., *Lifelong Learning Among Jews: Adult Education in Judaism from Biblical Times to the Twentieth Century,* New York: Ktav Publishing House, Inc., 1975.

Goldwurm, Hersh, *Chanukah: Its History, Observance and Significance,* Brooklyn: Mesorah Publications Ltd., 1989.

Goody, Jack, ed., *Literacy in Traditional Societies,* Cambridge: Cambridge University Press, 1968.

Gould, Alan, ed., *What Did They Think About the Jews?* Northvale, N.J.: Jason Aronson, 1991.

Graff, Harvey J., *The Legacies of Literacy,* Indianapolis: Indiana University Press, 1991.

———, ed., *Literacy and Social Development in the West: A Reader,* Cambridge: Cambridge University Press, 1981.

Grant, Michael, *From Alexander to Cleopatra: The Hellenistic World,* New York: Charles Scribner & Sons, 1982.

———, *The Jews in the Roman World,* London: Weidenfeld & Nicolson, 1973.

———, *Myths of the Greeks and Romans,* London: Weidenfeld & Nicolson, 1964.

———, *The World of Rome,* London: Weidenfeld & Nicolson, 1962.

Green, Alberto, *The Role of Human Sacrifice in the Ancient Near East,* Missoula, Mont.: Scholars Press, 1975.

Green, Ronald M., *Religion and Moral Reason,* Oxford: Oxford University Press, 1988.

Greenberg, Simon, *The Ethical in the Jewish and American Heritage,* New York: Ktav Publishing House, Inc., 1977.

Guillaume, Alfred, *Islam,* Baltimore, Md.: Penguin, 1969.

Guttentag, Marcia, *Too Many Women? The Sex Ratio Question,* Beverly Hills, Calif.: Sage Publications, 1963.

Halbertal, Moshe, and Margalit, Avishai, *Idolatry,* translated by Naomi Goldblum, Cambridge, Mass.: Harvard University Press, 1992.

Hale, John, *The Civilization of Europe in the Renaissance,* New York: Atheneum, 1994.

Haller, William, *The Rise of Puritanism,* New York: Harper & Row, 1957.

Halm, Heinz, *The Fatimids and Their Traditions of Learning,* London: I. B. Tauris & Co. Ltd., 1997.

Hands, A. R., *Charities and Social Aid in Greece and Rome,* London: Thames & Hudson, 1968.

Hanson, Marcus L., *The Atlantic Migration 1607–1860,* New York: Harper & Row, 1940.

Harris, William V., *Ancient Literacy,* Cambridge, Mass.: Harvard University Press, 1989.

Hassig, Ross, *Aztec Warfare—Imperial Expansion and Political Control,* Norman, Okla.: University of Oklahoma Press, 1988.

Heather, P. J., *Goths and Romans,* Oxford: Clarendon Press, 1991.

Heschel, Abraham, *The Earth Is the Lord's,* Woodstock, Vt.: Jewish Lights, 1995.

Hesiod, *The Homeric Hymns and Homerica,* translated by Hugh G. Evelyn-White, Cambridge, Mass.: Harvard University Press, 1977.

Homer, *The Iliad,* translated by Richard Lattimore, Chicago: University of Chicago Press, 1967.

Hulley, John, *Comets, Jews and Christians,* Jerusalem: Root & Branch, 1996.

Hunt, Morton M., *The Natural History of Love,* New York: Knopf, 1959.

Innes, Stephen, *Creating the Commonwealth: The Economic Culture of Puritan New England,* New York: W. W. Norton & Company, 1995.

James, Peter, *Centuries of Darkness: A Challenge to the Conventional Chronology of Old World Archeology,* Rutgers, N.J.: Rutgers University Press, 1993.

Jansen, G. H., *Militant Islam,* New York: Harper & Row, 1979.

Johnson, Paul, *A History of Christianity,* New York: Simon & Schuster, 1976.

————, *A History of the Jews,* New York: Harper & Row, 1987.

————, *Intellectuals,* New York: Harper Perennial, 1988.

Jones, Prudence, and Pennick, Nigel, *A History of Pagan Europe,* London: Routledge Press, 1995.

Josephus, Flavius, *The Jewish War,* London: Penguin Books, 1981.

Kahan, A. Y., *Taryag Mitzvos,* Brooklyn: Keser Torah Publications, 1987.

Kaplan, Mordechai, *The Purpose and Meaning of Jewish Existence: A People in the Image of God,* Philadelphia: Jewish Publication Society of America, 1964.

Katsh, Abraham I., *The Biblical Heritage of American Democracy,* New York: Ktav Publishing House, Inc., 1977.

Kaufman, Yehezkel, *The Religion of Israel: From Its Beginnings to the Babylonian Exile,* Chicago: University of Chicago Press, 1960.

Keller, Werner, *Diaspora: The Post-Biblical History of the Jews,* New York: Harcourt, Brace & World, Inc., 1966.

Kelly, Marjorie, ed., *Islam—The Religious and Political Life of a World Community,* New York: Praeger Publishers, 1984.

Kierman, Frank A., *Chinese Ways in Warfare,* Cambridge: Rainbow-Bridge Book Co., 1974.

Kitov, Eliyahu, *The Book of Our Heritage,* Jerusalem: Feldheim Publishers, 1978.

Kobler, Franz, *Letters of Jews Throughout the Ages from Biblical Times to the Middle of the Eighteenth Century,* London: The East and West Library, 1952.

Koch, Adolf G., *Religion of the American Enlightenment,* New York: Thomas Y. Cromwell Company, 1968.

Kochan, Lionel, *The Jew and His History,* London: Macmillan Press Ltd., 1977.

Kohl, Martin, ed., *Infanticide and the Value of Life,* Buffalo: Prometheon, 1977.

Kraye, Jill, ed., *Renaissance Humanism,* Cambridge: Cambridge University Press, 1996.

Kurinsky, Samuel, *The Eighth Day: The Hidden History of the Jewish Contribution to Civilization,* Northvale, N.J.: Jason Aronson, 1994.

Lamson, Herbert Day, *Social Pathology in China,* Shanghai: Commercial Press Ltd., 1935.

Lancaster, H. O., *Expectations of Life,* New York: Springer-Verlag, 1990.

Lancaster, Roger N., and di Leonardo, Micaela, eds., *The Gender Sexuality Reader,* New York and London: Routledge, 1997.

Leach, Edmund, Mukherjee, S.N., and Ward, John, eds., *Feudalism: Comparative Studies,* Sydney: University of Sydney Press, 1984.

LeGoff, Jacques, *The Medieval World,* London: Collins & Brown, 1990.

Leonard, Emile A., *History of Protestantism: The Reformation,* London: Nelson and Sons Ltd., 1965.

Lew, Myer S., *The Humanity of Jewish Law,* New York: Soncino Press, 1985.

Lewis, Bernard, *The Middle East and the West,* New York: Harper & Row, 1964.

Licht, Hans, *Sexual Life in Ancient Greece,* London: Routledge, 1932.

Lieber, Moshe, ed., *The Pirkei Avos Treasury: Ethics of the Fathers,* Brooklyn: Mesorah Publications Ltd., 1995.

Lincoln, Bruce, *War and Sacrifice: Studies in Ideology and Practice,* Chicago: University of Chicago Press, 1991.

Linder, Amnon, ed., *The Jews in Roman Imperial Legislation,* Detroit: Wayne State University Press, 1987.

Maimonides, Moses, *The Guide for the Perplexed,* translated by M. Friedlander, London: Routledge & Kegan Paul Ltd., 1904.

Mallett, Judith P., and Skinner, Marilyn B., eds., *Roman Sexuality,* Princeton, N.J.: Princeton University Press, 1997.

Malone, Joseph, ed., *The Shaping of the Arab World,* New York: Aspen Institute of Humanistic Studies, 1978.

Manuel, Frank E., *A Portrait of Isaac Newton,* Cambridge, Mass.: Belknap/Harvard University Press, 1968.

Marcus, Jacob R., ed., *The Jew in the Medieval World,* New York: Atheneum, 1973.

Markoff, John, *Waves of Democracy—Social Movements and Political Change,* Boston, Mass.: Pine Forge Press, 1996.

Massey, Michael, *Women in Ancient Greece and Rome,* Cambridge: Cambridge University Press, 1988.

McCabe, Joseph, *A History of Popes,* London: Watts & Co., 1939.

McCarthy, Kathleen D., ed., *Philanthropy and Culture,* Philadelphia: Rockefeller Foundation/University of Pennsylvania Press, 1984.

McEvedy, Colin, and Jones, Richard, *Atlas of World Population History,* London: Penguin, 1978.

McKeen, Richard, ed., *The Basic Works of Aristotle,* New York: Random House, 1941.

McKitterick, Rosamnod, *The Uses of Literacy in Early Medieval Europe,* Cambridge: Cambridge University Press, 1990.

Meeks, Wayne A., *The Origins of Christian Morality: The First Two Centuries,* New Haven: Yale University Press, 1993.

Mercer, Derrik, ed., *Chronicle of the World,* London: Dorling Kindersley Ltd., 1996.

Meyer, Michael A., *Ideas of Jewish History,* New York: Behrman House, Inc., 1974.

Miller, Avigdor, *Behold a People,* New York: Balshon, 1968.

Mitamura, Taisuke, *Chinese Eunuchs,* Tokyo: Charles E. Tuttle Co., 1970.

Montanelli, Indro, *Romans Without Laurels,* New York: Pantheon Books, 1959.

Montross, Lynn, *War Through the Ages,* New York: Harper & Brothers, 1944.

More, Louis T., *Isaac Newton—A Biography,* New York: Charles Scribner and Sons, 1934.

Murstein, Bernard I., *Love, Sex and Marriage Through the Ages,* New York: Springer Publishing Co., 1974.

Neider, Charles, ed., *The Complete Essays of Mark Twain,* New York: Doubleday, 1963.

Netanyahu, B., *The Origins of the Inquisition in Fifteenth-Century Spain,* New York: Random House, 1995.

Nicholls, William, *Christian Antisemitism: A History of Hate,* Northvale, N.J.: Jason Aronson, 1995.

Oates, Whitney J., and O'Neill, Eugene, eds., *The Complete Greek Drama,* New York: Random House, 1938.

Oldenziel, Ruth, "The Historiography of Infanticide in Antiquity," collected in Blok, Josien, and Mason, Peter, eds., *Sexual Asymmetry: Studies in Ancient Society,* Amsterdam: J. C. Gieben, 1987.

Padfield, J. E., *Hindu at Home,* Delhi, India: B. R. Publishing Corp., 1907.

Pakuda, Bachya ibn, *The Duties of the Hearts,* translated by Yaakov Feldman, Northvale N.J.: Jason Aronson, 1996.

Parkes, Henry B., *Gods and Men: The Origins of Western Culture,* New York: Knopf, 1959.

Phelps-Brown, Henry, *Egalitarianism and the Generation of Inequality,* Oxford: Oxford University Press, 1988.

Potter, David; Goldblatt, David; Kiloh, Margaret; Lewis, Paul, eds., *Democratization,* Cambridge, Mass.: Open University Press, 1997.

Powers, Richard, "Eyes Wide Open," *New York Times Magazine,* April 18, 1999.

Prager, Dennis, and Telushkin, Joseph, *Why the Jews?* New York: Simon & Schuster, 1983.

Princeton Language Institute, *21st Century Dictionary of Quotations,* New York: Bantam Doubleday Dell Publishing Company, 1993.

Pritchard, James B., ed., *Ancient Near Eastern Text Relating to the Old Testament,* Princeton, N.J.: Princeton University Press, 1950.

Pryce-Jones, David, *The Closed Circle: An Interpretation of the Arabs,* London: Paladin, 1990.

Rabinovich, Abraham, "Repository of History," *Jerusalem Post Magazine,* January 10, 1997.

Rapoport, Anatol, *Peace: An Idea Whose Times Has Come,* Ann Arbor: University of Michigan Press, 1992.

Rausch, David A., *Friends, Colleagues and Neighbors: Jewish Contributions to American History,* Grand Rapids, Mich.: Baker Books, 1996.

Ritmeyer, Kathleen, *Secrets of Jerusalem's Temple Mount,* Washington, D.C.: Biblical Archeology Society, 1998.

———, *Temple Mount: Reconstructing Herod's Temple Mount in Jerusalem,* Washington, D.C.: Biblical Archeology Society, 1990.

Roback, A. A., *Jewish Influence in Modern Thought,* Cambridge, Mass.: Sci-Art Publishers, 1929.

Robello, Alfredo Mordechai, *The Legal Condition of the Jews in the Roman Empire,* Jerusalem: Hebrew University Press, 1980.

Roger, Just, *Women in Athenian Law and Life,* London: Routledge, 1989.

Rohl, David M., *Pharaohs and Kings: A Biblical Quest,* New York: Crown, 1995.

Rose, H. J., *Religion in Greece and Rome,* New York: Harper and Row, 1959.

Roth, Cecil, *A History of the Jews,* New York: Shocken Books, 1961.

———, *The Jewish Contribution to Civilization,* London: The East and West Library, 1956.

———, *A Short History of the Jewish People,* London: The East and West Library, 1953.

Rouselle, Alice, *Porneia: Desire and the Body in Antiquity,* translated by Felicia Pheasant, Cambridge, Mass.: Blackwell, 1988.

Royle, Roger, *Mother Teresa,* San Francisco: HarperCollins, 1992.

Runes, Robert, ed., *The Hebrew Impact on Western Civilization,* New York: Philosophical Library, 1951.

Sachar, Howard M., *A History of Israel,* New York: Knopf, 1979.

Scherman, Nosson, and Zlotowitz, Meier, eds., *The Family Haggadah,* Brooklyn: Mesorah Publications, 1995.

Schoeps, Hans-Joachim, *The Religions of Mankind,* New York: Doubleday, 1966.

Schousboe, Karen, ed., *Literacy and Society,* Copenhagen: Akademick Forlag, 1989.

Seneca, *Moral Essays,* Vol. I, translated by John. W. Basome, London: William Heinemann, Ltd., 1943.

Sheldon, Garett Ward, *The Political Philosophy of Thomas Jefferson,* Bombay, India: Popular Prakashan, 1991.

Simms, Marion P., *The Bible in America,* New York: Wilson-Ericson, 1936.

Sivan, Gabriel, *The Bible and Civilization,* Jerusalem: Keter Publishing House, 1973.

Smalley, Beryl, *The Study of the Bible in the Middle Ages,* Oxford: Basil Blackwell Publishers, 1952.

Smith, Huston, *The Religions of Man,* New York: Harper & Row, 1958.

Southerland, Stewart, et al., eds., *The World's Religions,* London: Routledge, 1988.

Stager, Lawrence E., "Eroticism and Infanticide at Ashkelon," *Biblical Archeology Review,* July/August 1991.

Stark, Rodney, *The Rise of Christianity,* Princeton: Princeton University Press, 1996.

Stern, Menachem, ed., *Greek and Latin Authors on Jews and Judaism,* Vols. 1 & 2, Jerusalem: Monson Press, 1974.

Sternberg, Meir, *The Poetics of Biblical Narrative and the Drama of Reading,* Bloomington: University of Indiana Press, 1985.

Sullivan, Lawrence E., *Death, Afterlife and the Soul,* New York: Macmillan Publishing Co., 1987.

Sutherland, A., *The Origin and Growth of the Moral Instinct,* Longmans, 1898.

Tanakh, Philadelphia: The Jewish Publication Society, 1985.

Taylor, Insup, and Martin, M., *Writing and Literacy in Chinese, Korean and Japanese,* Philadelphia: John Benjamins Publishing Co., 1995.

Telushkin, Joseph, *Biblical Literacy,* New York: William Morrow & Co., 1997.

———, *Jewish Literacy,* New York: William Morrow & Co., 1991.

————, *Jewish Wisdom*, New York: William Morrow & Co., 1994.

Thomas, Hugh, *A History of the World*, New York: Harper & Row, 1979.

Thompson, Frank Charles, ed., *Thompson Chain—Reference Bible*, Indianapolis: B. B. Kirkbridge Bible Co, Inc., 1988.

Troyanksy, David G., Cismaru, Alfred, and Andrews, Norwood, eds., *The French Revolution in Culture and Society*, New York: Greenwood Press, 1991.

Tuchman, Barbara, *The Bible and the Sword*, New York: New York University Press, 1956.

————, *A Distant Mirror: The Calamitous 14th Century*, New York: Knopf, 1972.

Vaillant, George C., *Aztecs of Mexico—Origins, Rise and Fall of the Aztec Nation*, New York: Doubleday and Co., Inc., 1948.

Van den Haag, Ernest, *The Jewish Mystique*, New York: Dell, 1969.

Vanggaard, Thorkil, *Phallus: A Symbol and Its History in the Male World*, London: Jonathan Cape, 1972.

Wein, Berel, *Echoes of Glory: The Story of the Jews in the Classical Era 350 B.C.E to 750 B.C.E.*, Brooklyn: Shaar Press, 1995.

Weinfeld, Moshe, *Social Justice in Ancient Israel and in the Ancient Near East*, Jerusalem: Hebrew University Press, 1995.

Weissman, Moshe, *The Midrash Says*, Vols. 1–5, Brooklyn: Benei Yakov Publications, 1980.

Williamson, Ronald, *The Jews in the Hellenistic World: Philo*, Cambridge: Cambridge University Press, 1989.

Wilson, A. N., *Jesus: A Life*, New York: W. W. Norton & Co., 1992.

————, *Paul: The Mind of the Apostle*, New York: W. W. Norton & Co., 1997.

Wistrich, Robert S., *Anti-Semitism: The Longest Hatred*, London: Thames Mandarin, 1992.

Woodhouse, A. S. P., *Puritans and Liberty*, London: J. W. Dent & Sons, 1938.

Yerushalmi, Joseph H., *Zakhor: Jewish History and Jewish Memory*, Seattle: University of Washington Press, 1982.

Yherikover, Victor, *Hellenistic Civilization and the Jews*, New York: Atheneum, 1970.

Index

About the Author

Ken Spiro is a historian and a rabbi. A graduate of Vassar, he studied at the postgraduate level at the Pushkin Institute of Moscow and holds a master's degree in history from the Vermont College of Norwich University. A dynamic speaker, he lectures throughout the world on Jewish history and values, and is the originator of the WorldPerfect Seminar. He lives with his wife and five children in Israel, where he teaches at the Aish HaTorah College of Jewish Studies. His writings and seminars can be accessed on *www.aish.com.*

LaVergne, TN USA
13 February 2011
216303LV00004B/3/A